WASHING
and
POLISHING
for
FREEDOM

*A soldier in love,
war and peace*

By Eileen Edwards

New Generation Publishing

In Loving Memory
of my dear Dad
William Frederick Powell
and
of my dear Mum
Gladys Hilda (Elliston) Powell

"So proud to call
you my parents"

Acknowledgements

I wish to express my sincere thanks to my friend, Maureen Stagg, for her endless help with this book. Also to Lieutenant Colonel (Retired) Andrew (Andy) J.A. Main, Royal Logistic Corps who gave me so much valuable information regarding the army.

First of all I would like to dedicate this book to my brother, Bob. One fact we always shared was our enormous love for our parents. This book is also dedicated to my four children, my two nephews and niece who all had so much love and approbation to their grandparents: and to their equally loving partners and their own children. I know that reading about my parents' early life together, and apart, will only strengthen their fondest memories of a devoted couple.

Also my eternal thanks to my husband, Alan, for his love and support: not only to me but to my parents. Alan had so much respect to my Dad and Mum who both loved him unconditionally. My parents never once referred to Alan as their 'son-in-law'. Alan was always their 'son-in-love'.

Most of all my sincere love and thanks go to my parents. To my Dad for keeping a diary and writing his letters to Mum during the years 1940-1946 to give us the opportunity to know his personal thoughts. And to my Mum for keeping those precious diaries and letters and to then entrust them to me.

CONTENTS

Foreword

I always knew my Dad and I were so alike: we shared a special love. Perhaps this began on the day I was born. On the morning of Wednesday, 6th February 1952, King George VI died. The strain of the Second World War and the tensions of the post-war period had taken their toll on the King's health. The King failed to recover from a lung operation and died in his sleep while at Sandringham: he was aged 56. This initiated a time of mourning and most of the public services had stopped as a sign of respect. My Mum had gone into labour at their home in the early hours of Monday, 11th February. Dad frantically managed to contact the midwife who promised to arrive as soon as possible. However, I would not wait. Exactly 9.00 am Dad was alone with Mum when he delivered me into this world. When the midwife eventually arrived having had to cycle to their home, Mum was holding me: we were still attached by the umbilical cord. In the meantime Dad had boiled plenty of water knowing this was used during the procedure for a birth. Proudly producing the endless supply of boiled water, Dad then admitted to the midwife he never knew exactly what he had to do with it. She simply told him: "Make a nice cup of tea"!

I can imagine actually delivering your own baby will only make that bond stronger.

It was a far cry from when my older brother, Robert, was born in Epsom Hospital five years earlier on Monday, 10th March 1947. Mum had been admitted into hospital before the birth was due and Dad would constantly telephone to enquire on her current condition. He was always given the same information: "Mrs. Powell is still awaiting the birth and doing well". One usual telephone call Dad was told by the nurse: "Mother and child are doing well". Dad thanked the nurse and then he put the receiver down before he realised what he had just been told. He didn't even know if the 'child' was a son or a daughter! It was a son my parents desperately desired. And just a son was all they ever wanted and planned to have. Five years later they had a daughter: me.

Dad was once told by his father-in-law: "You can rule the boy [Robert], but you'll never rule the girl [me]." Grandad was right. I could always get away with far more than my brother did or dared. Yet, while I could easily manipulate my Dad, I never ever lost my sincere admiration and love for him. Throughout our years together my Dad became an inspiration to me and he was always full of words of wisdom. When my dear Dad died on Monday, 31st January 2000 it seemed as though my whole world fell apart. To me my Dad was always very special – he was the first man I ever loved. Today clocks in my home are left at 7.25 – the hour in the morning when Dad sadly died. That was a time when a part of me also stopped.

Five years later my husband, Alan, and I had a short break to Rome in May 2005. We showed my Mum our photos taken. She looked at them in horror. Mum had almost the identical photos taken of Dad when he was in Rome during the war in May 1945. Unknowingly, Alan had posed in the exact places as Dad had 60 years earlier. Mum showed me the photos of Dad and with them were letters he had written to her during World War II. Mum gave me those photos and Dad's letters to read and keep. She knew I would lovingly look after them.

It was not until after my Mum's sad death in March 2009 when I finally read those letters Dad had written to her. I was impressed at his neat handwriting and also amazed at how someone so young could think the way he did with views well beyond his years. Immediately it whetted my interest in Dad's service action with the R.A.S.C. during the war. The result is this book.

Even before I read Dad's diaries and letters I always knew how much in love with each other my parents were. Their actions were simply stronger than words. Having read my Dad's diaries and his letters to my Mum, these beliefs are proved beyond doubt. Their words were simply stronger than actions.

Once I read those letters, there was only one title to use for this book – *'Washing and Polishing for Freedom'*. Perhaps an odd title: but there is a reason. In one of my Dad's letters to my Mum he wrote: *"Boy, what a story I will be able to tell when I get my cards. I think I will write a book, 'Washing and Polishing for Freedom', sounds a nice title doesn't it?"* Dad never did accomplish that book. Well, Dad – I wrote it for you and I called it what you had suggested.

I hope you approve, Dad – and I did you proud.

September 1919 – December 1939

1919 is a year to rejoice. Finally it is the end of World War I: the Treaty of Versailles signed in June. Historically 1919 brought the Housing Act where the State for the first time helped local authorities to provide housing subsidies; the first regular passenger air service in the world (from London to Paris) and Lady Aston, although American by birth, is the first woman to take her seat in the House of Commons as member for Plymouth. In September Adolf Hitler, a 29 year old Austrian-born German and a decorated veteran of World War I, is working as a spy for the police and is ordered to monitor the German Workers' Party.

William Frederick Powell and Matilda (known as 'Tilly') Louise Fraser knew each other before the First World War had started. It was inevitable that Great Britain would be involved in a war soon so they decide to get married as quickly as possible. Both aged 24, William Frederick and Tilly marry at Christ Church, the parish church of Battersea in London on Saturday, 1st August 1914.

There is no honeymoon. Just one day after they are married William Frederick leaves Tilly to join the army. On Sunday, 2nd August an assurance is made that if the German fleet attacks the French channel ports the Royal Navy will intervene with the demand from Germany to respect the neutrality of Belgium. Their main obligation to defend Belgium is precise following an undertaking in a treaty which was made in 1839. With Germany's final refusal not to invade Belgium, Great Britain is compelled to declare war on Tuesday, 4th August 1914.

William is immediately sent to France where he works as

1

a lorry driver.   Vehicles are still unfamiliar to the majority of people so driving is classed as a skill.   Anyone able to drive a lorry is automatically assigned to a war vehicle at an enhanced rate of pay of six shillings a day [£29.31p in 2013].   Tilly's 20 year old brother, Percy Fraser, emigrated to Australia before the outbreak of war, but he returns to his home country to fight and he earns more from the Australian Government than William Frederick from the British Government.

While William Frederick is in France he receives the news that Tilly is expecting their first child.   She is living at 56 Gwynne Road, Battersea.   William is able to return to England in time for the birth of the son they name William, born on Sunday, 27th June 1915 at the General Lying-in (a term for childbirth) Hospital, York Road, on the north side of Westminster Bridge Road in the Borough of Lambeth, London.   Sadly, only two days later on Tuesday, 29th June their baby son dies of infantile convulsions.   William has the grim task of registering his son's birth and his death together on Thursday, 1st July 1915 at Lambeth.

William Frederick returns to France to continue fighting in the war.   Tilly is looked after by her father, Robert Fraser, living nearby at 32 Hibbert Street with his daughters, ten year old Lilian Edith and five year old Dulcie Rose.   Tilly was the fifth of eleven children.   Her mother, Elizabeth Rose, had died aged 43 on Tuesday, 4th July 1911 when Dulcie Rose was only 17 months.   When the war finally ends on Monday, 11th November 1918, William Frederick and Percy Fraser safely return to England.   Seven days before Christmas on Wednesday, 18th December 1918, William's mother, Rebecca Ann, dies of an aortic disease and cardiac dilatation exhaustion at her house, 11 Reform Street.

In 1919 Tilly's father, Robert Fraser, catches bronchitis and seven days later on Tuesday, 9th September, dies aged

57. He had been a widower for eight years. Four days after Robert's death and nine months after Rebecca Ann's death, Tilly gives birth to her second child and second son on Saturday, 13th September. Again they name their son William, adding Frederick. William Frederick Junior is also born at the General Lying-in Hospital then taken to the family home at 20 Freedom Street, Battersea, London. Percy, now aged 25, soon departs to return to his adopted country in Australia and takes with him his younger sister, Lilian Edith, now aged 14. The Fraser family still had to decide the future of nine year old Dulcie Rose. Tilly, despite just giving birth to her own child, agrees to care for her young sister. With only nine years difference in their ages, Bill would later look upon Dulcie Rose more of an older sister than a young aunt.

On Sunday, 2nd November William Frederick Junior is baptised St. Mary Parish Church, Battersea, London.

William and Tilly have their third child: a daughter, Ivy Louise, born on Friday, 11th November 1921, giving William (Bill) Frederick Junior a sister.

In 1924 Bill joins Latchmere Road School, Battersea, remaining there until he joins the junior school in 1926.

In 1925 Tilly's friend, Mrs. Alston, gives birth to a baby girl named June. Mental problems develop so she enters hospital to be cared for. Her husband, William Alston, is unable to cope on his own with a baby, so Tilly fosters June. Both Dulcie and June remain with the Powell family for many years.

In 1929 Bill contracts scarlet fever, aged 10. 1929 also sees Ramsey MacDonald's second Labour government and the start of the Great Depression. Bill's Aunt Dulcie marries milkman Will(iam) Wallace on Saturday, 3rd August. Will often takes Bill to watch Chelsea, their favourite football team, play.

In 1930 Bill moves to Battersea Central School. He

enjoys football, playing in his local church youth club football team and with various local teams. He is also keen on boxing and becomes a promising professional boxer himself.

In 1932 Bill contracts diphtheria, aged 13. On Monday, 30th January 1933 Adolf Hitler becomes the Chancellor of Germany. Benito Mussolini becomes the 27th Prime Minister of Italy and, with his fascist followers, consolidates their power into a one-party dictatorship. Mussolini sets his sight on creating a new Roman empire, so a brief colonial war fought between the Kingdom of Italy (Regno d'Italia) and the armed forces of the Ethiopian empire (also known as Abyssinia) begins in October 1935 and ends in May 1936. Emperor Haile Selassie of Ethiopia is forced to flee the country. But, more importantly, it exposes the weakness of the League of Nations as a force to preserve peace. Both Italy and Ethiopia are member nations, but the League of Nations fails to intervene.

A month after his 14th birthday on Friday, 27th October 1933 Bill leaves Battersea Central School. At Hoyts Metal Foundries in Putney Bill starts his first job, but after only six months he is sacked for falsifying his piecework. Bill's second job at Lewis Credit Draper is to last even less time: two months.

In 1934 Bill contracts jaundice, aged 15. Bill's next job is delivering accumulators throughout south London for Accumulator Supply Company. William believes his son's job offers no future prospects so he arranges for Bill to be a millwright apprentice with G. Fraser and Company when he is 16 years old. As a millwright Bill learns the craft engaged with the construction and maintenance of machinery. Early millwrights were specialist carpenters who erected machines used in agriculture, food and lumber processing and paper and their skills were pressed into service building the earliest powered textile mills.

William and his older brother, Charles James, are strongly involved in politics. At 16 years old Bill also shows an interest and joins the North Battersea Labour Party. Charles and his nephew would often discuss politics in detail. As a borough councillor and electrician, Charles has his name engraved on a plaque in 1927 at the electric showroom, Electric House, situated in Battersea, London.

In Europe Italy and Germany are becoming stronger. The fascist movement in Italy is led by Benito Mussolini, nicknamed 'Il Duce' ('the Leader') and Adolf Hitler continues as Chancellor and now Fuhrer (Leader) of Germany. Mussolini and Hitler lend military and financial support to the nationalist insurrection led by General Francisco Franco in Spain. Russia is supporting the existing government, the Spanish Republic, with their leftist tendencies. Over 30,000 foreign volunteers from different countries, known as the International Brigades, travel to Spain to fight for the Second Spanish Republic in the Spanish Civil War fought between 1936 and 1939. Bill tries to join the brigade, but is arrested and sent back home.

Oswald Mosley, once a Conservative M.P., had 'crossed the floor' to join the Labour government in 1924. The Labour Party rejects his proposals known as the Mosley Memorandum and Mosley starts his own New Party in February 1931. Inspired by the example of Benito Mussolini in Italy, Mosley forms the British Union of Fascists in 1932 which at its peak numbered 20,000 black shirted members. They propose to march through London during the weekends. On Sunday, 4th October 1936 Bill joins an estimated 100,000 anti-fascists in the Battle of Cable Street. The demonstrators succeed, but Bill is fined 40 shillings [£199.61p in 2013] for obstructing the police when refusing to move. The Battle of Cable Street is a major factor leading to the Public Order Act 1936 which requires police consent for political marches and forbids the wearing of political uniforms in public.

In April 1937 Guernica, a province of Biscay, Spain, is deliberately bombed by Germany in what is thought to be an opportunity to test improved weapons and tactics. Japan captures Beijing in China resulting in the Marco Polo Bridge (an eleven arch granite bridge) Incident, a battle between the Republic of China's National Revolutionary Army and the Imperial Japanese Army. The capital, Nanking, is captured on Monday, 13th December resulting in mass murder when hundreds of thousands of Chinese civilians and disarmed soldiers are murdered by soldiers of the Imperial Japanese Army. The soldiers rape an estimated 20,000 women including infants and the elderly who are mainly killed immediately afterwards often with horrific mutilation. Young girls are cut open to enable soldiers to rape them. The Spanish Civil War is now in its second year and Europe is very unsettled with cause to worry.

Neville Chamberlain, Great Britain's Prime Minister, and Édouard Daladier, the French Prime Minister, meet with Adolf Hitler and agree to the cession of the Sudetenland. In March 1938 Germany invades Austria with little response so Hitler sets German claims on the Sudetenland, an area of Czechoslovakia with a predominantly ethnic German population. In June the Japanese advance into the west and south of China. In an attempt to stall in order to prepare for their defence the Chinese flood the Yellow River near Zhengzhou and the Chinese government relocates inland to Chongqing and continues to fight. American magazine, Time, awards Adolf Hitler the Man of the Year. Italy wins the World Cup in football. On Friday, 29th July 1938 Japan invades Russia with the Battle of Lake Khasan (Changkufeng Incident). Although the Russians claim the victory, the Japanese dismiss this as an inconclusive draw.

Bill's radical political views are now his primary objective. He had joined the Labour Party Trade Union in 1936 and, at 17 years old, becomes the youngest ward secretary. Bill also becomes chairman, sports secretary and organising secretary of North Battersea Labour League of Youth from 1936-1939; delegate to Battersea Trade Council and General Committee Labour Party from 1937-1939 and secretary of Latchmere Ward Association from 1938-1939 with 11 years membership to the Transport and General Workers' Union. Charles remains a Labour Councillor until his early death at 51 years old on Sunday, 10th July 1938.

During the Munich Crisis Bill enlists for service into the Royal Army Service Corps (R.A.S.C.) Territorial Army (T.A.) and is embodied, to represent in bodily form, into the army on Thursday, 25th August 1938. On Saturday, 17th September, four days after Bill's 19th birthday, he has a medical examination in Putney, London. Considered 'fit' Bill accepts and signs for four years to 'serve and defend His Majesty King George VI against all enemies'. Instead of his father, Bill names his mother, Tilly, as his next of kin.

Thursday, 22nd September 1938 – Bill is attested into the R.A.S.C. in the rank of a driver. Attested is the first duty Bill has to perform before joining – i.e.: a ceremony to swear his oath of allegiance to the King and take the King's 'shilling' and sign on the dotted line. When that is completed Bill would then wait for orders to proceed to an army barrack to begin his training. Bill is immediately posted for duty at Wandsworth Barracks, London. His personal army number is T/69083.

Monday, 26th September 1938 – Bill is called on military service, section 13/2/B with the Territorial and Reserve Forces Act 1907.

Thursday, 29th September 1938 – Bill is attested on embodiment. On the same day Neville Chamberlain and

Édouard Daladier attend a meeting with Adolf Hitler and Benito Mussolini. The outcome is the Munich Agreement with Czechoslovakia surrendering their Sudeten borderlands with their carefully prepared defences into German hands clearing their final obstacle into Europe. The Czechoslovak government, not involved with the talks and against their wishes, is told of the agreement on Friday, 30th September. Neville Chamberlain believes he has secured peace of the world and, on his return from Munich, said to a cheering crowd at Downing Street: "I have returned from Germany with peace in our time." The German occupation of the Sudetenland begins the following day.

Saturday, 8th October 1938 – Bill returns from his military service.

Wednesday, 15th March 1939 – Germany invades the remainder of Czechoslovakia and Hitler makes further demands. Great Britain and France pledge their support to Poland. When Italy conquers Albania in April, the same guarantee extends to Romania and Greece.

Saturday, 1st April 1939 – The Spanish Civil War comes to an end when republican forces finally surrender after Dictator Francisco Franco gains power in Madrid. Despite the crisis around the world on Saturday, 29th April 1939, Wembley holds the 1939 F.A. Cup Final where favourite Wolves are beaten 4-1 by struggling Portsmouth. The cup is presented by King George VI, but it is the last final held until the conflict ends on Saturday, 27th April 1946.

Monday, 22nd May 1939 – After the Anglo/French pledge to Poland, Germany and Italy formalise their own alliance with the Pact of Steel Agreement.

Less than a year after the Munich Agreement aggression continues and on Friday, 1st September 1939 Germany invades Poland and Europe is plunged into World War II. Great Britain and France call for the withdrawal of all

German forces and Great Britain announces a general mobilisation. A day later the National Service Act is passed. Norway, Finland, Sweden, Switzerland, Spain and Ireland each declare their neutrality. However, as Germany has rejected the Anglo/French ultimatum, on Sunday, 3rd September Britain, along with France, Australia and New Zealand declares war on Germany at 11.00 am with Neville Chamberlain announcing: "This is a sad day for all of us and to none is it sadder than to me. Everything that I have worked for, everything that I have believed in during my public life has crashed into ruins. There is only one thing left for me to do: That is, to devote what strength and powers I have to forwarding the victory of the cause for which we have to sacrifice so much..........I trust I may live to see the day when Hitlerism has been destroyed and a liberated Europe has been re-established."

Thursday, 7th September 1939 – King George VI agrees to the National Registration Act introduced by the government for the issue of identity cards to be produced on demand.

Saturday, 9th September 1939 – Neville Chamberlain's cabinet plans for a three year war. In the next few days Nepal, South Africa and Canada join forces declaring war against Germany. America declares its neutrality in the war.

Wednesday, 13th September 1939 – Bill is 20 years old.

Sunday, 17th September 1939 – After signing a cease fire with Japan, Russia invades eastern Poland and the territory is divided between Germany and the Soviet Union. The Polish refuse to surrender, establishing an underground state and an underground home army, and continue to fight with the Allies on all fronts outside Poland.

Tuesday, 19th September 1939 – The first British casualty list is published.

Wednesday, 27th September 1939 – Liberal M.P. Sir John

Simon, as Chancellor of the Exchequer for Neville Chamberlain, produces his first war budget with income tax up to 7s 6d [£20.73p in 2013] in the pound (£).

Sunday, 1st October 1939 – It is announced that the conscription age for British men is to be between 20 and 22 years of age.

Saturday, 11th November 1939 – Queen Elizabeth (later the Queen Mother) broadcasts a message calling for women of the Empire to join the war effort.

Tuesday, 21st November 1939 – Prime Minister Neville Chamberlain imposes an embargo on all German trade with goods currently in Britain, but destined for shipment to Germany to be confiscated.

Monday, 18th December 1939 – Canadian troops arrive in Britain.

(Above left) William, Matilda, Ivy & Bill Powell

(Above right) Bill Powell, aged 17, September 1936

(Above left) Matilda ('Tilly') Louise Powell (nee Fraser)

(Above right) Ivy Louise Powell

January 1940 – March 1941

With the beginning of a new decade the Germans capture Paris and, after the Japanese invasion into Indochina, America place an embargo against Japan on iron, steel and mechanical parts.

In a phase nicknamed the Phoney War by the British and the Sitting War (Sitzkrieg) by the Germans, neither side launch any major operations against the other until April 1940 when Germany invades Denmark and Norway. Despite the Allied support, Norway is conquered within two months.

Monday, 22nd April 1940 – Bill is admitted to Queen Alexandra's Military Hospital at Millbank, London, with impetigo. With a highly contagious skin infection, Bill is isolated in the hospital and discharged on Sunday, 26th May.

In May 1940 British troops, unopposed, land in Iceland to prevent a possible German invasion. On Friday, 10th May 1940 Neville Chamberlain resigns as Prime Minister and is replaced by Winston Churchill. Germany invades France, Belgium, the Netherlands and Luxembourg and Adolf Hitler launches his western front.

Monday, 27th May 1940 – British troops are forced to evacuate the continent at Dunkirk abandoning their heavy equipment by early June. When Italy enters World War II in June 1940 the war quickly spreads to North Africa where her colony of Libya borders the vital British protectorate of Egypt.

Monday, 10th June 1940 – Italy declares war on Great Britain and France and invades France: twelve days later France surrenders and is divided into German and Italian occupation zones. The German Luftwaffe begins bombing raids signalling the start of the Battle of Britain.

Sunday, 30th June 1940 – Germany invades the Channel Islands serving no purpose other than the propaganda value in occupying some British territory.

Wednesday, 3rd July 1940 – The British attack the French fleet in Algeria to prevent its possible seizure by Germany.

Saturday, 13th July 1940 – Bill is posted to the 900 Anti Aircraft Company as a driver and is soon to become best friends with fellow T.A. soldier, Fred Stagg who is in transport. Fred is a year younger than Bill, with blonde hair and is a constant smoker. He always has a smile on his face and is very popular with all the soldiers who know him well. If anyone wants anything, Fred is able to provide it for them at a profit, with no questions asked. Like Bill, Fred is also a keen sportsman. Whereas Bill is a competitive boxer, Fred is a competitive cricketer and also plays his sport for the army. Fred tends to be in as much trouble with the army as Bill constantly is, and probably the reason why they immediately become such good friends. [It could also explain why the army later transferred Fred to another barracks away from Bill.]

Wednesday, 17th July 1940 – Bill is again admitted to Queen Alexandra's Military Hospital at Millbank, London, with impetigo and stays in military isolation until he is discharged on Monday, 22nd July.

The Battle of Britain continues. In the House of Commons on Tuesday, 20th August 1940 Winston Churchill praises the Allied pilots who fought against the German pilots: "Never in the field of human conflict was so much owed by so many to so few." Friday, 30th August 1940 is the climax of the Battle of Britain.

Saturday, 7th September 1940 – The start of the blitz (lightning war) named blitzkrieg by the Germans.

Friday, 13th September 1940 – With much to fear around the world, only one guest arrives to celebrate Bill's 21st birthday held at his parents' house: 3 Reform Street, Battersea, London.

Friday, 27th September 1940 – The Tripartite Pact, a treaty signed in Berlin, Germany, establishing the Axis Powers of World War II, unites Nazi Germany, Fascist Italy and Imperial Japan to formalize the Axis Powers to stipulate that any country, with the exception of Russia, not in the war which attacks any Axis Power would be forced to go to war against all three. During this time America agrees to a trade of American destroyers for British bases and continues to support Great Britain and China.

Monday, 28th October 1940 – Italy invades Greece.

While stationed at Ewell Barracks, Surrey, Bill attends a dance held at the T.A. drill hall on Saturday, 19th October 1940. A young girl walks in alone. Immediately she catches Bill's attention and he asks her for a dance. Her name is Gladys Hilda Elliston. Gladys originally arranged to meet her friend at a bus stop near the drill hall and to go to the cinema together. When her friend fails to arrive Gladys instead enters inside the hall to the dance. From the moment he first saw her, Bill knew he would marry Gladys.

When the bombing of London had started Gladys and her younger sister, Eileen, moved to safety to live at the home of her father's sister, Elsie and her husband, Syd Haycox, at 92 St. Clair Drive, Worcester Park, Surrey. Gladys' younger brother, George (known as 'Sonny'), has already been evacuated from London to Evercreech, Somerset. With her new home, came a new job for Gladys working for Whatcliffe Works at Epsom and Gladys soon discovered where to go for entertainment. One of the places is the dance hall at the T.A. drill at Ewell with many young soldiers frequenting the hall each Saturday night.

Wednesday, 20th November 1940 – The Axis Powers expands when Hungary, Slovakia and Romania join the

Tripartite Pact.

Monday, 9th December 1940 – Operation Compass; the British counter-attack the Italian forces and they retreat in chaos and a human tide of surrendering soldiers impedes the Allied advance making movement of tanks difficult. With Italian positions crumbling Adolf Hitler, shocked by the Italian failure, dispatches the German Afrika Korps commanded by General Erwin Rommel. Throughout December bombing raids are exchanged between Germany and Great Britain.

The war is giving young people the impatience of youth. Only weeks after meeting Gladys, Bill proposes marriage and Gladys accepts. Gladys' father, George, is not so quick to accept Bill. To protect his daughter from heartache, he insists on seeing Bill's army pay book which would show his marital status and prove Bill is single. Then, after giving Bill a 'once over', George decides "Why not?" and gives his permission for them to marry.

Only two months after their meeting Bill and Gladys are officially engaged on Saturday, 28th December 1940 at 92 St. Clair Drive, Worcester Park, Surrey, home of Gladys' aunt and uncle where she is living with her sister. The engagement ring Bill has bought Gladys cost £6 0s 0d [£283.93p in 2013] all the money he has to his name. A signet ring for Bill cost £2 15s 0d [£130.13p in 2013] bought at Sanders and Company in Sutton. They plan to marry *"as soon as possible"*, originally on Saturday, 20th September 1941, *"I hope"*, Bill writes in his 1941 diary, but that is crossed out with *"Perhaps"* written down for Saturday, 6th September 1941.

Wednesday, 1st January 1941 – Bill calls for Gladys in the evening. Gladys seems *"even lovelier than ever. I wish we could get married at once, I love her so."*

Thursday, 2nd January 1941 – Bill spends the whole day *"slapping paint around. Painted myself as well, by the state I am in."* He also writes a letter to Gladys.

Friday, 3rd January 1941 – Bill finishes painting then has a bathing parade. A bathing parade is swimming when on duty. The reason it is a parade is every soldier has to do a 25m swim, pick a brick up from the swimming pool floor and swim one length in uniform. Later Bill and Fred see 'It's a Date', a musical, and 'The Way of All Flesh', a drama, at the Morden Odeon cinema.

Saturday, 4th January 1941 – Bill is on fatigues duty. Fatigues duty is essentially housekeeping (i.e.: it could be picking up litter, peeling potatoes, washing up in the kitchen or any general tasks that need doing around camp and this time of year would involve sweeping up leaves). Sometimes a soldier could be on fatigues as a punishment for a minor misdemeanour and then it is referred to as R.O.P. (Restriction of Privileges) or jankers, a term for an official punishment. Bill is to paint lines on a football field at Dulwich with Eric Birr. As there is no paint available, they return to their barracks. In the evening Bill is invited to a stag party with free beer available.

Sunday, 5th January 1941 – Bill is on gate police duty until 12.00 noon. Gate police duty checks those entering the premises, also conduct random vehicle searches. Gate police guard their posts all day and night, in all types of weather. Bill takes Gladys home to meet his mother, with *"now all formalities over."*

Monday, 6th January 1941 – Bill is on gate police duty from 12.00 noon until 9.00 pm where it is *"same as usual on this job, bored stiff."*

Tuesday, 7th January 1941 – Bill is on a driving duty. Breaking down on the way, Bill is towed back to his barracks. He has a bathing parade in the afternoon and later takes Gladys to St. Anthony's Hospital, London Road, North Cheam, Surrey, as Gladys' mother has had an accident. Bill takes Gladys to see her mother in hospital the next day and then spends the evening with Gladys.

Thursday, 9th January 1941 – Bill sees his mother who has herself had an accident, slipping and breaking her arm. It *"seems strange both Mum and Hilda."* Bill then writes a letter to Gladys.

Friday, 10th January 1941 – Bill is on detail duty with Fred. Detail duty is similar to fatigues duty. A daily detail is published every day outlining the jobs or details need doing around camp the next day and could refer to a parade, inspection, or a driving detail; any job to be done is known as a detail. The detail duty manages to return early so that Bill could see Gladys, but instead Bill is put on charge for having a dirty rifle while on duty. As a punishment Bill has to stay in his barracks.

Saturday, 11th January 1941 – Bill is still on charge in the orderly room and has lost his 24 hour pass. *"Not too bad. Reported sick and spent the rest of the day in bed."* Fred calls to tell Gladys that Bill would not be allowed out of barracks to see her as planned.

Sunday, 12th January 1941 – Bill is on fatigues duty cleaning up the hall for a concert. He then calls to see Gladys: *"She is as sweet as ever. Wish I could stay here for good."*

Monday, 13th January 1941 – Bill is still on fatigues duty unloading coal and coke all afternoon. He is also *"not feeling too good."*

Tuesday, 14th January 1941 – Bill is still on fatigues duty then has detail duty carrying troops and kits. He returns too late to see Gladys and it *"seems ages since I saw her last."*

Wednesday, 15th January 1941 – Bill is on gate police duty all day. *"What a day, snowing and cold. Nearly froze stiff by the time it ends."* Bill writes to Gladys and is *"looking forward to seeing her soon. Tomorrow I hope."*

Thursday, 16th January 1941 – Bill is on detail duty before he calls home. He then sees Gladys in the evening; *"How I have missed her these last few days."* Gladys is *"the only girl in*

17

the world for me."

Friday, 17th January 1941 – Bill is on detail duty taking supplies to the headquarters and then he plays cards in the evening.

Saturday, 18th January 1941 – Bill is on fatigues duty having to *"push a broom again. What an exciting war."* Gladys' mother, Hilda, calls to see Bill at his barracks to tell him they are moving the next day.

Sunday, 19th January 1941 – Bill is on fatigues duty in the morning then moves kits to Cheam, Surrey. He meets Gladys in the afternoon to see 'The Under-pup', a musical, at the Worcester Park Odeon cinema; *"A good show with a wonderful girl."* Gladys informs Bill that she is still to live at the same address.

Monday, 20th January 1941 – Bill is on army maintenance duty all day. Army maintenance consists of engineers, technicians and military organizations responsible for the expert repair and maintenance of army vehicles, weapon systems and other equipment. It is too wet and cold to do a lot of maintenance work. In the evening Bill plays Ewell Social Club at darts losing 2-1, but he has a good time.

Tuesday, 21st January 1941 – Bill is on gate police duty until 12.00 noon then has a 24 hour pass. Bill and Gladys see 'Strike up the Band', a musical, at the Granada cinema in Cheam. Bill stays the night with Gladys and he *"would rather stay for good, but let's hope that will come soon."*

Wednesday, 22nd January 1941 – Bill is only on gate police duty for 30 minutes, *"the shortest guard I've ever done"* when his duty is cancelled. He is then on fatigues duty and general *"messing around all day."* British and Australian forces capture Tobruk, Libya, from the Italians.

Thursday, 23rd January 1941 – Bill is on maintenance and fatigues duty *"looking as if I'm working."* He has a bathing parade after dinner then sees Gladys who is *"the only thing to look forward to now."*

Friday, 24th January 1941 – Bill's lorry collapsed; *"Unlike me, it couldn't take it."* The lorry has *"got to have a new body now."* Bill is looking forward to seeing Gladys the next day and *"hope to get away early to see her."*

Saturday, 25th January 1941 – Bill takes his lorry into repair and returns to his barracks in a staff car. Bill is able to leave early to meet Gladys from work and they see 'Manhattan Madness', a comedy, at the Odeon cinema at Epsom.

Sunday, 26th January 1941 – Bill attends church parade. After dinner he writes to Gladys and has a quiet afternoon and evening reading and also moves his bed and kit from Cheam Barracks, Surrey.

Monday, 27th January 1941 – Bill is on detail duty doing *"a good job for a change."* Bill calls home to see his mother and it is *"a nice change to be with her again."* In the evening Bill has a darts match in the barracks canteen against Ewell Social Club.

Tuesday, 28th January 1941 – Bill is on detail duty doing the *"same job as yesterday. Lousy day, pouring with rain all day"*, but Bill receives a letter from Gladys *"as good as a tonic to hear from her"* and *"looking forward so much to seeing her soon."*

Wednesday, 29th January 1941 – Bill is on gate police duty then has a 24 hour pass to see 'He Stayed for Breakfast' and 'Gold Rush Maisie', two comedies, at the Granada cinema at Cheam before he meets *"the finest, sweetest girl in the world. Just like heaven to be with Gladys again."* Bill stays the night with Gladys.

Thursday, 30th January 1941 – Bill is up at 8.30 am to cook his breakfast as Gladys' mother (*"Mum Elliston"*) has gone home. Bill then leaves to report at Ewell Barracks, Surrey, for his gate police duty.

Friday, 31st January 1941 – Bill is on fatigues and maintenance duty all day *"greasing, cleaning and painting the lorries, the Major coming to inspect them on Sunday."* Bill is also looking forward to seeing Gladys at the dance the next evening.

Saturday, 1st February 1941 – Bill passes a workshop inspection then has more greasing and painting on his lorry. He takes Gladys to the dance and introduces her formally to Fred.   Bill hopes to see Gladys the next day.

Sunday, 2nd February 1941 – Bill is on fatigues and maintenance duty.   There is also the major's vehicle inspection, driving around all morning.   Bill passes the inspection and then is able to meet Gladys to see 'Dead Man's Shoes' and 'The Gracie Allen Murder Case', two dramas, at the Worcester Park Odeon cinema.

Monday, 3rd February 1941 – Bill is on detail duty having to move loads of straw all day which is a *"lousy job, straw everywhere, down my neck and back as well."*   Bill writes to Gladys hoping to see her very shortly.

Tuesday, 4th February 1941 – After gate police duty Bill has a bathing parade.   He then visits friends, Mr. and Mrs. Prince.

Wednesday, 5th February 1941 – Bill been on fatigues and maintenance duty all day and is *"just about browned off oiling and greasing lorries.   It would not be so bad if the lorry went out more often."*   For the first time in a long while Bill is on night guard duty at his barracks.   He receives a letter from Gladys.

Thursday, 6th February 1941 – Having answered Gladys' letter Bill is off night guard duty at 6.30 am, but is on fatigues duty until 12.00 noon and then on gate police duty. Despite *"feeling dead beat, can hardly keep my eyes open"* Bill still sees Gladys.   The British rapid advance causes the Italian 10th Army to evacuate Cyrenaica on the east coast of Libya in late January.   In the Battle of Beda Fomm the British destroy the Italian 10th Army and conquer Benghazi, Libya.

Friday, 7th February 1941 – Bill is on fatigues duty and

then detail duty. There is *"another big mess up. Nobody knows what we are to do or why."* Bill calls home and sees his Aunt Maud and Uncle Bert who are visiting his parents. Maud Ellen is Bill's mother, Tilly's, younger sister, born in 1899; Bert is her husband.

Saturday, 8th February 1941 – Bill is on a convoy driving detail. Everything goes smoothly with no hitches anywhere. In the evening Bill is almost caught slipping out to see Gladys without first obtaining a pass.

Sunday, 9th February 1941 – Bill works on his barracks boiler and later has a pass so is able to see Gladys and stays for dinner. Bill then takes Gladys to see his mother for tea. Taking her back home Bill has a *"lovely day, spent with a lovely girl."* Today in a worldwide broadcast Winston Churchill tells the Americans to show their support by sending needed arms to the British: "Give us the tools and we will finish the job."

Monday, 10th February 1941 – Bill is on fatigues duty and has a bathing parade in the afternoon. Feeling *"dead tired"* he falls asleep in the drill hall after tea. Waking too late to report to Cheam Barracks, Bill stays at Ewell Barracks.

Tuesday, 11th February 1941 – Bill has a dental appointment at East Surrey Barracks, then *"messed around in cookhouse"* all afternoon and later sees Gladys.

Wednesday, 12th February 1941 – Bill is on detail duty taking tents, etc., back to the mob stores and having to hang about all day. In the evening Bill is on a sparring practice against boxer Tony Cutts. Lieutenant General Erwin Rommel, known as the Desert Fox, is appointed commander of the Afrika Korps.

Thursday, 13th February 1941 – After gate police duty Bill has a medical examination for boxing. In the evening Bill calls for Gladys to see 'The Golden Fleecing', a comedy, and 'Sea Raiders', an action film, at the Rembrandt cinema in Ewell which is *"a good show and a glorious evening."*

Friday, 14th February 1941 – Bill is on fatigues duty all morning then gate police duty. Still a keen boxer, Bill is in the army team and dislocates his thumb boxing Tony Cutts at White City and is admitted to hospital, but is not kept in.

Saturday, 15th February 1941 – Bill is on guard duty, a military assignment watching over or protecting a person or place or supervising prisoners, at night although he did manage to call on Gladys for an hour, but *"wish it was for life."*

Sunday, 16th February 1941 – Bill is on fatigues duty and cleans his service dress. With a 24 hour pass he sees Gladys and they listen to the radio. Bill *"almost learnt how to waltz."* To Bill it is *"a lovely day, as is every day with Gladys."*

Monday, 17th February 1941 – Bill takes over despatch riding duty. It is a nice change to get back on a motor cycle again with no long runs, just a steady job. His section is moving back to the headquarters which would prevent Bill from seeing so much of Gladys.

Tuesday, 18th February 1941 – There is an ammunition emergency which Bill has to take. He also calls to see Gladys wishing *"I never had to leave her."*

Wednesday, 19th February 1941 – Bill is on section despatch riding duty, which is *"a cushy job, but boring."* Bill is stationed at Epsom Barracks, Surrey, in case of an emergency with nothing to do except sleep. He believes he is to be posted to 'B' section which he hopes for as he would stay at Ewell Barracks.

Thursday, 20th February 1941 – Bill writes to Gladys and his mother then has a 125 miles despatch run to Kent in the afternoon where he almost froze.

Friday, 21st February 1941 – Bill waits all day for a despatch riding duty and amuses himself drawing. Bill is informed he would be staying at Ewell Barracks for certain. He later calls to see Gladys which *"seems ages since I saw her last."*

Saturday, 22nd February 1941 – While on despatch riding duty Bill calls in to see his mother. He also sees Gladys' grandmother, Mrs. Gilby, living in Wrotham, a village in Kent. It has been pouring with rain and Bill is soaked through.

Sunday, 23rd February 1941 – Bill is on gate police duty until 12.00 noon. There has been a section changeover with 'B' section moving to Ewell; 'C' section moving to Dulwich, London. With the afternoon off Bill sees Gladys: *"The sweetest girl in the world, Gladys of course."*

Monday, 24th February 1941 – Bill is on despatch riding duty where it is *"a perfect day for motor cycling"* and he calls in to see his mother. In the evening Bill is on official practice for a boxing contest as a selected representative. Bill slips and injures his foot causing bruising and a strain of the metatarsal phalangeal joint on his left toe. Bill is placed on the sick list by the medical officer and excused all duties with a sore and swollen foot. It is predicted that progress would be slow with difficulty in walking and wearing his army boots.

Tuesday, 25th February 1941 – Bill sits around all day, but still manages to see Gladys which is *"as good as a tonic."*

Wednesday, 26th February 1941 – Bill is still on the sick list. He sees the medical officer to discuss duties. After an x-ray Bill is sent home and he sees Gladys, wishing *"every week was like this."*

Thursday, 27th February 1941 – Bill is on 105 mile despatch riding in the pouring rain. He later calls for Gladys and they see 'Gasbags', a comedy, at the Worcester Park Odeon cinema; *"Been perfect this week seeing Gladys every night."*

Friday, 28th February 1941 – Bill returns to Kingston Hospital for an x-ray on his foot.

Saturday, 1st March 1941 – Bill is fit enough to clean his service dress then calls for Gladys to take her to his barracks for their dance that night. Bill wishes he could dance properly although he is improving slowly.

Sunday, 2nd March 1941 – Bill and Gladys see 'They Came by Night', a crime film, and 'Barricade', an adventure film, at the Epsom Odeon cinema.   Bill later returns to his barracks at 11.30 pm.

Monday, 3rd March 1941 – Bill waits to see the medical officer, his foot still painful.   He then sees his mother when on his despatch riding duty.   In the evening Bill is able to see Gladys again and *"it is wonderful to see her so often."*

Tuesday, 4th March 1941 – Bill is on guard and later gate duty then he drives two sergeants to Highwood Barracks, Essex.

Wednesday, 5th March 1941 – Bill sees the medical officer, his foot still no better; in fact it is feeling worse than ever.

Thursday, 6th March 1941 – There is no despatch riding, a relief to Bill as it is pouring with rain.   Instead he sees Gladys: *"Still the sweetest girl in the world."*

Friday, 7th March 1941 – Bill sees the medical officer again as his foot is still painful.   He is told it will take time before it will be better.   The medical officer predicts Bill may develop permanent chronic synovitis of the joint which will partially interfere with his efficiency as a soldier.   Bill sees Gladys that evening thinking *"it's a lovely war if it keeps this way."*

Saturday, 8th March 1941 – Bill has another despatch riding duty, a run over 150 miles to Kent.   As he finishes work early, Bill meets Gladys from work and they see 'The Great Dictator', a comedy, at the Epsom Odeon cinema. There is another bombing raid in London: Buckingham Palace is hit.

Sunday, 9th March 1941 – With an already injured foot, Bill has an accident on his way to see Gladys while driving along Belmont Rise in the direction of Cheam.   Bill overtakes a MG sports car when, without warning, the driver brakes suddenly and swerves to turn into

Northdown Road in front of Bill's bike. Although Bill brakes, he could not prevent hitting into the back of the sports car. Sustaining slight cuts and bruises, Bill is still able to return to the section office where he is sent to the R.M.P. (Remote Medical Practice), an outstation from the Atkinson Morley Hospital at Wimbledon. The medical officer confirms Bill has a large haematoma over the lower end of his left tibia which may ultimately result in an inflammation and impair his military efficiency. Bill has an x-ray in Putney Hospital and returns to the R.M.P. [In his statement sent to Bill's army barracks, the driver of the sports car, Mr. G.T. Hannon, claims that he was turning off Belmont Rise at an approximate speed of 15 mph. He had made the necessary signals and, on turning, Bill tried to pass him on the off-side, misjudged his speed and ran into the back of his sports car.]

Monday, 10th March 1941 – Bill remains in bed all day feeling terrible with cuts and bruises everywhere. He writes to Gladys, but *"wish I was with her. Ok in here, but miss my little sweetheart too much to want to stay long."*

Tuesday, 11th March 1941 – Bill is allowed out of bed in the afternoon. He writes to his mother and a passing ambulance driver delivers a letter to him.

Wednesday, 12th March 1941 – Bill has not heard from Gladys and he hopes that nothing is wrong, and *"boy how I wish I was with her."* However, Bill has been informed that he is to be discharged the following day.

Thursday, 13th March 1941 – Despite being told he is to be discharged today the medical officer wants Bill to stay in hospital another day. Bill is disappointed as *"a day seems like a month when I am away from Gladys."* But he knows he is to have three days sick leave so expects to see plenty of Gladys soon, *"I hope."*

Friday, 14th March 1941 – Discharged from hospital, Bill returns to his barracks with two letters from Gladys waiting for him; *"Seems as if there's been a mess up."*

Saturday, 15th March 1941 – Bill attends Dulwich Barracks, London, for a pass. He meets Gladys from work to see 'The Mark of Zorro', an adventure film, and 'Yesterday's Heroes', a drama, at the Epsom Odeon cinema. The films did not matter as it is *"like heaven being with Gladys again. A week has seemed a year."*

Sunday, 16th March 1941 – Bill takes Gladys to Willesden, London, to visit his mother; *"Another perfect day with a perfect girl. Wish this leave would never end."*

Monday, 17th March 1941 – Bill takes Gladys by tube to the West End and the Dominion Theatre to see 'All This, and Heaven Too', a drama/romance film. Using their war coupons they later shop inside Selfridges then Bill walks around the West End with *"the sweetest girl in the world."*

Tuesday, 18th March 1941 – Bill takes Gladys to Canning Town where her mother shows them her new home. On Bill's last day on sick leave *"it's been wonderful being with Gladys for nearly four whole days, but I wish it were for life."*

Wednesday, 19th March 1941 – Bill returns to his barracks still unable to walk. *"What an exciting war, perhaps it will start one day."* When back at his royal engineer drill hall at Ewell Barracks, Surrey, Bill writes a letter to Gladys.

Bill is 21 years and 6 months old: Gladys is 18 years and 10 months old.

(Above) Gladys in her aunt & uncle's front garden, 92 St. Clair Drive, Worcester Park, Surrey, 1941

(Above) Gladys in her aunt & uncle's front garden & (Right) in the back garden with Fred Stagg, 1941

My own darling Gladys.

I arrived back at barracks safe and sound last night, and much to my surprise I found that they had managed to keep the war going during my little holiday. Somehow I was half afraid that I would be told that, as I was not there to keep things going, they could not manage without me and had turned it all in. As it is, well they have done so good without my help I am thinking of asking for my cards, as I am not necessary to the war. Things have altered a lot though, some for the better and some worse. First and foremost, leave restarted on Sunday, as our colonel has left us (are we pleased) I believe he is going to Libya, although

(Above) Bill's letter to Gladys written on Wednesday, 19th March 1941

Miss Gladys Elliston
92 St. Clair Drive
Worcester Park
Surrey

W.F. Powell, T/69083
R.E. Drill Hall
Ewell

Wednesday 19 March

My own darling Gladys,

I arrived back at barracks safe and sound last night, and much to my surprise, I found that they had managed to keep the war going during our little holiday. Somehow I was half afraid that I would be told that, as I was not there to keep things going, they could not manage without me and had turned it all in. As it is, well they have done so good without my help I am thinking of asking for my cards, as I am not necessary to the war. Things have altered a lot though, some for the better and some worse. First and foremost, leave restarted on Sunday, as our colonel has left us (are we pleased). I believe he is going to Libya, although he has a reputation as a slave driver, the rumour he has gone out there to make the A.N.Z.A.C.s. [1] sweep the sand off the desert is without confirmation at present. My own idea is that he is going to take charge of the sandbag parties as they are running short of sand down there. Sergeant Barber is back here again, but as there was not much difference between him and the sergeant who has gone, that does not interfere or help.

There is a lot tighter check on going out at night, you have to book in and out and be back by ten at night. I can

29

see myself having to start to say goodnight immediately on my arrival or else doing a few days C.B. [2] every week. What is even worse, there is a roll call [3] every evening at nine o'clock and everyone who is not out on pass must be present, or else – so that seems to have put paid to my little escapades without a pass at night. I said seems, because who knows, maybe I'll find a way round that difficulty. At least I would not be a bit surprised if I managed to.

One other alteration that is very disappointing, my Sunday pass is cancelled as all leave and passes have to be taken in rotation. This means I will have twenty-four hours leave every ten days or so. I will be off duty from 4.30 one evening until ten o'clock the following night. This may not be too bad, as I will have a Sunday afternoon pass as well about once a month and perhaps a few odd evenings whenever I can manage to scrounge a pass. I am afraid I can't say when I will get my first one yet, as even I have not got the nerve to ask for a pass on the first day back in barracks.

Anyway, I hope it is very soon as I don't think I could stand another week away from you, darling. The last week was bad enough, but that had its recompense in nearly four whole days with you, dear. Four days which were like heaven, days in which you were by my side all the time. How I long for the time when we will be together, not just for days, or even weeks, months or years, but for life. Darling, life can offer nothing more beautiful and perfect than just the sight of your sweet face looking up into mine when you are in my arms. How I wish those moments would never end. One thing I do know, that at least the memory will always be in my heart. Memories, even in the short time we have been together. I have so many, memories that are like treasure, something to help to cheer my days of loneliness when I am away from you, my sweet.

The day I met you at the dance, the handshake at your

door when we said goodnight, our first date and the ensuing walk through North Cheam to Cheam Barracks, where I discovered you were interesting to talk to as well as lovely to look at, then the introduction to your mother and Elsie and, above all, our first kiss. From that moment onwards, darling, I was yours, absolutely and completely. From then I grew to love you more each day until you became my very life, when you are as necessary to me as the sun is to the world, both separate spheres but the world dependent solely on the sun for life. That is what I am, darling, entirely dependent on you for everything that makes life worthwhile.

Whenever I am with you, dearest, I am terribly happy no matter what we are doing. Yet away from you even the most pleasant things have lost interest to me and become irksome and monotonous. I don't think even you would recognise me if you knew what I was like when I am away from you, darling. I feel moody and depressed and just about fed up with everything in general, just longing for the time when we will be together again and planning and dreaming of the time when we will be together always as husband and wife. The very thought of that, sweetheart, makes me hope and pray that soon we can make a real start on this war, so that we can be finished with that altogether. Then, if all goes well, as I hope it will, I can start work on getting a home and livelihood for us both.

People often comment on the impatience of youth. I am impatient and willingly admit it, impatient and eager to be with you and who can possibly blame me for wanting to be with such a sweet, adorable, lovely and wonderful girl. Darling, were it possible tomorrow would not be a day too soon for me, as it is though I would, if necessary, wait for eternity for you. I know we are both young and can afford to wait for each other, yet it seems such a waste of youth that we are compelled by the criminal insanity of our so called civilization to spend years killing and being killed, when life offers so much that is so beautiful. How wrong it all is that men and women should continue to undergo such horror and barbarity.

Yet even in peace time people have been denied the opportunities that everyone has the right to expect, the rights to live decently, to eat good food and live in a sound house, even the chance to work, to earn the money necessary to live on was denied to nearly two million men prior to the war. Then they were all absolved into the war machine, for what, only to be thrown back on the scrap heap when their period of usefulness is at an end. Millions of pounds being spent daily on the upkeep of a nation engaged solely in destruction, when before the war money to help to educate, house, clothe and feed the people could not be obtained. Then we have the nerve to call ourselves civilized. One day perhaps people will awaken and know what fools they are. Then we will be on the way towards seeing that the next generation will not have to sacrifice their youth to satisfy a nation's greed.

We were told that the last war was to preserve democracy, to end war for all time, to make Britain a land fit for heroes to live in and for freedom. We were very gullible when that ended, just hoped for the best and the heroes sold matches in the streets and we are at war again for that same democracy and freedom. I hope people are not such fools this time and when this is over take steps to see that the cause of this and all wars are erased from our life, greed, hate and lust for power and money. When they are gone so will go wars and all social evils. Thus every one can enjoy life to the full, life as it was meant to be.

Sometimes I am a little scared when I think of all that could be achieved if only people would think a bit. How great life could be if freed from worry of hunger, unemployment and destitution. Knowing that you will always have the necessary means to live and raise a family and that the children will be assured of a good education, a trade and employment, knowing also that in sickness both you and your dependants will be cared for. All this is possible if people would only realize the fact.

Well, dear, I think that is enough of that. I don't know what made me bore you with my political ideals and beliefs, but honestly I believe they are interwoven into life so much that almost every topic is an invitation to give a political solution. By the way, I saw the M.O. [4] this morning and he gave my leg a pretty thorough examination and now I have to go to Kingston Hospital for the necessary treatment. I start tomorrow at nine o'clock. What a life I will have going to hospital at nine each morning, hanging about for two or three hours, then returning to barracks. I think it would be as well if they gave me my cards for all the good I will be to them for the next few weeks. My leg has been very sore today. The M.O. ripped that plaster off this morning and half my leg came off with it. Still, I hope by tomorrow it will be alright again, at least not so sore. I have not done any work today as I am still excused duty, but it is ever so monotonous just hanging about, nowhere to go and nothing to do. If I am lucky I hope to get the doctor at the hospital to allow me to carry on light duty. I think a little exercise will do my leg a world of good. Anyway, I don't think it will do it any harm and it will help to ease the boredom of sitting about looking like something the cat has just dragged in.

I am all on my own almost now, every lorry is out on a job. Sergeant Barber, the officer in charge, and all the corporals are attending a lecture at Dulwich and Fred is on guard duty at Cheam. Only the cook, the office staff and gate police are left in here, so you can guess the place is very lonely. But I am afraid I feel lonely even in a crowd, darling, if you are not with me. All the day I have been thinking of you, seeing you in my mind even as I sit writing this letter, so lovely and charming, with your beauty reflected in your eyes and in your smile. The fire light glinting on your hair as we used to sit together hearing you say you love me, never could I tire of hearing those words, darling. I love you with all my heart and soul, dear. You are so sweet. I want you never to change. Just the thought of you sends my heart pit-a-pat with delight. Sweetheart – how I love just to sit beside you with your hand in mine and admiring your loveliness and adoring you always. Thinking of the time when all this war is over and we are together for all time, when we can be with each other every day.

If I had been told six months ago that I would take pleasure in sitting beside the fire with a girl, no matter how lovely, I would have thought they were crazy. Perhaps I am. At least I am crazy about you, darling, crazier than I ever thought it possible for anyone to be about anybody. I am sure that no one else has ever experienced such a consuming love for a person as I feel for you, sweetheart. Love which I feel sure is returned by you. That is the wonderful part about it. It is understandable for me to love you so very much, as you are so radiantly lovely, but to have that love returned, that is beyond even my wildest dreams. Yet it is so. I felt it more these last few days when we were together, than ever before.

I am sure that our enforced absence from each other affected you almost as much as me. I think that time away from each other helped in a way to further our love for each other. Much as I know I loved you and adored you that showed me just how much I miss you when I can't see you at all. Lovely as you are at all times, darling, you never looked better to me than on Saturday afternoon when I called for you at your firm. Never in my life have I been so pleased and delighted to see anyone and, after a whole week away from you, that afternoon you looked even more beautiful than ever before. For all that though, I hope I never have to be away from you so long again. I would nearly go mad, I am sure of that. Still, I would far rather not think of anything like that happening.

Well, dear, sometime this week so I have been told, I have got to go to Dulwich to have a nice quiet chat with our new major. I feel sure he will be very pleased to have an introduction to me. No doubt the sergeant major has told him I am a regular visitor there. Anyhow, I have to go and explain why on Sunday the 9th of March I did knock a car over with my bike or something like that. One of our fellows was before him this morning charged with careless driving and he made him pay for the cost of repairs, which was £2 [£85.34p in 2013]. They are stopping two shillings and sixpence a week [£5.33p in 2013] until it is paid for. Well, my damage to my bike alone is reckoned to be fifty six pounds [£2,389.56p in 2013], so if he does the same for me, I am in a job for life almost. It will take about eight and a half years to pay that off. If they include the car damage in the bill as well, it looks as if I'll be collecting that pension for twenty two years service after all.

Will you still love me, darling, if I am discharged from the army with a long white beard? I don't expect I'll still be driving lorries then, a bath chair will be nearer the mark, I think. One thing, I am not worrying about seeing the old man, for a change I am in the right. The only trouble is, usually I have been in the wrong and have managed to get away with it. I wonder, if now I am in the right, perhaps it will work the other way and I will get stung for the damage. Still, I will find out very soon now, I suppose.

We are holding a dance here again on Saturday, 5th of April [there is no dance that evening; instead Bill stayed in at his barracks and played cards] so we are not losing any time now our beloved colonel is leaving us. I hope by then my foot will be sufficiently well to enable me to try your patience again by trying to dance with you. Perhaps I will manage to learn one day. Also, I have made enquiries about my seven days leave, Jerry [5] permitting. The date is as before, from 4.30 Thursday evening (May 1) until twelve o'clock Thursday night (May 8). So here's hoping Jerry does not see fit to start any invasion until May 9th at the earliest.

Well, dear, I will draw to a close now, hoping to see you very soon darling. Give my love to your Mum and Eileen and remember me to Syd. I hope he enjoys his stay at Evercreech. It seems pretty good weather for him anyway.

All the best, dear, and write very soon as I look forward to hearing from you so much, sweetheart. Goodbye, dear, see you again soon, I hope. All my love and fondest regards, I am yours with love forever,

Bill

xxx

LOVE AND KISSES DARLING

xxxxxxxx

S.W.A.L.K.
[Sealed With A Loving Kiss]

[1] A.N.Z.A.C.s – Australia and New Zealand Army Corps.
[2] C.B. – Confined to Barracks, normally for a minor punishment.
[3] Roll call is the calling of names of soldiers to check attendance.
[4] M.O. – medical officer.
[5] Jerry is a World War II-era nickname for German soldiers.

(Above left) Bill Powell, aged 21, 1941
(Above right) Gladys Hilda Elliston

(Below) Gladys aged 18, 1941

March – May 1941

In early 1941, with Italian forces having been pushed back into Libya by the Commonwealth, Winston Churchill orders a dispatch of troops from Africa to support the Greeks. Adolf Hitler sends German forces to Libya resulting in the Commonwealth forces retreating back into Egypt.

Thursday, 20th March 1941 – Bill visits Kingston Hospital to see doctors and surgeons and have x-rays on his injured leg. The Nazi German/Yugoslav Pact is signed to end 11 days of futile resistance against the invading Germans.

Friday, 21st March 1941 – Bill works on his barracks boiler in the morning then returns to Kingston Hospital in the afternoon. He calls to see Gladys in the evening: *"It's great to see her again."*

Saturday, 22nd March 1941 – While out on despatch riding duty Bill's bike breaks down so he returns to the section headquarters. He meets Gladys from work to see 'Old Bill and Son' and 'The Bride Wore Crutches', two comedies.

Sunday, 23rd March 1941 – Bill is fit enough for fatigues duty and later has a walk to Nonsuch Park with Gladys which is *"a lovely place, a lovely day, lovely time, with a lovely girl."*

Monday, 24th March 1941 – Bill is on fatigues duty dry scrubbing the drill hall. Totally despondent, Bill writes how the *"war was more boring than ever."* Lieutenant General Erwin Rommel, the Desert Fox, launches his first offensive in Cyrenaica, the eastern coastal region of Libya, and German troops occupy El Agheila, a coastal city at the bottom of western Cyrenaica, Libya.

Tuesday, 25th March 1941 – Bill is on section despatch

riding duty. He has a run to Kent so takes the opportunity to see Gladys' grandmother, Mrs. Gilby. Then, on his bike, Bill sees *"my sweetheart – still completely crazy about her."* The kingdom of Yugoslavia joins the Axis Powers in Vienna.

Wednesday, 26th March 1941 – Bill is on cookhouse and fatigues duty which is *"a nice, steady job."* In the evening he slips out to see Gladys and it is *"perfect to be with her. Wish I never had to leave her."*

Thursday, 27th March 1941 – After section despatch riding duty Bill calls to see Gladys. Bill thinks he may as well be living with Gladys as he stays so often with her. And, no matter how bad things are for him during the day, they are perfect when he sees Gladys most evenings and it is a *"lovely war – so far."*

Friday, 28th March 1941 – Bill returns to the headquarters then travels by bus to Kingston Hospital for another examination on his foot. As usual Bill sees Gladys in the evening.

Saturday, 29th March 1941 – Bill is on fatigues duty all day. He is *"fed up, nothing to look forward to today"* as Gladys is away for the weekend. Instead Bill travels to the Granada cinema to see 'The Man Who Talked Too Much', a drama, and 'The Ape', a horror film.

Sunday, 30th March 1941 – While he is on section despatch riding duty Bill calls to see his friend, Bill Batch living at Southfields, London, with it *"like old times again."* Bill later sees Gladys and it *"seems ages since I saw her last."*

Monday, 31st March 1941 – After section despatch riding duty Bill sees Gladys and stays. *"Might as well live here, I'm here so often these days."* The Afrika Korps counter-offensive continues the German offensive in North Africa; Mersa Brega, north of El Agheila, Libya, is taken.

Tuesday, 1st April 1941 – Bill is on section despatch riding duty. *"What a lousy start to a month – pouring with rain, soaked right through. Seems I'm the April Fool."* The British retreat after losses at El Agheila, Libya. Although surprised at the retreat, Rommel still decides to continue his offensive.

Wednesday, 2nd April 1941 – After another wet day section despatch riding duty Bill is with Gladys. It *"doesn't matter how bad things are during the day, they are perfect when I'm with Gladys."* After taking Ajdabiya, the capital of the Al Wahat District northwest of Libya, Rommel decides to take all of Libya and moves his troops toward Benghazi. All of Cyrenaica in Libya seems ready for the taking.

Thursday, 3rd April 1941 – Today for Bill it is *"fatigues, fatigues and more fatigues, bored to tears."* Things are brighter for Bill in the evening when he and Gladys see 'Hold that Woman!', a comedy, and 'Four Sons', a drama, at the Rembrandt cinema. Rommel takes Benghazi, Libya; Tobruk will remain a threat for the next seven months.

Friday, 4th April 1941 – After being on cookhouse duty all day and despatch riding duty in the evening Bill sees Gladys and *"even this war is ok while I can see Gladys as often as this."* In early April, following Bulgaria's signing of the Tripartite Pact, the Germans invade Greece and Yugoslavia. Rommel is now about 200 miles east of El Agheila, heading for Tobruk and Egypt.

Saturday, 5th April 1941 – After cookhouse duty Bill has a 24 hour pass so he meets Gladys and they walk around Kingston shops. Bill later plays cards with Gladys' father, George, and her Uncle Syd, whose house Gladys is staying at.

Sunday, 6th April 1941 – Bill and Gladys see 'Tilly of Bloomsbury', a comedy, and 'On Dress Parade', a drama, at the Granada cinema. The northern wing of Rommel's forces takes Derna on the Libyan coast. The southern wing moves toward Mechili, a small village in Cyrenaica, Libya, and takes it two days later on 8th April. Major General

Michael Gambier-Parry, the British General Officer Commanding 2nd Armoured Division, is captured in Mechili and sent to Florence, Italy, as a prisoner of war.

Monday, 7th April 1941 – Bill returns to fatigues duty but is already wishing for his seven day leave.

Tuesday, 8th April 1941 – Bill is on cookhouse duty in the morning before returning to Kingston Hospital in the afternoon. In the evening he and Gladys see 'Spring Parade', a musical/comedy.

Wednesday, 9th April 1941 – Bill is on cookhouse duty all day then despatch riding duty in the evening. He visits Gladys and has to leave in a hurry as he has a despatch call to make.

Thursday, 10th April 1941 – Bill is on section despatch riding duty. *"What a life, thank God I have got Gladys. Fed up with everything else."* German troops conquer Cyrenaica, Libya.

Friday, 11th April 1941 – Bill is on section driving duty when he calls in to see his father and sister, Ivy. His mother is at work. He sends out an Easter card to Gladys, his mother and Gladys' mother. Germany blitzes Coventry, England.

Saturday, 12th April 1941 – Bill is on section driving duty in the morning before he has a 24 hour pass. He calls for Gladys and they have a walk before staying in together at her aunt and uncle's home for the rest of the evening.

Sunday, 13th April 1941 – Bill takes Gladys to Romford, Essex, to see her friends, Lily, Doreen and Doris Kaufman. He returns to his barracks late that night. There has been a heavy German assault on Tobruk, Libya.

Monday, 14th April 1941 – Bill is on fatigues duty in the morning then on section despatch riding duty in the afternoon. In the evening he plays darts and writes a letter to Gladys. Rommel attacks Tobruk, but is forced to turn back.

Tuesday, 15th April 1941 – Bill is on section despatch riding duty in the morning and then returns to Kingston Hospital. He visits his mother before returning to section despatch riding duty at night. It is the first time he stays in his barracks at night for some time. He receives a letter from Gladys.

Wednesday, 16th April 1941 – Bill visits his Aunt Dulcie; *"Quite strange to see her* [Dulcie]. *Will* [William, Dulcie's husband] *is going into R.A.F. on Monday."* That evening there is a bad air raid so Bill stays with Gladys.

Thursday, 17th April 1941 – Bill is on section despatch riding duty all day and is so tired he is in bed at 7.00 pm.

Friday, 18th April 1941 – Bill again calls to see Dulcie to arrange to be with her when she sees Will off on Monday. Bill pops in to see Gladys then returns to his barracks and writes a letter to Gladys.

Saturday, 19th April 1941 – Bill is getting fed up with motor cycling every day. He has a pass in the evening so is able to see Gladys again who to Bill is *"still the sweetest girl in the world."* London suffers one of the heaviest air raids in the war and St. Paul's Cathedral is mildly damaged; other Christopher Wren churches are heavily damaged or destroyed.

Sunday, 20th April 1941 – Bill has a 24 hour pass and calls for Gladys to see his mother and her friends, Mr. and Mrs. Prince, before returning home.

Monday, 21st April 1941 – Bill keeps his promise to be with his Aunt Dulcie to see her husband, Will, off at Euston Station to join the R.A.F. and then takes Gladys to the Rembrandt cinema to see 'The Son of Monte Cristo', an adventure film. It is not a good ending to Bill's leave. He feels he upset Gladys.

Tuesday, 22nd April 1941 – Bill is on fatigues and cookhouse duty in the morning. He should have returned to Kingston Hospital in the afternoon, but instead Bill ignores his appointment to see 'Down Argentine Way', a comedy, and 'A Modern Hero', a drama, at the Granada cinema. On his way home he visits Gladys and spends the evening with her.

Wednesday, 23rd April 1941 – Bill is on section despatch riding duty to the headquarters getting dizzy going back and forward over the same round all day. To Bill the war is *"getting even more boring than ever. Maybe over one day (I hope)."*

Thursday, 24th April 1941 – Bill writes that the colonel is *"raising hell again"* and leave is now to start at 6.30 pm instead of 4.30 pm. Bill has a late pass so he spends *"another lovely evening with Gladys. Perfect evening, in fact."*

Friday, 25th April 1941 – Bill is on cookhouse and fatigues duty all day and cleans his equipment in the evening. Writing to Gladys, Bill is looking forward to soon spending a week with her. Rommel wins an important victory at Halfaya Pass, Egypt, near the border with Libya.

Saturday, 26th April 1941 – Bill is on section despatch riding duty when he calls in to see Gladys' mother and takes a message to her mother in Wrotham, Kent, where he also sees Gladys who is visiting her grandmother. Rommel attacks the Gazala defence line and crosses into Egypt; Tobruk continues to hold.

Sunday, 27th April 1941 – Bill is on section despatch riding duty when he calls home to see his mother. Gladys returns from Wrotham, Kent.

Monday, 28th April 1941 – Bill is on section despatch riding duty all day, giving the opportunity to enjoy himself shopping and touring around London.

Tuesday, 29th April 1941 – Bill and Gladys' mother see 'No Time for Comedy' and 'The Farmer's Wife', two comedies, at the Granada cinema. In the evening he has a ride around in a car with Gladys before returning to Ewell Barracks.

Wednesday, 30th April 1941 – Bill reports sick with an ear ache and is sent to the R.M.P. at Wimbledon for treatment. When he returns, Bill cleans his kit for his seven day leave. He discovers that *"some dirty swine helped themselves to my kit and Gladys' present yesterday."*

Thursday, 1st May 1941 – Bill is on cookhouse and fatigue duty, the day lasting for ages. Bill is *"excited as boy going on Sunday school treat"* before he leaves to see *"my lovely fiancée."* The Germans make an assault on Tobruk, Libya.

Friday, 2nd May 1941 – Bill starts his seven day leave and takes Gladys on her 19th birthday to dinner at the Corner House, Oxford Street, London, followed by an evening at the London Palladium to see a variety show with Max Millar, Florence Desmond and Vera Lynn. Bill describes his day with Gladys as a *"perfect day with a perfect girl."* Martin Bormann succeeds Rudolf Hess as Adolf Hitler's deputy and later named as head of the Nazi Party Chancellery in Germany.

Saturday, 3rd May 1941 – Bill and Gladys see 'The Ghost Train' and 'Arise My Love', two comedies, at the Metropole cinema. After seeing two films, Bill and Gladys then go to the Strand Theatre to see 'Women Aren't Angels', a comedy play starring Robertson Hare, famous for his "Oh, Calamity!" catch phrase. It is *"another lovely day, a good start to my leave."* The Anglo/Iraqi war begins with British combat operations against the rebel government of Rashid Ali in the Kingdom of Iraq. There is a German air raid on Liverpool, England.

Sunday, 4th May 1941 – Bill has a bad start to the day as Gladys is upset over something. After seeing a Sunday matinee, Bill and Gladys return home where Gladys is a lot happier so *"all ends well."*

Monday, 5th May 1941 – Bill takes Gladys to Evercreech, three miles from Shepton Mallet in Somerset, to see her younger brother, Sonny, who has been evacuated there.

They walk around the village and meadows. To Bill the day is *"really lovely being in such surroundings with a wonderful girl like Gladys."*

Tuesday, 6th May 1941 – Bill and Gladys walk across the fields at Shepton Mallet before returning home. Bill has a glorious time wishing *"this war was over."* Joseph Stalin becomes premier of Russia.

Wednesday, 7th May 1941 – Bill and Gladys return from Evercreech, Somerset, and visit Canning Town, London. Here they see the results of the bombs having been *"knocked around a lot by Jerry"* and that *"some fool said the war would be over by Christmas. But he forgot to say which Christmas, or where it would be all over. All over the world, I expect."* In the House of Commons there is a 477-3 vote in favour of Winston Churchill.

Thursday, 8th May 1941 – Bill and Gladys see 'Black Vanities'; *"A really fine show"*, at the Victoria Palace then went to the Metropole cinema to see 'So Ends Our Night', a war drama, and 'Trial of the Vigilantes', a western comedy.

Friday, 9th May 1941 – After *"a wonderful week ends"* Bill returns to his barracks. He has been fined £4 [£170.68p in 2013] for damages over his motorbike accident; *"Lovely welcome home from leave."* He thinks he could buy two new bikes for that hefty fine. Bill leaves his barracks with Fred to see 'Pride of the Blue Grass', a drama, and 'Comrade X', a comedy/romance, at the Rembrandt cinema. When he returns to his barracks Bill writes a letter to Gladys.

Saturday, 10th May 1941 – Bill is so enraged about his fine he returns his driving licence to the army and refuses future despatch riding duties. Bill insists he *"would not drive for this rotten mob again."* Instead Bill is assigned to work in the cookhouse and the orderly room. With a late pass Bill sees Gladys. On a mission to open peace negotiations, Rudolf Hess, Adolf Hitler's ex-deputy, is captured in Scotland after parachuting out of his plane. The House of Commons is damaged by the Luftwaffe in an air raid.

Sunday, 11th May 1941 – Bill is still on cookhouse duty and *"hope to keep this job away from all driving."* He is totally demoralised at *"being a toy soldier in a boy scouts uniform."* If Bill did not have Gladys he believes he would desert.

Monday, 12th May 1941 – Bill's rebellion towards the army has him constantly in the orderly room and is *"thinking of taking my bed and sleep there."* Bill believes he is *"leading the field for bad marks, just like being in school, only worse."* Seeing Gladys that evening things brighten up for Bill.

[In the meantime the army have recognised Bill's potential as a tradesman and his name has been submitted to the war office to train as a motor mechanic fitter.]

Tuesday, 13th May 1941 – With a further cookhouse duty Bill has *"more bad marks. Hope teacher lets me go home tomorrow. Wonder if I'll get the cane and book. We're supposed to be soldiers – tin ones."*

Wednesday, 14th May 1941 – Bill thinks the army is *"like a schoolroom. Only thing that makes me put up with this tripe is because I'm so crazy over Gladys."* With a 24 hour pass Bill visits Gladys and is *"out of this hole at last."* He then has a walk with Gladys and they have a drink at the Drill Inn pub.

Thursday, 15th May 1941 – While Gladys is at work Bill meets Gladys' parents and they see 'So You Won't Talk', a comedy/crime film, and 'Escape', a war film, at the Odeon cinema at Worcester Park. He then meets Gladys at Cheam Granada cinema and they see 'Flowing Gold', an adventure/drama, and 'Ma, He's Making Eyes at Me', a musical/comedy/romance film. Bill has watched four films in one day and has had *"another nice day with my Gladys (I hope)."* The British make their first attempt to attack Halfaya Pass, a steep slope located in Egypt near the border with Libya about two miles inland from the Mediterranean in Operation Brevity. Rommel counter-attacks and the

British later withdraw. In the same named Operation Brevity, Fort Capuzzo near the Egyptian/Libyan border, is also attacked in Libya. It changed hands for two days and then remained in German/Italian possession when the operation failed.

Friday, 16th May 1941 – Remaining in the cookhouse is a monotonous job for Bill, but *"at least I am out of everyone's way."* After playing in a darts match against Sutton Garage Home Guard, Bill returns to his royal engineer drill hall to write a letter to Gladys.

Bill is 21 years and 8 months old: Gladys has just turned 19 years on 2nd May.

R.E. Drill Hall
16 - May 1941

My own darling Gladys.

Already ages seem to have gone by since I saw you last, ages of hopelessness and boredom. God only knows what it will be like if I am away from you for weeks at a time, I can hardly wait days now, even hours seem like years when we are apart, it is like losing your memory, I still walk and talk but my mind is a complete blank when you are away from me. Yet it does not seem over a week ago that I was on leave and

(Above) Bill's letter to Gladys written on Friday, 16th May 1941

48

Miss Gladys Elliston
92 St. Clair Drive
Worcester Park
Surrey

W.F. Powell, T/69083
R.E. Drill Hall
Ewell

16 May 1941

My own darling Gladys,

Already ages seem to have gone by since I saw you last, ages of hopelessness and boredom. God only knows what it will be like if I am away from you for weeks at a time, I can hardly wait days now, even hours seem like years when we are apart, it is like losing your memory, I still walk and talk but my mind is a complete blank when you are away from me. Yet it does not seem over a week ago that I was on leave and with you every day. Never in my life have I enjoyed such a wonderful week, to be able to take you where you wanted to go and to be with you all the time. You have no idea how happy I was just to see you smiling and enjoying yourself just knowing I had made you happy and that for a short while we had managed to overthrow all worries and troubles of war, air raids and other such cares. I believe, darling, you were happy too, happy as I was, just the nearness of ourselves to each other. My darling, I love you with all my heart and soul, love you passionately and completely. Perhaps I even love you too much, rather selfishly but, sweetheart, I need you so much, I am lost without you. I know I hardly give you a moment to yourself. I am waiting for you when you return home from work and will not leave you until very late at night. I also realize that you have many little jobs you want to attend to and you have a long and tiring day at work and should get a good long nights rest. Believe me, my love, it is almost beyond my control to stay away from you at all, even for the hours we are apart.

While I am so near to you as I am at the moment, I just can't resist the desire to see you and be with you. So I am afraid, darling, selfish or not, I must continue to see you every time I get the opportunity and I only wish you were not at work when I would be planning how I could see you in the daytime as well as in the evening. I could never see too much of you, dear. It would be far easier to get fed up with the sun, stars, moon, air and even life itself than it is to get tired of being with you, darling. You are so sweet and charming, even after a long day at work, it is almost unbelievable that anybody could be so lovely as you are, sweetheart. Often I have to kick myself to see if it is only a beautiful dream that such a lovely girl should fall in love with me and I know you do love me, darling, you said so twenty one times in your last letter. Those words were ringing in my head all day 'I love you, darling', 'I love you, darling'. It was like music to me, music that has never been excelled even by such master musicians as Strauss, Chopin, Wagner and Mendelssohn. I only hope that I will be worthy of you and your love and will continue to hold it always. I am confident that together we can face and overcome any difficulties that may arise after this filthy war is over. Whatever its outcome and no matter what is the system and conditions that will face us, together we will win through and be happy.

Sometimes I wonder just what we will have to face when this party is over. Whatever it is, fascism, capitalism, or any other such oppressive systems of government, I feel sure that my real work will begin then. It might not be rosy and plain sailing to try and bring a socialist state to this country, but I know the result will be worth any sacrifice and struggle, a world in which war, hate, poverty, hunger and employment are unknown. Where everyone works for their benefit of the people and not for gain, where things are made for use by all and not for profit for the few. A system which gives every single person a chance and opportunity to marry and rear a family, not haunted by the fear of being out of work, children being well fed and educated and able to take their part in the world as they get older, where positions of trust are given to those with ability instead of those with an Oxford accent. I believe this is possible and will eventually come about and the job for those who believe this is to show the rest of the people the way it can be obtained. It may not be in our time, anyway we have had our war, the thing is now to prevent the next generation being faced with a war which will make even this one seem like a vicar's tea party.

Our fathers fought to save us from a war, but I am not kidding myself, the outcome of this was, whether it is won by us or by Germany, will not settle any future wars. It only means if Germany wins, socialism will be harder to obtain, but fascism and capitalism are almost identical and will eventually rise again to fight amongst themselves. When people are crazy with greed and lust for power, they first drain the workers of all they have then when they find there is nothing left to take, even then they are not satisfied. They quarrel with each other, rob each other, then – another war for democracy, freedom, right, Christianity, or what have you. Any excuse does, we always fall for it, never stopping to consider what freedom or rights we have worth fighting for. Never mind, one day it will end, people will regain a little sanity and stop acting like a lot of half crazy schoolboys, each banging the others for all they're worth, not stopping to wonder why. What a life and we are supposed to be a civilized race.

Well, dear, things are still about the same here, just like a flock of sheep chasing our leader. So far I have not collected any bad marks today, although I got one for yesterday. How, I don't know, as I was not here. Still, I don't like to spoil their fun, so I am not grumbling – much.

Royal Army Service Corps – they put the wrong name in our initials, it should read 'Rubbing and Scrubbing Corps'. I always thought a soldier's job was to fight a war. Still, I don't know what gave me the idea I was a soldier. Male charlady in a khaki suit is a more appropriate description. Never mind, I can always pretend I am a soldier when I get out of school in the evenings. Boy, what a story I will be able to tell when I get my cards. I think I will write a book, 'Washing and Polishing for Freedom', sounds a nice title, doesn't it?

By the way, the driving licence episode is developing into a serial and seems to be continued every day. They gave me another one today. I tore it up, but did not say anything about it. Then they asked to see it, so I told them what I had done – so now to be continued tomorrow. Don't miss this exciting serial. Episode 2 will be even exciting – for someone. I bet Hitler and his gang would give their right arm to know the way our army is carrying on. Lying under lorries with a tin of metal polish, walking about the yard picking up matchsticks, weeding the fields and digging for victory (I don't know if they have found it yet, but they are still digging). I was going to suggest we scrape the paint off the railing and polish those, but thought better of it as they might take me seriously and make us do it. If we decided to fight this war with brooms and mops, boy, Jerry wouldn't stand a chance. We can all wield a broom and are almost experts at polishing. The only trouble is this war is waged with rifles, guns, tanks and bombs and we don't know anything about those things.

The only thing we can do with a rifle is to clean it and lean on it when on guard duty. A bayonet, well it cooks a nice slice of toast, but is otherwise useless. My one would not cut butter even if it was hot, let alone hurt anybody. Perhaps the idea behind it all is our sense of sportsmanship. We want to give Jerry a chance first, let him play for a little while, then beat him up and shake hands and then be pals evermore. Well, I think he's had a good run now and it's about time we made a start on this war and tried to get it over.

Today was my great day, it was pay day. I slipped away and dodged the parade. Then I called in the office and asked for my money, of course they asked why I was not on pay parade [6]. I said if they expected me to line up for half hour, salute twice and click my heels about a dozen times for seven shillings [£14.93p in 2013] I'd want the rest of the week off as I'd earned my pay on the parade only. Still, it is not too bad. I am getting ½d [9p in 2013] an hour. I was thinking of putting in some overtime at the same rate of pay.

Well, dear, I am hoping to see you tomorrow at three o'clock. It will be a good show – I hope. If you are working though, I will try and get round in the evening as I don't think I could stand another whole day away from you, darling. Two days is more than enough to have to be away from you. Anyway, try to come down tomorrow afternoon in case I can't get away in the evening.

I have had a stroke of good luck today. They have rearranged the duty sections and leave rota and my next 24 hours is Sunday. So, instead of just coming round on late pass for Sunday afternoon, I will be off all the afternoon and all day Monday. Not bad, eh, then on Thursday I will be on late pass, so some things work out nicely for me. When I was told they almost apologised to me about it. They said, "Sorry Powell, we have had to alter your leave a bit, you won't be able to go now until Sunday. I hope it does not upset any arrangements you may have made." Well I just answered, "I suppose it will have to do" and that was that.

We are playing the Home Guard at darts tonight. I hope to be in the team as it will help to pass away the time, as already the evening seems to have lasted for ages, yet it is only six o'clock now. I have been nearly an hour and a half writing this letter and my wrist is beginning to ache like blazes. So, I think I had better draw to an end. There is not much to write about, anyway, as my life away from you just consists of washing dishes and sweeping up. We did relieve the monotony a little this afternoon. We had a bathing parade to Epsom Baths and I amused myself swimming. It was lovely, so cool and fresh. I was very sorry when I had to come out and return to school (sorry, barracks, I mean).

Well, my love, I will have to say goodbye for now. I hope very much that I will see you tomorrow at our social. If not, then I will see you Sunday about two o'clock and will be staying the night. Give my love to Mum, Dad, Eileen and Syd and all my love to you, darling. Just one thing before I close. I believe you now owe me a letter, so will you please oblige by settling the account at the earliest possible moment. As I am dying to hear from you again, darling, your last letter was a treat to read. When it arrived I was just about fed up to the teeth with everything, but after reading it, sweetheart, even the army seemed to be alright. So write soon please, my loved one. If you are in doubt as what to say, you won't go far wrong if you repeat the last one, as I could never grow tired of either hearing it or seeing it written on paper. I believe, darling, it is only the knowledge that you love me and care for me that stops me from throwing this job up altogether and getting out of it. As it is, well darling, I am madly in love with you, sweetheart and need you more than anything else in life. But for now, darling, I will say goodbye until Saturday or at the very latest Sunday. Put that way it seems ages, but I mean either tomorrow or the day after and even that is far too long to be away from you.

All the best, my love. Remember I love you and will always do so.

Yours with all my love forever,

Bill

xxx

I LOVE YOU DARLING
S.W.A.L.K.

[6] Pay parade is when soldiers would assemble and march up one at a time to the officer who would count out the cash to every soldier individually.

May – September 1941

Saturday, 17th May 1941 – Bill takes charge of teas at the T.A. dance. Gladys arrives but, for Bill, the frustration of the week causes *"niggles all around, but soon over, thank God."*

Sunday, 18th May 1941 – Bill has a 24 hour pass and takes Gladys to Epsom Downs. Later he sees Gladys' parents, Hilda and George. In his diary Bill writes how he hopes to get married in the next seven days. Bill wishes Gladys is his wife now as he is *"really crazy about her."*

Monday, 19th May 1941 – Bill meets Gladys from work to see the drama, 'Dr. Kildare's Crisis'.

Tuesday, 20th May 1941 – Bill and Gladys talk about getting married on Bill's next seven day leave. Bill is impatient to marry Gladys and wants nothing else; *"I hope we can as I am crazy about her and want nothing else."*

Wednesday, 21st May 1941 – Bill is on *"cookhouse duties as usual and the evening with my little girl – soon to be my wife if all goes well. Here's hoping and praying it will be ok."* Bill writes to his mother.

Thursday, 22nd May 1941 – After his cookhouse duty Bill has a late pass so he calls to see Gladys. He is *"getting a habit"* of seeing Gladys so often and Bill wonders with the war what he would do if he is away from Gladys.

Friday, 23rd May 1941 – Bill sees Gladys after his cookhouse duty. He plans to ask Hilda and George if they object to them getting married soon, hoping they would agree.

Saturday, 24th May 1941 – While in the performance of military duty Bill is cleaning the cookhouse windows at the Drill Hall at Ewell when he slips, his hand going through the window pane and is sent to Horton Hospital, Epsom, Surrey. The medical officer writes that the slight injury of a superficial cut to his forearm is unlikely to interfere with any future efficiency Bill has as a soldier. His injury is a minor concern. That evening Bill and Gladys see her parents and Bill mentions they are getting married in October. Gladys' parents, George and Hilda, have no objections so *"everything set now, am I pleased."*

Sunday, 25th May 1941 - Despite his arm still sore Bill attends church parade and is on cookhouse duties. He is able to see Gladys and *"just longing for October when Gladys will be my wife."*

Monday, 26th May 1941 - Bill speaks to his military officer about his injury to his arm. With a 24 hour pass he sees his mother and tells her the details of his forthcoming wedding.

Tuesday, 27th May 1941 - Bill plays cards with Syd waiting for Gladys to return home from work then they walk to the Drill Inn pub. *"Boy it is good to see her. Am really crazy about her"*, but Bill has to leave early as he has a *"lousy headache."* The British sink the German flagship, Bismarck, in the Atlantic.

Wednesday, 28th May 1941 - Gladys writes to Bill telling him how she loves Bill as much as he loves her. Very soon they will be married. Bill is *"really pleased with life"* and is far too excited to work in the cookhouse that day.

Thursday, 29th May 1941 - Bill takes Gladys to the Granada cinema to see 'The Fighting 69th', an action film, and 'The Bank Detective', a drama. His friends, Fred and Tony, call round to see them for tea.

Friday, 30th May 1941 - There is a big detail duty so all are up at 4.30 am. As Bill is on cookhouse duty it does not concern him. Instead Bill and Gladys see 'The Ghost of St. Michael's', a comedy, and 'San Francisco Docks', a drama/crime film, at the Odeon cinema.

Saturday, 31st May 1941 - After his cookhouse duty with Fred, Bill and Gladys have a walk through Nonsuch Park.

To Bill *"Gladys looks even lovelier in the sunset."* Their plan to marry in October has been put forward to September but with no date decided. They meet Hilda, George and Fred in the Drill Inn pub and all return to Elsie and Syd's house at 92 St. Clair Drive.

Sunday, 1st June 1941 – It is arranged for Bill's parents and his sister, Ivy, to meet Gladys' parents for the first time. Bill is so *"pleased my Ma and Pa have met my future Ma and Pa in-law."* Back at Bill's barracks all the lorries have left on a four day job. Meanwhile the Royal Air Force successfully resists the Luftwaffe's assault in the Battle of Britain and the German bombing campaign ends in May.

Monday, 2nd June 1941 – Bill is still working in the cookhouse. He has a darts match against the A.F.S. (Air Formation Signals) held in the canteen. Bill is still *"fed up with this tin pot rotten war."*

Tuesday, 3rd June 1941 – Having not seen Gladys yesterday, Bill *"never knew I could miss anyone so much. Must be even more in love than I thought."* The convoy that left his barracks on Sunday returns earlier than expected.

Wednesday, 4th June 1941 – The day of their wedding has now been fixed: Sunday, 14th September which is *"only 4½ months and Gladys will be my wife. I only wish it could be tomorrow."*

Thursday, 5th June 1941 – Bill travels to Ewell and then to Worcester Park, Surrey, and is disappointed with the prospect of postponing the wedding planned on 14th September as they could not get married on that Sunday. It is suggested for the following Saturday, 20th September 1941. That evening Bill and Gladys see an adaptation from Jane Austen's novel 'Pride and Prejudice' drama at the Rembrandt cinema.

Friday, 6th June 1941 – After his cookhouse duty with Fred, Bill and Gladys have another walk through Nonsuch Park and it is *"lovely with flowers all in blossom and Gladys looking even lovelier."*

Saturday, 7th June 1941 – There is another T.A. dance where Gladys arrives with her mother, Hilda, and her Uncle Syd. Also with them is Fred and, to Gladys' disapproval, the men *"celebrate too much."*

Sunday, 8th June 1941 – Bill is *"not feeling too bad considering all things"* having cleared up last night's mess and with Gladys *"everything is perfect again."*

Monday, 9th June 1941 – Bill is still unwell, sick and unable to eat. He sees Gladys and they stay in together.

Tuesday, 10th June 1941 – Bill arranges for his next seven day leave for Saturday, 18th September and his planned wedding on the 20th September. Certain everything is set, Bill calls to tell Gladys the news.

Wednesday, 11th June 1941 – Even the weather is better with the sun out making *"quite a change."* Bill and Gladys see 'Arizona', a western, and 'Convicted Woman', a crime film, at the Rembrandt cinema.

Thursday, 12th June 1941 – After his cookhouse duty Bill calls to see Gladys who also has her grandmother and aunt with her.

Friday, 13th June 1941 – Bill plays cards with Syd who gives Bill and Gladys permission to open his house at 92 St. Clair Drive for their wedding reception. When Gladys finishes work they see 'Back Street', a drama, and 'Sandy Gets Her Man', a comedy, at the Odeon cinema.

Saturday, 14th June 1941 – After his cookhouse duty Bill reports sick and is sent to Wandsworth Barracks to see the medical officer who gives him some ointment for his ear. Bill sees Gladys who is *"the only lovely part of this lousy war."* Today is also Bill's mother's 51st birthday.

Sunday, 15th June 1941 – After his cookhouse duty Bill takes Gladys to watch 'B' section play cricket against the A.F.S. Fred scores 121, not out. After the match Bill takes Gladys to the Drill Inn pub to join Fred, Syd and her parents. British Operation Battleaxe attempts and fails to relieve the Siege of Tobruk, Libya. The British are heavily defeated at Halfaya (nicknamed Hell-fire) Pass in Egypt.

Monday, 16th June 1941 – Bill asks his sergeant to give him a haircut which is *"not before time, it was long enough for a perm."* He then spends the evening with Gladys and is *"still completely crazy about her."*

Tuesday, 17th June 1941 – Bill completes his cookhouse duty then meets Gladys to take her to see his friend, Mrs. Prince, and tells her about their forthcoming marriage which is *"not long to wait now, thank God."*

Wednesday, 18th June 1941 – Bill is on cookhouse duty then plays in a cricket match against M.C.C. (Marylebone Cricket Club) losing by 46 runs. *"Lovely day. Summer is really here at last."*

Thursday, 19th June 1941 – Bill is put on charge for being improperly dressed the day before when playing at the cricket match against M.C.C.: his punishment is not being allowed out to see Gladys. Bill is totally despondent. *"What fools we are, we call ourselves civilized, yet kill each other wantonly and take pride in our slaughter. When will we learn that no matter which side wins any war, the people always lose."*

Friday, 20th June 1941 – Bill drives the staff car to Dulwich Barracks, London, to change some clothes then washes out the orderly room. He later has a bathing parade which is *"just what the doctor ordered swimming on a day like this."* With a 24 hour pass Bill calls for Gladys.

Saturday, 21st June 1941 – Bill meets Gladys and they travel to Kingston by bus and walk around the shops. They then meet Gladys' parents and Syd in the Drill Inn pub. *"Lovely leave, wish it lasted for ever."*

Sunday, 22nd June 1941 – After his cookhouse duty Bill calls for Gladys and they sunbathe in her aunt and uncle's back garden: *"Love her [Gladys] more than anything else. I could not live now without her."* Today Germany, along with other European Axis members and Finland, invades Russia in Operation Barbarossa, a code name after Frederick

Barbarossa, the medieval Holy Roman Emperor. Adolf Hitler's objectives are to eliminate Russia as a military power and exterminate communism. It is the largest military operation in history and would also result with the largest casualty numbers. Winston Churchill, often outspoken on his opinions of the U.S.S.R., promises to give all possible technical and economic help: "I will unsay not a word that I have spoken about it," he said, "but all this fades away before the spectacle which is now unfolding. Any man or state who fights against Nazidom will have our aid. Any man or state who marches with Hitler is our foe..........We have but one aim and one irrevocable purpose. We are resolved to destroy Hitler and every vestige of the Nazi regime." Figures published today reveal that since the start of the war the British armed forces have lost 18,627 killed, whereas civilian casualties are 35,756 killed. Proportionally the Royal Air Force has lost more than either the Royal Navy or the Army.

Monday, 23rd June 1941 – Winston Churchill states: "The Russian danger is our danger and the danger of the United States, just as the cause of any Russian fighting for his hearth and home is the cause of free men and free peoples in every quarter of the globe." *"What a war, one day it might start. Russia in the part now, so things might start."*

Tuesday, 24th June 1941 – The Foreign Secretary, Anthony Eden, announces an Anglo/Soviet mutual aid agreement. *"War news same as ever, both sides winning, only the people losing. Why don't they get wise to themselves?"* Then Bill *"called for Gladys, thank God I can see her often."*

Wednesday, 25th June 1941 – Bill reports sick and is sent to Kingston Hospital for a dental treatment. In the evening Bill is on cookhouse duty so could not see Gladys. Missing her, Bill writes a letter to Gladys which Fred delivers.

Thursday, 26th June 1941 – Bill is on cookhouse duty in the morning then in the afternoon he attends a cricket match against the Peckham police, Bill playing for the police. The 'B' Section won by 99 to the police 83; Fred with 56, not out. Gladys meets Bill at the cricket match and then Bill and Fred return to her home to see her aunt and uncle. Hungary and Slovakia declare war on the Soviet Union. Finland enters the war against Russia.

Friday, 27th June 1941 – Bill is on *"cookhouse. Pretty well fed up with this job and with this lousy war. Wish we could get some action, maybe Jerry would know he's been in a fight then."* Stalin accepts Churchill's offer of an alliance to fight Hitler.

Saturday, 28th June 1941 – Bill is still in the *"cookhouse. War still dragging on, this ought to be called the Bore War. Let's hope U.S.S.R. does not know the meaning of strategic withdrawal."* Despite his pessimistic view on the war Bill is pleased to confirm his wedding date has been altered again, but for the better: Saturday, 6th September, two weeks earlier than last suggested. However, Bill still wishes it is two months earlier as Gladys is *"the only fine and lovely thing in this lousy war."*

Sunday, 29th June 1941 – Bill takes Gladys to see his parents and sister, Ivy. He is pleased to see them all again, but more pleased to know how Gladys gets on so well with his family.

Monday, 30th June 1941 – Bill has an interview regarding his marriage and arranges to see his commanding officer. All night he is on cookhouse duty where he writes a letter to *"my own Gladys. Love her so very much that one day away from her is almost unbearable."*

Tuesday, 1st July 1941 – With only 9½ weeks before the wedding, Bill thinks *"it is almost too good to be true."*

Wednesday, 2nd July 1941 – Bill and Fred meet Gladys and all three go to the Rembrandt cinema to see 'Monkey Business', a comedy, and 'Boom Town', an adventure film. Bill is pleased Fred agrees to be his best man at his wedding. *"Guess I'm a pretty lucky guy having a girl like Gladys and a mate like Fred."*

Thursday, 3rd July 1941 – Bill has an interview with his commanding officer. His wedding for Saturday, 6th September is approved and Bill is *"glad when the day arrives. I'm just living for that now."* Bill is on cookhouse duty that night.

Friday, 4th July 1941 – When Bill takes Gladys to the Drill Inn pub the pub has sold out of beer. *"What a war"* is Bill's unimpressed opinion *"spit and polish, paint and white-wash, scrubbing and sweeping, dusting and brushing seems to be the victory aim of our mob. No wonder we are called toy soldiers. One day we may fight, then – God help us."*

Saturday, 5th July 1941 – Bill is on cookhouse duty all day then calls to see Gladys in the evening. He plays cards with George and Syd and *"it is just heaven being with my Gladys, love her so much."*

Sunday, 6th July 1941 – Bill and Fred meet Gladys, Bill's parents and sister, Ivy. Gladys is upset over something and Bill has a lousy day wishing he knew why. His mother and Ivy stay with Bill, but his father returns home.

Monday, 7th July 1941 – Bill, Gladys, his parents, Gladys' mother and both sisters, Ivy and Eileen, travel to Canning Town, London, to buy the wedding dress, the bridesmaid dresses and shoes. With most details now settled, all is back to being perfect for Bill and *"what a change from yesterday, everything perfect."*

Tuesday, 8th July 1941 – When he returns to his barracks Bill has to take charge of cookhouse duty. He leaves his ring behind and when he returns for it, the ring is gone. Bill feels lost without it on his finger and wishes he could find the *"swine who's got it."*

Wednesday, 9th July 1941 – Bill has been sent help in the cookhouse. There is still no sign of his ring and is *"all at sea without it. It means an awful lot to me."*

Thursday, 10th July 1941 – Bill finishes writing out the wedding invitation cards, only eight weeks before his wedding.

Friday, 11th July 1941 – Gladys is leaving for Romford, Essex, so Bill writes her a letter as he is already missing her. Fred tells Bill he thinks he knows who has his ring.

Saturday, 12th July 1941 – While his boss is on leave Bill is in charge of the cookhouse. To his delight, Fred finds and returns Bill's ring to him and he *"felt pleased as hell."* Bill takes Fred to the Organ Inn pub. Great Britain and Russia form a military alliance against Germany.

Sunday, 13th July 1941 – Bill is on cookhouse duty followed by church parade. With a 24 hour pass Bill meets Gladys' parents and Aunt Elsie in the Drill Inn pub. When they return home Gladys is waiting having returned from her visit to friends at Romford, Essex.

Monday, 14th July 1941 – Bill goes to Epsom, Surrey, to enquire about wedding photos. When he sees Gladys later they have *"a little quarrel. Feeling fed up to the teeth."* However, they *"made up again, so everything was ok."*

Tuesday, 15th July 1941 – Bill receives a letter from Gladys and his mother. Their banns are to be called at Harlesden Church, a London Borough of Brent.

Wednesday, 16th July 1941 – Bill reports sick and is sent to Wandsworth Barracks, London, to see the medical officer. In the evening Bill and Gladys see 'Here We Go Again', a comedy, and 'Four Mothers', a drama/romance film, at the Granada cinema.

Thursday, 17th July 1941 – Bill and Gladys attend St. Phillips Church, North Cheam, Surrey, to arrange their wedding and to put up their wedding banns. Bill is counting down his seven weeks before their wedding with *"all details settled now. Only just over seven weeks to wait now."*

Friday, 18th July 1941 – Bill is told to pack his kit: he is being sent to Spennymoor Barracks for a gun fitting course, but later the course is postponed. Instead Bill and Gladys see 'Come Live with Me', a comedy, at the Rembrandt cinema.   It has been a mixed week *"from wonderfully happy to acute despondency.   Fed up and dreading next Friday.   God only knows how I will get on without my Gladys with me.   I hope it will not interfere with my wedding.   I am living for that now."*

Saturday, 19th July 1941 – Bill and Gladys travel to Sutton, Surrey, to buy their wedding rings.   This is Bill's *"happiest day of his life – so far."*

Sunday, 20th July 1941 – Bill is on gate police duty all day; *"Just my luck to be on duty for my last Sunday here."*   Gladys waits with Bill until he is off duty when they return home to see her aunt and uncle and also join Gladys' parents.

Monday, 21st July 1941 – After an easy day Bill calls for Gladys in the evening with *"only a few more days left with her now, so must make the best of them."*

Tuesday, 22nd July 1941 – After fatigues duty in the morning and gate police duty in the afternoon Bill collects the bridesmaid dresses and visits his parents.

Wednesday, 23rd July 1941 – Bill meets Gladys from work to see 'Kitty Foyle', a drama, at the Capital cinema then they join Gladys' parents and Elsie at the Drill Inn pub.   Bill has a *"frank talk with Gladys afterwards"* that *"eases my mind a lot."*

Thursday, 24th July 1941 – Bill is out on detail duty with Fred on his lorry and *"it was a lovely day with plenty of fun."*   Florrie [Fred's fiancée] arrives for Fred and with Bill they meet Gladys.   Bill is worried that this may be the last time for six weeks he will be able to see Gladys and is *"feeling pretty rotten."*

Friday, 25th July 1941 – Bill packs his kit ready to attend Dulwich Barracks, London, for a kit inspection and he is given all his papers for the railway and will be leaving tomorrow from King's Cross Station.   Bill writes a letter to Gladys.

Saturday, 26th July 1941 – Bill leaves Dulwich Barracks and arrives at Spennymoor Barracks, County Durham.   *"What a journey and this place looks lousy."*   Bill writes to Gladys, but *"wish I was with her.   Seems as if I've left my life behind."*

Sunday, 27th July 1941 – Bill is on parade then inspection before having the rest of the day to himself. He walks around the town and sees a sadly appropriate titled 'My Love Came Back', a musical/comedy/drama. He then writes to Gladys. After ten weeks of peace German bombers attack London.

Monday, 28th July 1941 – Bill has an interview with his commanding officer who grants him three days leave for his wedding. Bill is still despondent and thinks about leaving the army and would decide his future in a day or two. He wishes he is with Gladys.

Tuesday, 29th July 1941 – Bill writes to Gladys and receives two letters from her. *"It's grand to hear from her and know she cares so much about me"* and *"even work was a lot more interesting today."*

Wednesday, 30th July 1941 – Bill writes to Gladys and June Alston, his foster sister, and receives a parcel from Gladys. *"Guess I am the luckiest guy in the world having such a wonderful girl. Not doing so bad at work, but would sooner be at Ewell and be able to see Gladys."*

Thursday, 31st July 1941 – Bill is *"feeling lousy"* as he has yet to receive any letters *"Miss her* [Gladys] *terribly, aim to get back as soon as I can."* He writes to Gladys then has supper in Cambridge.

Friday, 1st August 1941 – Bill feels better having received two letters from Gladys. *"Gee I never knew anyone could mean so much to me, I am crazy about her."*

Saturday, 2nd August 1941 – Bill writes to Gladys and receives another letter from her; *"She loves me to write every day."* Bill is *"fed up"* with being away from Gladys, but will stick it for her sake. Gladys wants Bill back though *"so nothing on earth will keep me here. Amor Vincit Omnia"* [Love Conquers All]. Bill sees the manager at the centre about returning and everything seems settled. That evening Bill sees 'Spare a Copper' a musical/comedy, at the Acadia cinema.

Sunday, 3rd August 1941 – Bill writes another letter to Gladys. *"Miss my Gladys more than ever, I can't stand this separation."*

Monday, 4th August 1941 – With nothing to do as it is pouring with rain Bill writes yet again to Gladys and receives a letter from her. *"This is all I have to wait for every day, a letter from Gladys telling me she loves me."*

Tuesday, 5th August 1941 – Bill receives three letters from Gladys. *"Boy I wish I was with her."* Bill sees 'Young People', a drama, at the Cambridge cinema.

Wednesday, 6th August 1941 – Bill writes to Gladys. *"One day I will wake up and find this war is just a horrible nightmare."*

Thursday, 7th August 1941 – Bill sees the liaison officer about returning to his unit and is informed he will be leaving tomorrow. Delighted, he attends a party at Cambridge knowing he will be seeing Gladys again soon, but is a little worried over not hearing from her.

Friday, 8th August 1941 – Bill is so keen to leave he is up at 5.30 am and reports to the drill hall to collect his tickets and two letters from Gladys. Bill catches the train from Spennymoor Station, County Durham, back to Surrey and goes straight to see Gladys. *"Boy, it is wonderful to see her again."*

Saturday, 9th August 1941 – Bill returns to Dulwich Barracks, London, and *"even this place is heaven after Durham"* and immediately requests a pass for tomorrow. Great Britain and America meet to jointly issue the Atlantic Charter setting post-war goals for the world.

Sunday, 10th August 1941 – Bill attends a church parade and all leave is cancelled. However, he still manages to leave his barracks to see Gladys, although it is not for long.

Monday, 11th August 1941 – Bill has an interview with his commanding officer for his wedding leave which is granted.

Tuesday, 12th August 1941 – Bill is on gate police duty all day and on guard duty all night.

Wednesday, 13th August 1941 – Bill starts on fatigues duty then gets ready for his 24 hour pass. He hitchhikes home where he sees Gladys who is *"lovelier than before"* and has *"a perfect evening with a perfect girl."*

Thursday, 14th August 1941 – Bill meets Gladys from work and they see 'Major Barbara', and 'I'm Nobody's Sweetheart Now', two comedies, at the Odeon cinema. Bill then catches the train from Worcester Park Station, Surrey, to his new barracks at Knockholt, Kent.

Friday, 15th August 1941 – It pours with rain all day so Bill cannot do any outside work so instead tidies the huts. After a bathing parade in the evening he plays cards. German spy, Josef Jakobs, is executed by a military firing squad at the Tower of London. With a broken ankle he is forced to sit on a chair.

Saturday, 16th August 1941 – Bill starts on fatigues duty then on gate police duty until 7.00 pm. He is looking forward to seeing his mother tomorrow knowing Gladys will also be there and *"only three weeks to my wedding day."*

Sunday, 17th August 1941 – Bill is able to get a late pass in the afternoon so travels by train to Waterloo Station, London, where he meets Gladys and also her Uncle Jack and Aunt Daisy. Great Britain and Russia protest to Iran about their large number of German 'tourists'.

Monday, 18th August 1941 – Bill is on fatigues duty all day the *"weather lousy"* and being *"fed up with everything"* especially as he has not received any letters since he has been stationed in Knockholt, Kent.

Tuesday, 19th August 1941 – Bill is on bathing parade staying in Sevenoaks, Kent. With others he sees 'The Trail of Mary Dugan', a drama, and 'Too Many Girls', a musical/comedy, at the Plaza cinema. A lorry picks them up later to return them all to their barracks at Knockholt,

Kent.

Wednesday, 20th August 1941 – Bill is on gate police duty with Fred and Bert Lord before seeing his medical officer at Chislehurst, Kent. Bill receives a letter from Gladys and *"in two weeks time I will be getting ready to go on my seven days. What a seven days it will be as well."*

Thursday, 21st August 1941 – Bill is on fatigues duty before he leaves at 5.30 pm to see Gladys. Also with her are his mother and sister, Ivy, which is *"a nice surprise to see them."* Bill takes them to the bus stop to see them off then he spends the rest of the evening with Gladys.

Friday, 22nd August 1941 – Bill meets Gladys from work and they see 'I Wanted Wings', a drama. *"Lovely to be with her* [Gladys], *wish I never had to leave her"*, but Bill has to return to his barracks at Knockholt, Kent.

Saturday, 23rd August 1941 – Bill is on fatigues, gate police and then on guard duty as they are short handed. He also volunteers to be on guard duty that night so he will be off duty tomorrow. It is only *"two weeks today and I will be married to the sweetest girl in the world."*

Sunday, 24th August 1941 – Bill is on fatigues duty then has a lift to see Gladys. *"To be with Gladys again is like being in heaven."* They see 'The Door with Seven Locks', a horror film, and 'The Spy in Black', a war thriller, at the Odeon cinema at Worcester Park. Bill then returns to his barracks at Knockholt, Kent.

Monday, 25th August 1941 – Bill is on fatigues duty *"feeling dead tired, can hardly keep my eyes open."* He writes a letter to his mother and receives a letter from June Alston, Bill's foster sister. He then has an early night.

Tuesday, 26th August 1941 – Bill has been in the army *"two years too long."* He is on fatigues duty and attends a mechanical transport lecture and then is on a bathing parade. The British and Russia invade Iran to secure the oil fields.

Wednesday, 27th August 1941 – Bill is on fatigues duty

then attends another lecture as there is *"not much to do down here. Life pretty boring, but soon be on a 24 hour with my Gladys. One day this war will be all over then I will be with Gladys for always."* Bill receives a letter from Gladys.

Thursday, 28th August 1941 – Bill is on gate police duty until 6.00 pm then on guard duty and it is raining again. *"Only one more week now then my seven days. Looking forward to that more than anything else in the world. Then Gladys will become my wife."*

Friday, 29th August 1941 – Bill has been on fatigues duty all day expecting to be on a 24 hour pass, but it is postponed until tomorrow as he has to attend hospital. Instead he sees 'Target for Tonight', a documentary, at Sevenoaks before returning to his barracks at Knockholt, Kent.

Saturday, 30th August 1941 – Bill attends Woolwich Hospital in the morning before he has his 24 hour pass. He meets Gladys and they visit his parents where he also sees his foster sister, June; *"Great to see her again after over a year."*

Sunday, 31st August 1941 – Bill and Gladys travel to Canning Town to see her parents, Lily, Laurie and Mrs. Kaufman. Lily is Gladys' friend and Laurie is her husband. Bill leaves Gladys at London Bridge Station to return by train to his barracks at Knockholt, Kent.

Monday, 1st September 1941 – Bill is on detail duty with Bert Lord with only short jobs. He writes a letter to Gladys, his *"last letter to my fiancée (I hope)."*

Tuesday, 2nd September 1941 – Bill is on gate police and guard duties with *"only two more days then my seven days. Four more days and I will be a married man. Looking forward to that more than anything else."*

Wednesday, 3rd September 1941 – Bill is on fatigues duty all morning then detail duty with Fred in the afternoon.

Thursday, 4th September 1941 – Bill is in the cookhouse all day before preparing for his seven day leave. First there is no pass and then the despatch rider has broken down so Bill is not able to leave his barracks until 7.30 pm not seeing

Gladys until 9.30 pm.

Friday, 5ᵗʰ September 1941 – Bill sees the vicar about the wedding service and helps to prepare the church. He meets Fred in the Stanley Arms pub then takes a taxi home afterwards. *"Hurry up tomorrow, then happiness at last."*

Saturday, 6ᵗʰ September 1941 – The wedding day finally arrives for Bill and Gladys. Bill is up at 8.00 am and he meets Fred, his best man. At St. Phillips Church, North Cheam, Surrey, Bill achieves his greatest ambition and he marries *"the sweetest girl in the world."* Gladys is given away by her father, George Elliston. Gladys wears a white lace gown with a lace veil, orange blossom head dress and white gloves and carries a bouquet of red carnations. The bridesmaids are Gladys' sister Eileen, Bill's sister Ivy and Bill's foster sister June Alston. They wear blue satin gowns and haloes of blue flowers with white gloves and all carry bouquets of pink carnations. Fred is Bill's best man. Organ music is played during the service and the hymns 'Love Divine All Loves Excelling' and 'Gracious Spirit Holy Ghost' are sung. The marriage is conducted by the Reverend F. Strong. The bridal pair leave the church to the strains of Mendelssohn's 'Wedding March'. Sixty guests attend the reception at 92 St. Clare Drive, Worcester Park, Surrey, the home of Gladys' Aunt Elsie and Uncle Syd Haycox, who Gladys has been living with for the past few months and the party continues all night and into the next day. Bill believes that *"everything was perfect and a really fine show. Party lasts all night and a grand time for all"* and to Bill his wedding day is *"the proudest, happiest day of my life."*

Sunday, 7ᵗʰ September 1941 – As paper is scarce, only two wedding photos are allowed. Bill and Gladys manage for a few more photos to be taken so they dress in their wedding outfits again to pose for extra photographic memories. Ivy and June oblige and also wear their bridesmaid dresses, but Eileen refuses.

Monday, 8th September 1941 – Bill and Gladys leave Worcester Park by train to start their honeymoon in Evercreech, Somerset, and stay at the Bell Inn pub. *"Gladys and I together alone at last."*

Tuesday, 9th September 1941 – Bill *"with my lovely wife"* spend one full day walking across the meadows.

Wednesday, 10th September 1941 – Returning to London Bill and Gladys spend the evening watching 'Me and My Girl' show at the Coliseum. Bill 'phones his squadron headquarters and is granted a one day extension to his leave.

Thursday, 11th September 1941 – Bill and Gladys visit his parents before they return to Worcester Park, Surrey.

Friday, 12th September 1941 – Bill's last day on leave and their last day on honeymoon. Bill and Gladys open a joint savings bank account to save for their own home. They also see 'A Woman's Face', a thriller, at the Rembrandt cinema. *"What a difference a year can make. A year ago today I was 21, since then I have met my Gladys, become engaged and got married all before I was 22."*

Saturday, 13th September 1941 – A week after their wedding is Bill's 22nd birthday. He receives *"a wonderful card from her"* [Gladys]. On his first day back Bill is on gate police duty all day and guard duty all night. From his 900 Anti Aircraft Company, c/o the General Post Office at Halstead near Sevenoaks, Kent, Bill writes to Gladys, now his wife. Gladys is 19 years and 4 months old.

This letter Bill gives Gladys a full description of their wedding and his thoughts of the future now they are married.

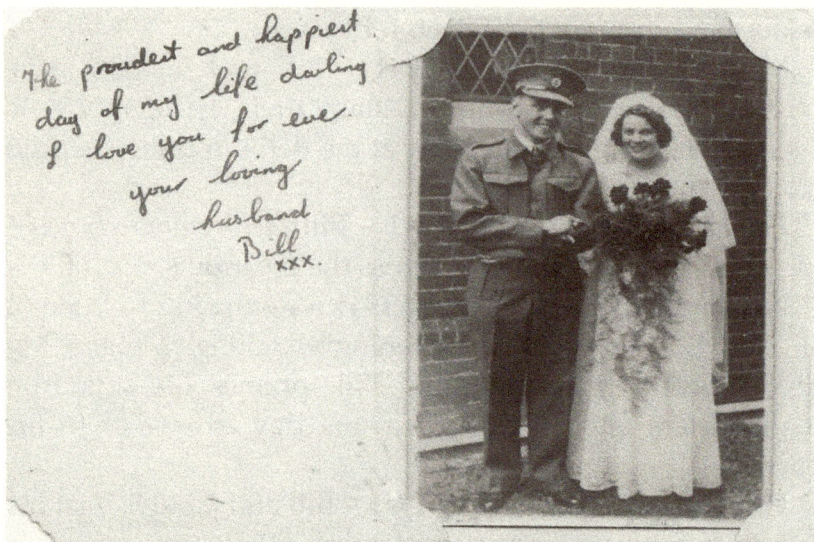

The proudest and happiest day of my life darling I love you for eve. your loving husband Bill xxx.

(Above) Bill's 'proudest and happiest day of my life' – his wedding to Gladys at St. Phillips Church, North Cheam, Surrey on Saturday, 6th September 1941

(Below left-right) William (Bill's father), Matilda (Bill's mother, Tilly), Ivy (Bill's sister), Fred Stagg (best man}, June Alston (Bill's foster sister), Bill, Gladys, George (Gladys' father), Eileen (Gladys' sister), Syd Haycox (Gladys' uncle), Hilda (Gladys' mother), Ellen Gilby (Gladys' grandmother & Hilda's mother) & George Jnr. 'Sonny' (Gladys' brother)

(Above) Bill & Gladys on Sunday, 7th September
1941 for extra wedding photos

(Below) with Ivy & June (also behind are Hilda & Elsie Haycox)
in the back garden of 92 St. Clare Drive

Driver Powell T/69082.
900 A.A. Coy. R.A.S.C.
℅ G.P.O. HALSTEAD
N8 SEVENOAKS
KENT.

Saturday Sept 13. 1941.

My own darling beloved wife,

A week of perfect and sublime happiness has just ended, a week which I will never be able to forget. Darling words will never describe the ecstacy I experienced when you became my own, the greatest and most thrilling day of my life would be only a poor description of that wonderful day. My feelings have been pretty mixed up all this week, perhaps you could understand what I mean if I described to the best of my ability what my thoughts were from last Thursday until today.

Thursday evening (how much has happened since then, it still seems too good to be true) I was cleaned up and ready to leave barracks by two-o-clock. I was thinking mostly about how I could dodge everybody so that I would keep clean and ready to leave at half past four. In that I was very successful; but at four-o-clock

---

(Above) Bill's letter to Gladys written on Saturday, 13th September 1941

Mrs Gladys Powell
92 St. Clair Drive
Worcester Park
Surrey

Driver Powell T/69083
900 A.A. COY. R.A.S.C.
c/o G.P.O. Halstead
Nr. Sevenoaks
Kent

Saturday Sept 13. 1941

My own darling beloved wife,

A week of perfect and sublime happiness has just ended, a week which I will never be able to forget. Darling words will never describe the ecstasy I experienced when you became my own, the greatest and most thrilling day of my life would be only a poor description of that wonderful day. My feelings have been pretty mixed up all this week, perhaps you could understand what I mean if I described to the best of my ability what my thoughts were from last Thursday until today.

Thursday evening (how much has happened since then, it still seems too good to be true) I was cleaned up and ready to leave barracks by two o'clock. I was thinking mostly about how I could dodge everybody so that I would keep clean and ready to leave at half past four. In that I was very successful, but at four o'clock I went over to the section office and enquired if my pass was ready. The answer was, "It will be down by despatch rider at six o'clock tonight." That spoilt my plans and made me a little annoyed, but I thought I would still be able to get round to see you by eight. At five thirty our sergeant major came down to give us a lecture on 'bombs and how to use them'. The lecture was supposed to last an hour and a half. I was told I would have to attend. By now I was beginning to get a little anxious about my leave.

Anyhow, at the lecture I started to lay the law down and the sergeant major gave me permission to leave as soon as my pass arrived. The despatch rider came in about six-fifteen. I just picked up my haversack, etc. and flew into the office where I waited very impatiently while they undid the case containing all the papers from our company headquarters. All the papers, that is except the one I was interested in, my pass was not there. I was in a lovely mood then. No pass, no ration card and no cash and the sweetest girl in the world waiting for me to arrive home. I told them all what I thought of them, their ancestors and their descendants. Believe me I have never been so furious before. Then when they rang up and made enquiries about the pass they told me the C.H.Q. [7] knew nothing about it. Well, that just about put the tin hat on it all.

Well, at long last, after a lot of arguing and threatening, I was allowed to leave without my pass and very soon I was on my way to you, sweetheart. While waiting for the bus at Morden, though, I experienced the greatest feeling. It felt as if someone was squeezing my stomach and my mouth felt terribly dry, at last my leave had started the leave which I had been looking forward to for so long. It was a wonderful thought and everything seemed perfect. Then, when I at last arrived indoors and was able to take you in my arms and hold you close to me, I forgot everything except how beautiful you were, how much I loved you and that in less than two days you would become my wife.

Friday was very uneventful, just dragging slowly by as if determined to keep you single as long as possible. But, I was wonderfully happy, that is until I called for Fred, he was not there. It seemed as if something was trying to stop our marriage, obstacle after obstacle that had tried to hinder us, we had overcome, but now it was my wedding eve and I had no best man. I waited for what seemed hours then decided to phone up. He was out on a job and they had no idea when he would be back. The officer said he would see he was relieved as soon as possible and about half past ten Fred came home. It was a little before that, I believe, because we went straight round to get a drink and arrived in the pub just as time was called. (They don't shut until 10.30 pm in Battersea.)

Still, we managed to have one drink together then I returned with Fred, collected my kit and set off for home. Only to find I had missed the last bus and it looked like a nice long walk home, so I started walking but had only gone few yards when I saw a taxi and decided that I could, as it was a special occasion, afford a taxi fare home. It saved a long walk and got me in at a reasonable hour, but at eight shillings [£17.07p in 2013], well, I still don't know if it was worth it. On arrival indoors I was shown all the presents and then sat down and wrote an account of the wedding. An account which, as events were to prove, did nowhere near give justice to the beauty of loveliness of my bride. It was three a.m. before I finally got into bed.

I woke in the morning with great anxiety, was I late, what time was it, was the weather fine and would everything go as we wished? Time seemed to be flying by as I was getting ready. It seemed as if I would never have time to get to the church. I was thinking of phoning Fred and telling him to go on to the church and I would meet him there, but it was not necessary, by ten thirty I was all ready. I had told Fred I would call for him at half past twelve and it would only take about three quarters of an hour to get to his home. I was left with over an hour to spare, how that hour dragged, it seemed longer than the rest of the day. I tried to read the paper, but although I seemed to have been reading for hours, the clock registered only a few minutes. I walked into the front room to check the clock, both clocks agreed, but still I was not satisfied. I put the wireless on and waited to get the time from that. Music While You Work [8] was on, so I knew I still had a long while to wait. I then walked up to the main road to get some cigarettes, but almost ran back as I was certain I had been out for at least an hour, but no, it was still only about quarter past eleven. I spent the rest of the time walking from one room into the other looking at clocks then after what seemed years, it was time for me to leave. I said goodbye to everyone, including my aunts and uncles who had come round for Mum and then set out to meet Fred.

It was an uneventful journey and Fred was waiting at the bus stop for me when I arrived. We called in his sisters and I dropped my kit then set out for the local. Fred's brother-in-law met us in there and, despite a lot of chaffing, I only had one drink and as I was sipping that. I was still casting anxious eyes at the clock. I was certain we had left it too late. In the end I got up, called to Fred and walked out. Fred followed, we then collected our kit again and I was then on the last stage of my journey to the altar.

Once we were on the tube I realized we were very early and for the first time that day I relaxed. My fear and anxiety had left, I know I would have plenty of time and I had nothing else to worry about. I was not a bit scared of the ceremony itself, I had been looking forward to it so long. I had pictured it all in my mind's eye time and time again. It was to be the greatest day of my life, I had been living for it and now it was here. I certainly had nothing to be scared about, I was far too wonderfully happy. The sweetest, loveliest, most adorable girl in the world, the person I loved more than anything or anybody else, was about to become my wife.   Darling, I was longing for the ceremony to begin, I was dying to hear you say "I will" and to know that all my wildest dreams were fulfilled and that at last we belonged to each other.

I arrived at the church to find Mr. and Mrs. Short [family friends] already there.   They were under the impression that the ceremony was at half past two.   After greeting them, Fred and I sat down in our respective seats waiting for everybody to arrive.   I could hardly keep a straight face as Fred was wisecracking all the time.   Slowly people began to trickle in and it seemed to be terribly slowly. Most of them I shook hands with and greeted.   A few slid into the back seats, so I left them.   At last everybody was there, everybody that is except the one person I was waiting for.   Again ages seem to have passed before I heard the strains of 'Here Comes the Bride' and I knew that my wife-to-be had arrived.   I stole a quick glance out of the corner of my eye, but all I could see was a lot of blue and I caught a faint glimpse of something white.   I rose and walked to the altar, longing all the time to look behind me and see how lovely you were, darling.   But, somehow I managed to continue to look in front of me.   How I managed that, I will never know myself, so I cannot tell you.

When you reached my side I could contain myself no longer, I just had to see you, from then onwards it was all I could do to look at the clergy occasionally.   As far as I was concerned, there were just us two present in the church.   I had eyes for no one else but you, my love.   I knew you were really beautiful, I have told you so many times, but even I was not prepared for that heavenly vision of loveliness that stood by my side, your face alight with a breathtaking radiance and your eyes shining like stars, reflecting the love you held for me.   Darling, I was spellbound that God could create a girl so lovely and that she should fall in love with me.   I had the hardest task I have ever experienced then, sweetheart, it was all I could do to stop myself throwing my arms around you, crushing you close to my bosom and then smothering you with kisses. I had to exercise every ounce of self control I ever had to fight against it and it was all I could do to manage it. Then he [the vicar] started to knitter and natter about confetti and other such junk, that's why I snapped out about getting on with his job. I knew that if he kept me there much longer I would have to kiss you. I would be able to control myself no longer. You yourself can see by the photos that you were wonderfully beautiful, but no camera could ever recapture that angelic loveliness that was radiating from you, sweetheart. I have never before in my life set eyes on anything so perfectly lovely. As you stood there beside me I felt and knew that never again would I experience such ecstasy and happiness. We belonged to each other for always, now nothing could or would ever come between us, we were man and wife.

As I escorted you from the church I felt as if the world was indeed a grand place and that I was the luckiest man alive to have such a wonderful girl for a wife. I was proud as well, proud of you, darling. How lovely you were, how charming and how beautiful you looked and as we posed for the photographs my pride excelled itself. I was showing the world what a beautiful wife I had just married. Darling, words could never tell how happy I was and how lovely you looked, it was magnificent and marvellous and I will never be able to forget it, my love. I knew then that our happiness together was only just beginning, that we had a lifetime before us and I knew you loved me almost as much as I loved you. I do love you, darling, but I will never be able to tell you how much, the English language was never meant to express the love I hold for you, there are no words to describe it. It is so all embracing and overwhelming that nothing else in life matters to me, my world consists of just us two, nobody else matters. I just live to be with you and to hold you close to me pressing my lips against yours and experiencing the ecstasy of your kiss. The whole world means nothing to me, darling. I just love and need you beyond all other things in life. I know that we will be happy, sweetheart. All I hope is that we will also be lucky. I want to give you the life you deserve.

Believe me, darling, I will do my best to achieve that, all I need is a little luck to get a start, then I can handle the rest. The rest of the day, darling, was pretty uneventful. We were together and I was too happy to think clearly and you know what was done as you were with me all the time. All I am trying to tell you here are the conflicting thoughts and emotions I explained this week.

Of Sunday also I am afraid I can say very little, except that on Sunday night I laid awake in bed for hours thinking and worrying about what you told me. Then and then only was the first time I was scared not for myself, my dearest, but about you. I love you far too much to risk anything happening to you, my love and I would not hurt you for anything if I can possibly avoid it. My whole life is centred on you, darling. If you are hurt, I also feel the pain. If you are happy and contented, I experience happiness myself. So, my sweet, please rest assured that I will do all in my power to protect you always. Remember, darling, you are my life. I love you and need you and will never do anything likely to cause you suffering or unhappiness.

The rest of the week, my loved one, was just deliriously happy for me. I have experienced happiness that I never before knew possible, except for once or twice when I remembered that soon I would be back at barracks and our wedding week just a beautiful memory. I experienced that more than ever on Friday, but I suppose it was only very natural that I would be a little downcast when it got to our last few hours together. Let us look forward, dearest, to the time when we will be together always, no goodbyes and a home of our own to share. It will happen, my precious and let's hope it will not take too long to come about. If and when this war does eventually end, we will be able to live together, enjoy life together and be happy together forever, my sweet.

How I wish it was all over now, that sanity returns to this murder crazy world which goes under the guise of so called civilization. If only the people woke up for a few minutes, just long enough to see where our pro-fascist leaders are taking us, then perhaps they would realize that our only hope for a world of peace is to support the heroic Red Army in its fight against fascist reaction and tyranny. To see that the people of the Soviet Union have all the assistance that such brave people deserve and that Socialism emerges triumphant over capitalist and fascist hierarchy and then the world will be really fit for heroes to live in.

Well, my little wife, I hope to have seen you again before you have this letter. I am hoping to be able to see you tomorrow afternoon. I am longing to be with you, my love, to tell you how much I miss you and need you, darling. I will be home on my next seven days on December the twenty third, not bad, eh! Christmas together, it is great news and I am nearly as excited as if it were only a few days away. The new seven days leave rota has just been published, you should have seen us all clamouring round the notice board trying to see when we all go.

Fred has left here now and I saw our section officer this morning to see if I could leave as well, but I want to go to Ewell, perhaps you may know why. Fred is now at Woolwich and the two Harrys are parted. It is a pretty lousy trick. They sent Harry Hamilton back here and sent Fred to Woolwich, thus they broke up Fred and myself and the terrible twins. Besides, I am fed up with this place and want to get back near you again, darling. I hope the officer does not try to stop me going, he may do but he will regret it if he does.

How have you enjoyed today, darling. I know you have missed me, but we will soon be together again, one day for good. Have you seen about those photos and what are you going to do about the cake? I am longing to hear from you, my love, as I have not yet had a letter from my wife. Write soon, darling and don't forget to tell me you love me.

I saw about the allowance this morning and that has gone through alright. God only knows when you will draw it, but it will come eventually.

Well, darling, I have not got much more to say now, but I will write again tomorrow if I can't get down seeing you. I love you, my sweetheart and miss you very much. I am longing to see you and hear from you, my darling, so until then I will say goodbye, my love. Give my love to all at home and keep on loving me always, dear and keep telling me you love me.

Your loving husband,

Bill

xxx

I LOVE YOU ALWAYS DARLING
AU REVOIR DEAR
I AM YOURS ALONE

xxxxxxxxx

P.S.
I love you now and forever, you are the best wife any man ever had. I'm crazy about you, darling.

S.W.A.L.K.

84

[7] C.H.Q. – Company Headquarters. Company and squadron both refer to sub-divisions of regiments: generally there are five companies to an infantry regiment or five squadrons to a tank regiment, transport regiment, cavalry regiment, etc.

[8] Music While You Work is a BBC daytime radio programme of continuous live popular music which started in June 1940 aimed to help workers become more productive.

(Above left) Bill, aged 22, (Above right) Gladys, aged 19, September 1941

September 1941 – May 1942

After his 22nd birthday, wedding and honeymoon, Bill is back on army duty and is posted to Knockholt Barracks, Kent. He is missing Gladys desperately, writing to her almost daily.

Sunday, 14th September 1941 – Bill is on fatigues duty and church parade before returning home to *"see my wife again. It's lovely to be with her, I believe I love her more than ever before."*

Monday, 15th September 1941 – Bill is on fatigues and detail duties. He sees his section officer regarding a transfer to Ewell Barracks, Surrey, and then takes over lorry no.241539, his first lorry since 12th February 1941.

Tuesday, 16th September 1941 – Bill is on detail duty in his lorry to Canning Town and visits Aunt Flo [Florence, Gladys' aunt, her mother's older sister]. Bill writes to Gladys, but *"wish I were with her. One day we will be together always."*

Wednesday, 17th September 1941 – Bill is on gate police duty with Fred and Ted Grant having a *"usual sort of day, nothing to do and all day to do it in. Fed up and hoping to see Gladys soon."*

Thursday, 18th September 1941 – Bill is on detail duty in his lorry all day. He visits friends to tell them he is now a married man.

Friday, 19th September 1941 – Bill is on fatigue duty at the company headquarters heaving coal all day. Fred drops him off to see Gladys and he later returns by train to Knockholt Barracks, Kent.

Saturday, 20th September 1941 – Bill is on fatigue duty at Woodmansterne, Surrey, heaving coal again and then

living quarters for a soldier, for the general's inspection then on his half day leave visits Gladys. *"All I live for now is to be with my wife for a few hours. One day I won't have to leave her."*

Friday, 10th October 1941 – Bill is taking supplies to Eltham and Kidbrooke, London, and is *"fed up with this job, taken hours to find the places."* To make matters worse he is fined for speeding at 41 mph; *"Suppose I will be hard up soon now."*

Saturday, 11th October 1941 – Bill takes supplies to Bromley, Kent, packs his kit for Halstead Barracks, Essex, and then takes Gladys to a dance before he has to return to his squadron headquarters at 12.30 am.

Sunday, 12th October 1941 – Bill is on fatigues duty all morning and then on guard duty all night. He misses Gladys, but *"must not grumble as I have seen her almost every Sunday, but would prefer every day."*

Monday, 13th October 1941 – Bill is on detail duty driving all around the country and is sent to the wrong place. When he does get to the proper destination they do not want him anymore.

Tuesday, 14th October 1941 – Bill is on fatigues and maintenance duty all day *"hiding myself."*

Wednesday, 15th October 1941 – After a detail duty at Kidbrooke, London, Bill spends the day sitting around a fire, but *"still, it's all part of the war effort."* Bill calls in at Wrotham Barracks, Kent, on his way back to his squadron headquarters and is told he is on a 24 hour pass that has been brought forward a day, so he returns home to Gladys at 11.30 pm.

Thursday, 16th October 1941 – Bill meets Gladys from work then in the evening they see 'One Night in Lisbon' and 'The Leather Pushers', two comedies, at the Odeon cinema.

Friday, 17th October 1941 – Returning to gate police duty Bill is *"bored stiff, what an exciting war."*

Saturday, 18th October 1941 – Bill is on cookhouse and

detail duty all day.

Sunday, 19th October 1941 – Bill is on detail duty with nothing to do except bring a fatigue party back in the evening. He sees his mother at home at Willesden, London, and then returns home to see Gladys.

Monday, 20th October 1941 – Bill is on fatigues and maintenance duty then has a lecture and is *"fed up with this lousy war, what a day it will be when it is all over."*

Tuesday, 21st October 1941 – Bill and Gladys move to their new home: 84a London Road, North Cheam, Surrey; a flat above a parade of shops and near to Gladys' Aunt Elsie and Uncle Syd. Bill calls in to see Gladys at their new home. Bill is now mustered as a T.T. (Technical Training) motor mechanic, grade 3. Mustered is to assemble for inspection, service, etc., as troops or forces.

Wednesday, 22nd October 1941 – Bill has a detail duty run to Mill Hill, London, and Gravesend, Kent, and also sees his mother after *"not a bad day's work."*

Thursday, 23rd October 1941 – Bill is on detail duty with enough *"general running about, not a lot to do, boring job."* The *"lights on the lorry were pretty bad, could hardly see a thing."* He calls in to see Gladys at their new home.

Friday, 24th October 1941 – Bill is on detail duty but manages to get the lights on his lorry working.

Saturday, 25th October 1941 – Bill is on gate police duty until 4.30 pm then has a 24 hour pass so returns to Gladys at their home. Germany attacks Moscow.

Sunday, 26th October 1941 – Bill and Gladys see 'Hit Parade of 1941', a musical/comedy, at the Granada cinema before Bill returns to his squadron headquarters.

Monday, 27th October 1941 – Bill is on detail duty to Dulwich, London, *"waiting about and getting frozen stiff."*

Tuesday, 28th October 1941 – Bill has *"another cushy run"* on detail duty before he sees his mother.

Wednesday, 29th October 1941 – Bill has a detail duty run

to White City, London, so he visits his mother at Willesden, London.

Thursday, 30th October 1941 – Bill is on fatigues duty having a *"nice job for a change. Enough to do to keep me busy without having to tear around."*

Friday, 31st October 1941 – Bill is on fatigues duty. He hopes to return home in the evening, but is only able to call in for one hour.

Saturday, 1st November 1941 – Bill is on fatigues and maintenance duty all day. Bill has an evening pass so he is able to see Gladys and also her Aunt Flo, Maud, Ron and Lil who were all part of Gladys' family.

Sunday, 2nd November 1941 – Bill is on detail duty and able to call home to see his parents and he takes them to see their friend, Mrs. Prince, before he returns home briefly to see Gladys.

Monday, 3rd November 1941 – Bill is on detail duty doing *"nothing again – except fire watching round the office fire. What a day and thousands dying in Russia."*

Tuesday, 4th November 1941 – Bill repairs a tail light in the workshop. He calls home and then returns to his squadron headquarters for a bathing parade and is then on guard duty all night.

Wednesday, 5th November 1941 – Bill is on detail duty to Dulwich, London, waiting all day to return to his squadron headquarters.

Thursday, 6th November 1941 – Bill is on detail duty *"running up and down Blackheath Common getting buckets of water – just about fed up."*

Friday, 7th November 1941 – Bill has a section inspection. Although he hoped to return home, instead has to drive a bathing parade to Sevenoaks, Kent.

Saturday, 8th November 1941 – Bill is on fatigues and maintenance duty and then on guard duty at night where it is *"pretty cold."*

Sunday, 9th November 1941 – Bill takes a detail convoy to

Paddington, London, before having an afternoon pass home to Gladys.

Monday, 10th November 1941 – Bill is on detail duty, another job doing nothing wondering *"why worry, we hope we will muddle through to victory. If we do it will be thanks to the U.S.S.R. not us."*

Tuesday, 11th November 1941 – Bill is on detail duty to Chelmsford, Essex; it is pouring with rain all day. Bill has a 24 hour pass so he leaves to return home to Gladys by train.

Wednesday, 12th November 1941 – Bill, Gladys, her mother, and sister Eileen, go to the Queen Victoria for the Whatcliffe Works dance in the evening. Bill has to leave for his squadron headquarters at 10.30 pm, arriving at 1.00 am.

Thursday, 13th November 1941 – Bill drives a staff car to the company headquarters getting a puncture on the way. He is then sent to the orderly room on charge for exceeding the speed limit and is fined two days pay and given guard duty with Fred and Dicky Cowell at his squadron headquarters.

Friday, 14th November 1941 – Not having a lot of luck with vehicles, the lights pack up on his lorry and Bill has difficulty returning the lorry to his squadron headquarters.

Saturday, 15th November 1941 – Bill is part of the fatigue party at the company headquarters for a week. In the afternoon Bill meets Gladys at Epsom, Surrey, and they see 'Underground', a war film, at the Capital cinema before he rides back to the company headquarters on Gladys' bike.

Sunday, 16th November 1941 – Bill is on fatigues duty all morning and on guard duty all night. It is *"not quite as easy as 'B' section, but not too bad"* and Bill is *"looking forward to seeing Gladys very often now."*

Monday, 17th November 1941 – Bill is on fatigues duty until 4.30 pm then cycles home to be with Gladys staying at home all night, returning to his barracks early in the

declares war on Finland.

Sunday, 7th December 1941 – Bill is on detail duty then he and Gladys visit his mother who is still looking unwell. Japan attacks the U.S. Fleet at Pearl Harbor to prevent them from interfering with any military action. In the two hour raid 18 warships, 188 aircraft and 2,403 servicemen are lost.

Monday, 8th December 1941 – Bill works on his barracks boiler then he is on detail duty to Morden Barracks, in Surrey. Bill and Gladys later see 'Sunny', a musical, and 'Men against the Sky', a drama, at the Rembrandt cinema. Today Great Britain, America, Canada, New Zealand and the Netherlands declare war on Japan. Japan declares war on Great Britain and America and the Japanese troops invade Malaya, Thailand and the Bataan Island in the Philippines.

Tuesday, 9th December 1941 – Bill is on gate police duty until 6.00 pm then stays at his barracks all evening. Australia and China declares war on Japan.

Wednesday, 10th December 1941 – Bill is on detail duty all day to Shoeburyness, Essex. The battleship H.M.S. Prince of Wales and the battle cruiser H.M.S. Repulse are sunk by the Japanese navy.

Thursday, 11th December 1941 – It is Bill's first day of his seven day leave. He meets Gladys from work and they see 'The Wagons Roll at Night', a drama, at the Capital cinema. Germany and Italy declares war on America: America in return declares war on Germany and Italy.

Friday, 12th December 1941 – Bill meets Gladys from work and they see 'Skylark', a drama, at the Odeon cinema. Romania and Bulgaria declare war on Great Britain and America: Great Britain and America in return declare war on Romania and Bulgaria.

Saturday, 13th December 1941 – Bill, Gladys, and her sister Eileen, travel to Tottenham Court Road. They walk around the West End then see Sydney Howard, Arthur

Riscoe, Vera Pearce and Richard Hearne in 'Thanks to Love, Fun and Games' show. Hungary declares war on Great Britain and America: Great Britain and America in return declares war on Hungary.

Sunday, 14th December 1941 – Bill and Gladys travel by train to Romford, Essex, to spend the day with Mr. and Mrs. Kaufman and their daughter, Doreen, sister of Gladys' best friend, Lily.

Monday, 15th December 1941 – Bill, Gladys and Eileen travel by tube to Leicester Square to see 'Get a Load of This' show starring Vic Oliver and Cecilia Lipton at the London Hippodrome.

Tuesday, 16th December 1941 – Gladys returns to work leaving Bill at home. *"Miss her* [Gladys] *an awful lot. Fed up nothing to do and all day to do it in."* That evening Bill and Gladys see 'Stars of Radio' show starring Evelyn Dall, Max Bacon and Jack Cooper. Rommel orders a withdrawal all the way to El Agheila, Libya, where he began in March 1941. He awaits reinforcements of men and tanks.

Wednesday, 17th December 1941 – Bill travels to Sutton, Surrey, to enquire about Gladys' income tax assessment, with nothing to pay.

Thursday, 18th December 1941 – Bill and his mother see 'Give Us Wings', a comedy, and 'The Case of the Black Cat', a crime film, at the Rembrandt cinema. Bill is *"a little fed up not having Gladys with me, still someone's got to win the war."*

Friday, 19th December 1941 – Gladys has the day off work so Bill takes her to Oxford Circus and the London Palladium to see 'Gangway' show with Ben Lyon, Bebe Daniels and Tommy Trinder.

Saturday, 20th December 1941 – Bill is up at 5.30 am to return to his squadron headquarters for gate police duty which is to become his permanent job from next Monday. He returns home to see Gladys, but does not stay the night.

Sunday, 21st December 1941 – Bill is on fatigues duty

before seeing Gladys at 2.00 pm when they visit his mother at Willesden, London. Bill notices she still looks unwell, but not as bad as the last time he saw her. He and Gladys have a little quarrel, but all turns out okay.

Monday, 22nd December 1941 – Bill is on gate police duty at his barracks at 6.00 am to *"a monotonous job and pretty chilly, but able to keep seeing Gladys every night, so it's well worth it."*

Tuesday, 23rd December 1941 – Bill is on gate police duty and it is *"pretty cold still, but considering the time of the year, we mustn't grumble."* Bill should have attended a lecture at the company headquarters, but manages to avoid attending and instead spends the evening with Gladys.

Wednesday, 24th December 1941 – Bill spends Christmas Eve on gate police duty at 8.00 am and it *"doesn't seem a bit like Xmas Eve, everything is dead, but one day the good old days will return – we hope."*

Thursday, 25th December 1941 – Bill is on gate police duty at 6.00 am until 12.00 noon. He has dinner at the company headquarters then home at 2.00 pm. Christmas is *"not a bad day, considering there's a war on."* Hong Kong surrenders to Japan. Allied forces retake Benghazi, Libya.

Friday, 26th December 1941 – Bill is still able to stay with Gladys at night and be on gate police duty at 8.00 am. They later see 'Nothing but the Truth', a comedy, at the Worcester Park Odeon cinema.

Saturday, 27th December 1941 – Bill is on gate police duty at 6.00 am. Bill remembers he and Gladys were engaged a year ago today.

Sunday, 28th December 1941 – Bill is on gate police duty from 8.00 am until 6.30 pm then he returns home to Gladys and *"only wish this war kept like this, able to see Gladys every evening and stay every night."*

Monday, 29th December 1941 – Bill is on gate police duty at 6.00 am and *"it is freezing cold, about the coldest day this winter so far."*

Tuesday, 30ᵗʰ December 1941 – Bill is on gate police duty at 8.00 am with it *not quite as cold as yesterday."* Bill writes to his mother and receives a letter from Fred to say he is getting married this Saturday. Bill should have attended a lecture, but he is able to avoid it and instead he returns home to Gladys again.

Wednesday, 31ˢᵗ December 1941 – New Year's Eve and Bill is on gate police duty at 6.00 am. He later meets Gladys from work to see 'West Point Widow', a comedy, and 'Aloma of the South Seas', an adventure film, at the Odeon cinema.

Bill and Gladys see 1942 in at the Charter Inn pub *"and so a wonderful year ends."* To Bill 1941 was *"the finest year I have ever had. Even better than last year. I only hope everything keeps the way they are now. Being able to see Gladys every night is like being in heaven, only better."*

Thursday, 1ˢᵗ January 1942 – With the arrival of 1942 *"another year of the war has started. I hope this one will be the last."* Gladys' Aunt Flo and Uncle Arthur visit with Bill's mother. Together they insure Gladys' engagement ring at Sutton, Surrey. Bill and Gladys spend New Year's Day at home all evening.

Friday, 2ⁿᵈ January 1942 – Bill is back on gate police duty. He returns home to Gladys and stays with her the night.

Saturday, 3ʳᵈ January 1942 – Bill is caught arriving at his barracks in the morning. He is sent to the orderly room and charged with 'Absent Without Leave', which is adjourned until the following Monday. Despite this, Bill and Gladys spend the evening at his barracks dance. With his A.W.O.L. charge earlier Bill did not want to risk sleeping at home again so he sleeps at his barracks that night for the first time in seven weeks, which he thinks strange. Fred marries Florrie today and Bill is disappointed not to have been able to attend their wedding and hopes all went well for his best friend.

Sunday, 4ᵗʰ January 1942 – Bill is on fatigues duty all

morning. He planned to visit his parents and sister, but could not now leave his barracks. Instead Gladys and her parents visit Bill's parents. Bill is *"disappointed, but it can't be helped."*

Monday, 5th January 1942 – Bill reports to Woodmansterne Orderly Room, Surrey. He has been charged for failing to book out (classed as 'Absent Without Leave') from 2nd-3rd January 1942. Bill is forfeited three days pay and one day's pay 'Under Royal Warrant'. However, Bill is still granted an evening pass so returns home to Gladys, who is surprised to see him.

Tuesday, 6th January 1942 – Bill is on gate police duty at 8.00 am, the weather *"seems as if winter has really started, freezing cold and a strong wind."* Despite the risk, Bill still slips home to see Gladys for an hour and *"only wish I could stay."*

Wednesday, 7th January 1942 – Bill is on gate police duty at 6.00 am, the weather *"still cold, but it's a lot colder in Russia."* Bill attends a lecture in the evening, but still manages to get a pass so meets Gladys to see 'South American George', a comedy, and 'The Phantom Submarine', a war film, at the Granada cinema.

Thursday, 8th January 1942 – Bill is on gate police duty at 8.00 am then has an interview for a permanent pass with the S.O. S.O. initials are classic military which could have multiple meanings. This one could represent 'Staff Officer', normally someone who works in a brigade or divisional Headquarter; 'Station Office', the office responsible for a geographical location with lodger units (i.e.: Donnington Station); or 'Senior Officer'. Permission is granted for Bill to have a coke brazier, a container used for an open fire, for the gate police duty so it *"makes things a lot better."* Again Bill manages to return home to Gladys for a couple of hours.

Friday, 9th January 1942 – Bill is on gate police duty at

6.00 am, the weather *"still cold but soon had fire going."* Bill receives a letter from Fred saying everything went well for him on Saturday [Fred's wedding to Florrie]. Bill has a pass so returns home in the evening.

Saturday, 10th January 1942 – Bill is on gate police duty at 8.00 am . He is feeling *"just about browned off, this is the world's most boring war."* He slips out again at 7.00 pm to be home with Gladys and did not like to have to return to his barracks at night.

Sunday, 11th January 1942 – Bill is on gate police duty at 6.00 am, the weather *"still very cold."* He leaves at 4.30 pm to return home to see Gladys, his parents and sister, Ivy. It is *"good to see them again. A very good and enjoyable day with all."*

Monday, 12th January 1942 – Bill is on gate police duty at 8.00 am. There are no passes tonight owing to a lecture at the company headquarters and Bill *"could not dodge it so I had to go."* However, he found it *"very interesting, but would far sooner be with Gladys. Miss her a lot and love her more."*

Tuesday, 13th January 1942 – Bill is on gate police duty at 6.00 am, the *"war still going strong. Russia continues to advance – and so do the Japs."* With an evening pass Bill takes Gladys to the Granada cinema to see 'Affectionally Yours', a comedy, and 'Adventure in Sahara', an action film.

Wednesday, 14th January 1942 – Bill is on gate police duty at 8.00 am. Leave is cancelled, but Bill still slips out in the evening to see Gladys. He is *"still madly in love with her."*

Thursday, 15th January 1942 – Bill is on gate police duty at 6.00 am. He is also told he is in a divisional boxing team to fight against 6AA division at Finchley. When he reports for the match he has been put down for the wrong weight so has to return to his squadron headquarters. He later visits Gladys.

Friday, 16th January 1942 – Bill is on gate police duty at 6.00 am then relieved at 2.00 pm to return to Finchley

Barracks, London, to register his correct weight. He has to box the following day despite having had no training. Bill returns home by tube and stays with Gladys.

Saturday, 17th January 1942 – Bill reports to Finchley Barracks, London, by tube and rests all afternoon before his boxing match. They lose their matches 2-3, with one rematch planned.

Sunday, 18th January 1942 – Bill is on gate police duty at 6.00 am. He is stiff all over and hardly able to move, the result of fighting without any training. He has a half day off so meets Gladys and stays at home the night.

Monday, 19th January 1942 – Bill is on gate police duty at 8.00 am. He is still feeling very stiff from his fight on Saturday, plus has a black eye, but still thinks it is worth it. In the afternoon Bill attends a lecture at the company headquarters on science in modern war.

Tuesday, 20th January 1942 – It is snowing hard and Bill is on gate police duty at 6.00 am. With an evening pass Bill meets Gladys to see 'Hi Gang!', a comedy, and 'Dressed to Kill', a crime film, at the Worcester Park Odeon cinema.

Wednesday, 21st January 1942 – Bill is on gate police duty at 8.00 am. There are still no 24 hour passes and Bill is *"fed up with this."* But Bill still manages to return home to see Gladys. Operation Crusader, the British 8th Army's initial plan to destroy the Axis armoured force before advancing its infantry in late 1941, forces Rommel to withdraw. Rommel receives reinforcements in men and tanks and today launches a surprise counter-attack. The outcome is the Battle of Gazala.

Thursday, 22nd January 1942 – Bill is on gate police duty at 6.00 am with the *"Japs still shoving us out of Malaysia."* With an evening pass Bill returns home. Gladys is not well and has not gone to work so Bill takes her to the doctors.

Friday, 23rd January 1942 – Bill is on gate police duty at 8.00 am. He has an interview with his staff officer regarding his 48 hour leave for the boxing last Saturday which is granted for tomorrow. After pay parade at 6.00 pm Bill has an evening pass to return to Gladys.

Saturday, 24th January 1942 – Bill is on gate police duty at 6.00 am. Eleven soldiers have been posted away, but Bill is still to remain. Bill is home at 5.00 pm to take Gladys to Mrs. Prince's house to attend her son Ron's 21st birthday party. Also there are Bill's parents and sister, Ivy. The party lasts all the night, Bill and Gladys leaving at 4.30 am. Later that day Bill is still on leave so he sees his mother who has stayed with Mrs. Prince. Bill leaves with his mother at 7.00 pm to return home to Gladys. Thailand declares war on Great Britain and America.

Monday, 26th January 1942 – Bill and Gladys travel by bus and tube to Leicester Square to the Tatler cinema to see 'Professor Mamlock' a Soviet drama. Then they see 'Jack and Jill', a pantomime with Arthur Askey and Florence Desmond, at the Palace Theatre. The first American troops arrive in Europe.

Tuesday, 27th January 1942 – Bill is on gate police duty at 8.00 am. There is still no 24 hour pass, but Bill manages to slip out of his barracks in the evening to accompany Gladys to be *"signed off the panel"* (doctor signing off).

Wednesday, 28th January 1942 – Bill is on gate police duty at 6.00 am. With a pass Bill returns home and takes Gladys to the Rembrandt cinema to see 'When Ladies Meet', a comedy, and 'Our Russian Allies', a war film. The prediction that Japan would conquer the Malay Peninsula before attempting an invasion of Singapore proves to be correct. The British army are cut off from their supply bases in southern Malaya and Singapore so withdraw to Singapore and prepare for the final siege, making the *"news from Malay very bad."*

Thursday, 29th January 1942 – Bill is on gate police duty at 8.00 am. With the disturbing news regarding Malaysia few people are requesting a pass so Bill is able to see Gladys with one of several spare passes.

Friday, 30th January 1942 – Bill is on gate police duty at 6.00 am. With another pass he is able to spend the evening with Gladys who is *"the only thing about this war that is just perfect is my wife."*

Saturday, 31st January 1942 – Bill is on gate police duty at 8.00 am then leaves to see a film show with Gladys and her parents at Epsom, Surrey. Bill makes sure that he is back at his barracks before roll call as he is without a pass and did not want to risk being caught again and another A.W.O.L. charge.

Sunday, 1st February 1942 – Bill is on gate police duty at 6.00 am then with Gladys he visits his parents. Bill is pleased to see his mother, but worried she still looks unwell. The Japanese are now just outside Singapore; *"What a war."* Taking a chance on being missed at his barracks, Bill still stays the night at home.

Monday, 2nd February 1942 – Bill is on gate police duty at 8.00 am. *"What a life and what a war – who knows, it may start one day."* Bill is *"fed up as usual, but feel fine when I see Gladys in evening."*

Tuesday, 3rd February 1942 – Bill is on gate police duty at 6.00 am then has an evening pass so takes Gladys to Epsom Rembrandt cinema to see 'International Squadron', a war film, and 'A Shot in the Dark', a comedy. Bill reports to his barracks to book in before returning back home for the night.

Wednesday, 4th February 1942 – Bill is on gate police duty at 8.00 am doing the *"same as usual, just exist throughout the day. Then begin to live as soon as I get home with my little girl."*

Thursday, 5th February 1942 – Bill is on gate police duty at 6.00 am and has a pass in the evening.

Friday, 6th February 1942 – Bill is on gate police duty at 8.00 am then returns home. He again reports to his barracks for roll call before returning home to Gladys and stays the night.

Saturday, 7th February 1942 – Bill is on gate police duty at 6.00 am. He later meets Gladys at Epsom, Surrey, at 5.00 pm to have a photo taken together. They then go to Cheam Century cinema to see 'My Son, My Son!', a drama, and 'He Found a Star', a musical, which Bill saw before in October the previous year. Again Bill stays at home with Gladys.

Sunday, 8th February 1942 – Bill is on gate police duty at 8.00 am and then returns home for the evening. Gladys has been to London and did not return home until 8.00 pm. Bill reports for roll call then returns home to stay the night with Gladys.

Monday, 9th February 1942 – Bill is on gate police duty at 6.00 am. At 4.30 pm he leaves his squadron headquarters to travel to Wandsworth Barracks, London, where he sees Fred. He then reports to Finchley Barracks, London, before he leaves in the staff car to Cheam Barracks, Surrey. After reporting in Bill returns home to Gladys.

Tuesday, 10th February 1942 – Bill travels by tube to report to Finchley Barracks, London, to train for another boxing competition against Simms Motors arranged for 21st February. The training is hard work, but Bill has good fun.

Wednesday, 11th February 1942 – Bill wakes feeling stiff all over, but still has more exercising, physical training, boxing and a five mile run. Bill receives a pass to return home to Gladys and stays the night.

Thursday, 12th February 1942 – Bill is up at 6.30 am and by tube he reports to Finchley Barracks, London, for more running, P.T. and a sparring practice. His stiffness is going off a little. He meets Gladys from work to see 'Honky Tonk', a crime/comedy, and 'Hello Sucker', an action/comedy at the cinema.

Friday, 13th February 1942 – Bill is up at 6.30 am to report to Finchley Barracks, London, for more training, not returning home until after midnight. Bill is looking forward to his weekend pass when his friend, Den, is expected.

Saturday, 14th February 1942 – Bill is up at 6.30 am to report to Finchley Barracks, London, for his usual run and exercises. He is *"feeling grand"* until he is informed that all passes have been cancelled owing to the 'five day mock war'. However, he still has an evening pass and returns home in time to see Gladys with his friend, Den, and his fiancée, Beatrice.

Sunday, 15th February 1942 – Bill is up at 6.30 am to report to Finchley Barracks, London, for a walk in the morning. In the afternoon and evening he stays in his barracks to read. *"Miss my Gladys. I will try to see her tomorrow."*

Monday, 16th February 1942 – *"What a life. Still busy running, skipping and exercising. Wish I could get home to see my lovely wife. Don't think much of this C.B. nonsense. A war on paper – well, what do you think?"*

Tuesday, 17th February 1942 – Bill is *"training and moping about longing to get home. Only three days away from Gladys but it seems a life time."* In the evening there is a darts match in the barracks canteen.

Wednesday, 18th February 1942 – *"Just the same as yesterday except I miss Gladys more than ever. Won't put up with much more of this. I'll get home somehow – I hope it will be tomorrow."*

Thursday, 19th February 1942 – Bill has more training and feels as fit as he could be. Bill pretends to go out for a walk for his training, but instead he returns home to Gladys and spends the night with her.

Friday, 20th February 1942 – Bill is up at 6.30 am to report to Finchley Barracks, London, for a walk and massage in the morning. He then leaves to meet Gladys at Cheam and stays at home.

Saturday, 21st February 1942 – Bill reports to Finchley

Barracks, London, for a massage. He rests until 7.30 pm when the boxing contest starts. Bill is winning easily, but then has to retire with a cut eye. Bill returns home at 2.15 am.

Sunday, 22nd February 1942 – Bill and Gladys travel to Willesden, London, to see his mother and has *"a very nice evening with them."* His eye is okay, but there is a nasty cut just above it.

Monday, 23rd February 1942 – Bill reports to Finchley Barracks, London. He is due to box again at Brompton Road, but is unable to fight because of his cut eye. Instead Bill is allowed to return home.

Tuesday, 24th February 1942 – Bill reports to Finchley Barracks, London, and packs his kit to return to Ewell, Surrey, and back to his squadron headquarters. He meets Gladys from work and they see 'A Yank in the R.A.F.', a war film, and 'The Smiling Ghost', a comedy, at the Capital cinema.

Wednesday, 25th February 1942 – Bill is on gate police duty at 8.00 am with *"no fire and about the worlds coldest job. Never more glad for a day to end."* Bill stays at his barracks all night as he overheard a plot to trap him from going home at night so he *"will try and stay in barracks more often at nights. It's not fair on Gladys to be home every day. I will let her have a little more time to herself – if possible."*

Thursday, 26th February 1942 – Bill drives another soldier to Horton Hospital, a psychiatric hospital in Epsom, Surrey, and then he later returns to his barracks for his 24 hour pass. At home he pays his first premium insurance as the agent calls for their signatures.

Friday, 27th February 1942 – Bill meets Gladys at the Queen Victoria Granada cinema to see 'Gert and Daisy's Weekend', a comedy, and 'Naval Academy', a drama. Bill has to leave Gladys to report to his barracks at 10.35 pm.

Saturday, 28th February 1942 – Bill is on gate police duty

at 6.00 am and manages to keep the fire burning for most of the day. Bill returns home, but does not have a very good evening and is *"fed up, feel like slinging this war over."*

Sunday, 1st March 1942 – Bill is on gate police duty at 6.00 am then returns home in the afternoon. With Gladys they see 'Tin Pan Alley', a musical, and 'The Gay Caballero', a western, at the Granada cinema.

Monday, 2nd March 1942 – Bill is on gate police duty at 6.00 am then attends a lecture at the company headquarters on 'Nazi Germany' at 7.00 pm. Bill then has a boxing practice with some of the boys.

Tuesday, 3rd March 1942 – Bill is on gate police duty at 6.00 am and is *"just waiting for the day to end so that I can be with Gladys again."* Bill returns home to Gladys and stays the night.

Wednesday, 4th March 1942 – Bill is on gate police duty at 6.00 am.

Thursday, 5th March 1942 – Bill is on gate police duty at 6.00 am.

Friday, 6th March 1942 – Bill is on gate police duty at 6.00 am. He then meets Gladys at North Cheam, Surrey, and they see 'Million Dollar Baby' and 'New York Town', two romantic comedies, at the Granada cinema.

Saturday, 7th March 1942 – Bill is on gate police duty at 6.00 am then he meets Gladys to travel by bus to see his mother and is disappointed that June, his foster sister, is not there. Bill then reports to his barracks.

Sunday, 8th March 1942 – Bill is on gate police duty at 6.00 am then posted to the company headquarters and on guard duty at night. It is *"not a bad night, it feels strange first guard duty in three months."*

Monday, 9th March 1942 – Bill is on fatigues duty all day and has a lecture in the evening. He finds it very interesting *"but would far soon be with Gladys. Miss her a lot, should be on a pass tomorrow."*

Tuesday, 10th March 1942 – Bill is on fatigues duty until 10.30 am then he is *"hiding myself until 4.30 pm"* when he has a pass to return home and able to see Gladys again.

Wednesday, 11th March 1942 – Bill is on fatigues duty uploading coke and petrol before he packs his kit and is able to be *"at long last home for seven long, lovely days with my little girl."*

Thursday, 12th March 1942 – Bill has a lousy cold and stays in bed all day. *"What a start to my leave, but it was a nice rest."*

Friday, 13th March 1942 – Still feeling unwell, Bill meets Gladys from work to see 'Kathleen', a comedy, and 'China Sea', an adventure, at the Odeon cinema. *"Not a bad day, but real leave will start tomorrow as Gladys will be with me all day."*

Saturday, 14th March 1942 – Bill and Gladys travel by bus to Prince's Head, Richmond, Surrey, to meet his mother and sister, Ivy. They have a walk around Clapham Junction, London, and then stay with Bill's parents.

Sunday, 15th March 1942 – Bill and Gladys leave his parents to travel by train to Romford, Essex, to see Gladys' friends, Lily and her husband Laurie, Doreen and her husband Jack Braiden, and Doris and her husband Reg Kaufman.

Monday, 16th March 1942 – Bill and Gladys travel by tube to the West End and have lunch at the Strand Corner House before they see 'Twenty To One' show with Lupino Lane at the Victoria Palace. Australia and New Zealand declares war on Thailand.

Tuesday, 17th March 1942 – Bill and Gladys travel by tube to the West End and walk around Oxford Street. They see 'Hippodrome', a comedy, starring Harry Korris, Cecil Frederick and Robbie Vincent at the Prince of Wales theatre. They then see 'Great Guns', a war comedy, and 'The Gay Falcon', a crime film, at the Morden Odeon cinema.

Wednesday, 18th March 1942 – Gladys is back at work so

Bill sees 'The Black Sheep of Whitehall', a comedy, and 'Behind the News', a drama, with his mother at the Rembrandt cinema before he reports back to his barracks and *"off to the war once more."*

Thursday, 19th March 1942 – Bill is on fatigues duty all day then on guard duty all night. *"Miss Gladys an awful lot, but hope to be able to get home again to see her tomorrow."*

Friday, 20th March 1942 – Bill is on fatigues duty in the morning and then packs his kit now attached to 'B' section at Wandsworth Barracks, London, to report to Colonel Poole and help with boxing training. He returns home by bus and tube staying the night. Bill has a *"lousy headache."*

Saturday, 21st March 1942 – Bill reports to Wandsworth Barracks, London, for running, boxing and skipping all morning. Bill returns home then with Gladys they see 'Santa Fe Trail', a western, and 'Bob's Your Uncle', a comedy, at the Granada cinema. Bill stays at home the night.

Sunday, 22nd March 1942 – Bill reports to Wandsworth Barracks, London, for sparring and running in the morning. In the evening Bill and Gladys see 'No, No, Nanette', a musical, and 'For Beauty's Sake', a comedy, at the Granada cinema.

Monday, 23rd March 1942 – Bill reports to Wandsworth Barracks, London, for *"more like real honest to goodness fighting than sparring."* He then stays in his barracks and plays cards.

Tuesday, 24th March 1942 – Bill reports to Wandsworth Barracks, London, for more sparring, skipping and running. He leaves his barracks and meets Gladys from work to see 'Dr. Jekyll and Mr. Hyde', a horror film, and 'The Border Legion', a western, at the Rembrandt cinema.

Wednesday, 25th March 1942 – Bill reports to Wandsworth Barracks, London, in the morning then meets Gladys from work. They see 'The Sea Wolf', a drama, and

'Time Out for Rhythm', a musical, at the Capital cinema.

Thursday, 26th March 1942 – Bill reports to Wandsworth Barracks, London, and does very little as Harry Poole, the boxer Bill is training, has injured his foot so Bill returns home. *"It's lovely being with Gladys so much, she is the finest, sweetest and loveliest girl in the world."*

Friday, 27th March 1942 – Bill reports to Wandsworth Barracks, London, and is on guard duty and also picket duty.

Saturday, 28th March 1942 – Bill attends a match at Seymour Hall, London, where the boxer he has trained is knocked out in the first round. With a 24 hour pass Bill goes to the Drill Inn pub while Gladys is at her firm's dance.

Sunday, 29th March 1942 – Bill and Gladys visit his mother at Willesden, London; she is still not looking too well. Bill stays the night with Gladys.

Monday, 30th March 1942 – Bill reports to Wandsworth Barracks, London, for fatigues duty and later cycles home then sees 'Alfredo and his Band' show.

Tuesday, 31st March 1942 – Bill reports to Wandsworth Barracks, London, for fatigues duty in the morning then bathing parade in the afternoon and picket duty at night. *"Wish I was home with my little girl, but I suppose I can't grumble – much."*

Wednesday, 1st April 1942 – Bill is on fatigues duty with the *"hardest job of all is to keep out of everybody's way."* In the evening Bill and Gladys go to the Morden Odeon cinema, but it is full so they walk back home.

Thursday, 2nd April 1942 – Bill reports to Wandsworth Barracks, London, for fatigues duty then later he meets Gladys from work and they see 'Buy Me That Town', a comedy, and 'Return of the Thin Man' film at the Odeon cinema.

Friday, 3rd April 1942 – Bill reports to Wandsworth Barracks, London, for fatigues duty and later is on picket duty. Picket duty is a soldier or small group of soldiers maintaining a watch. This may mean a watch for the enemy in the evening and Bill is *"rather pleased as it will give me the holidays clear, but I miss being with Gladys."*

Saturday, 4th April 1942 – Bill is on fatigues duty preparing the hall ready for a dance held there in the evening. Bill goes to the Rembrandt cinema to see 'The Big Blockade', a war film.

Sunday, 5th April 1942 – Bill reports to Wandsworth Barracks, London: the clocks go forward one hour. Bill and Gladys later see 'A Night Alone' a horror film, and 'Edison, the Man', a biographical film, at the Rembrandt cinema.

Monday, 6th April 1942 – Bill reports to Wandsworth Barracks, London, and is on fatigues duty. He attends a lecture at the company headquarters in the evening so is unable to return home.

Tuesday, 7th April 1942 – Bill reports sick to the R.M.P. at Wimbledon and needs to have an operation on his nose. With an evening pass Bill meets Gladys from work and they see 'Hell's Angels', a war film, and 'Let the People Sing', a comedy, at the Rembrandt cinema.

Wednesday, 8th April 1942 – Bill reports to Wandsworth Barrack, London, and is on fatigues duty in the day and picket duty in the evening.

Thursday, 9th April 1942 – Bill is on fatigues duty and *"longing for this rotten war to end so I can be with Gladys for always. The only good part of the army is when I am away from it."*

Friday, 10th April 1942 – Bill reports to Wandsworth Barracks, London, and is on fatigues duty in the morning. Bill has an evening pass, so with Gladys they see 'You'll Never Get Rich', a musical, and 'Thieves Fall Out', a comedy, at the Granada cinema.

Saturday, 11th April 1942 – Bill reports to Wandsworth Barracks, London, and is on fatigues duty all morning then reports to the company headquarters to collect coke in the afternoon. He is on picket duty in the evening and *"miss my Gladys a hell of a lot, wish I was with her."*

Sunday, 12th April 1942 – Bill is on gate duty and arranges for another soldier to work his afternoon shift so he can go home. With Gladys they visit his parents for tea.

Monday, 13th April 1942 – Bill reports to his squadron headquarters to start a two week course on P.T. and a lecture on map reading, rifle drill and foot drill. Foot drill is when soldiers march into battle, be expected to gather in a formation and react to words of command from their commanders once the battle commenced. Bill is dropped off at home on the way back where he stays the night with Gladys.

Tuesday, 14th April 1942 – Bill reports to Wandsworth Barracks, London, for a lecture, P.T. and a rifle drill. Rifle drill is given to a rifle which has been altered so it can no longer be fired. Instead it is used solely for drill purposes, training and teaching. In the afternoon Bill plays football at the company headquarters, losing 2-0. With an evening pass Bill takes Gladys to the Granada cinema to see 'The Scarlet Pimpernel', an adventure film, and 'Spooks Run Wild', a horror film.

Wednesday, 15th April 1942 – Bill reports sick at Wandsworth Barracks, London. With Fred and Harry Lockett, Bill sees the medical officer at Wimbledon, but is still on picket duty in the evening.

Thursday, 16th April 1942 – Bill has P.T., lecture and a rifle drill and foot drill all day and is on picket duty during the night. He is *"fed up with being in here, looking forward to seeing Gladys again tomorrow."*

Friday, 17th April 1942 – Bill has P.T. and attends a lecture. During the day Bill is on rifle drill and foot drill then has a pay parade and a bathing parade ending with an inspection.

Saturday, 18th April 1942 – Bill reports to Wandsworth Barracks, London, for a lecture and drill all morning then has a pass in the afternoon so returns home. He and Gladys visit Madame Tussauds, a museum in London displaying waxworks, and they have to walk nearly all the way back home.

Sunday, 19th April 1942 – Bill reports to Wandsworth Barracks, London, for fatigues and picket duties. He is able to swap duties with another soldier so Bill returns home. Bill and Gladys then spend the afternoon and evening at Hampton Court, Surrey.

Monday, 20th April 1942 – Bill has a lecture and P.T. and is then on fatigues duty and later is on guard duty at night at Wandsworth Barracks, London.

Tuesday, 21st April 1942 – Bill has P.T. and a lecture in the morning and foot drill and bathing parade in the afternoon. He meets Gladys at the Organ Inn pub in the evening then sees 'The Corsican Brothers', an adventure film, and 'Niagara Falls', a comedy, at the Rembrandt cinema. *"Grand to be with my little girl again."*

Wednesday, 22nd April 1942 – Bill has P.T., lectures and a drill all day. He should have been on picket duty in the evening, but manages to again arrange for another solder to cover for him so he can return home.

Thursday, 23rd April 1942 – Bill first reports to Wandsworth Barracks, London, then attends Queen Alexandra's Military Hospital at Millbank, London, to see a specialist regarding his nose. Bill reports back to Wandsworth Barracks, London, for picket duty in the evening. Gladys 'phones Bill to find out how he is. It is *"lovely to hear her even if I can't see her."*

Friday, 24th April 1942 – Bill receives treatment on his nose all day at the R.M.P. at Wimbledon then has a pass in the evening to return home to Gladys.

Saturday, 25th April 1942 – Bill reports to Wandsworth Barracks, London, then to the R.M.P. at Wimbledon before having a pass in the afternoon to return home. He and

Gladys go to Tooting Granada cinema to see 'The Man Who Came Back', a drama.

Sunday, 26th April 1942 – Bill reports to Wandsworth Barracks, London, for home guard exercises. From 1940 until 1944 the Home Guard acted as a secondary defence force in case of an invasion by Germany and their Allies. The Home Guard guarded the British coastal areas and important places, i.e.: airfields and factories. Bill is stopped seven times on the way back. He should have been on picket duty, but instead he meets Gladys at Putney and they visit his mother, who returns to Wandsworth Barracks with Bill. Fred and Florrie also join them.

Monday, 27th April 1942 – Bill reports to Queen Alexandra's Military Hospital at Millbank, London, for further treatment on his nose. He has a pass in the evening so meets Gladys and together they see 'Paris Calling', an action film, and 'Radio Revels of 1942' film at the Odeon cinema.

Tuesday, 28th April 1942 – Bill reports to Wandsworth Barracks, London, and then Millbank Hospital, returning to his barracks at night. A big detail has left with the two Harrys recalled in a general call out.

Wednesday, 29th April 1942 – Bill reports to Queen Alexandra's Military Hospital at Millbank, London. He sees friends Eric and Lil and their new son before reporting to Wandsworth Barracks, London, for picket duty in the evening. His sister, Ivy, visits him.

Thursday, 30th April 1942 – Bill reports to Queen Alexandra's Military Hospital at Millbank, London, and then returns home to Gladys. *"What a life – and they say there is a war on – somewhere."*

Friday, 1st May 1942 – Bill first reports to Wandsworth Barracks, London, and then returns again to Queen Alexandra's Military Hospital at Millbank, London. He is pleased to be on guard duty during the night as it would leave him free over the weekend.

Saturday, 2nd May 1942 – Bill reports to Queen Alexandra's Military Hospital at Millbank, London, and then later he has an evening pass to spend with Gladys on her 20th birthday. He takes Gladys to Wimbledon Theatre to see Harry Parry's sextet and comedian Ronald Frankau. It has been *"another lovely evening with my wonderful wife."*

Sunday, 3rd May 1942 – Bill first reports to Wandsworth Barracks, London, and then later to the Queen Alexandra's Military Hospital at Millbank, London. He has a pass in the afternoon so takes Gladys to Clapham Common and Hyde Park, London.

Monday, 4th May 1942 – Bill first reports to Wandsworth Barracks, London, then reports to Queen Alexandra's Military Hospital at Millbank, London. In the evening Bill is on picket duty then attends a lecture at the company headquarters and later cleans the respirator. A plan to construct the world's first oil pipeline under the English Channel between England and France is tested in the River Medway, known as Operation Pluto ('Pipe Line Under The Ocean').

Tuesday, 5th May 1942 – Bill reports to Queen Alexandra's Military Hospital at Millbank, London. He is *"getting a little fed up with this"*, but he has an evening pass to go home.

Wednesday, 6th May 1942 – Bill reports to Wandsworth Barracks, London, and tells his officer he has to return to the Millbank Hospital, but instead he goes for a ride on his bike. Bill has an evening pass so meets Gladys and together they have a walk around Morden, Surrey. Bill stays with Gladys.

Thursday, 7th May 1942 – Bill reports to Wandsworth Barracks, London, and then has another ride on his bike. He buys Gladys a late birthday present, plus some fish knives and tea spoons. Bill is on guard duty at his barracks all night with Fred and Bill Baker.

Friday, 8th May 1942 – Bill has another morning riding on his bike calling in at Willesden, London, to see his father. With a pass in the evening Bill takes Gladys to the Granada cinema to see the drama 'Manpower'.

Saturday, 9th May 1942 – In the morning Bill travels by bus and tube to return to Queen Alexandra's Military Hospital at Millbank, London, as he still feels so ill. He then calls to see his mother where he also meets Gladys. Returning to his section headquarters Bill feels terrible so the medical officer is sent for and Bill is taken by ambulance to the R.M.P. at Wimbledon.

Sunday, 10th May 1942 – Bill is in the R.M.P. at Wimbledon still feeling bad. Gladys visits Bill which makes him feel a lot better.

Monday, 11th May 1942 – Bill is in the R.M.P. at Wimbledon still feeling no better, but enjoys being in bed all day and sleeping, then waking up and then sleeping.

Tuesday, 12th May 1942 – Bill is still in the R.M.P. at Wimbledon and is feeling a little better. He is now missing Gladys and is bored being in bed all day. In the R.M.P. at Wimbledon Bill writes a letter to Gladys.

Bill is 22 years and 8 months old: Gladys was 20 years old on 2nd May.

(Above left) Bill, aged 22, & (Above right) Gladys, aged 20, February 1942

R. M. P.
the Wkm
9 Victoria Drive
Wimbledon. S.W.19.

12 May 1942.

My own darling beloved sweetheart,

Many thanks for your letter which came as a very welcome surprise on yesterday evening. It was lovely to hear from you and to know you love and miss me darling as I love you with all my heart and soul and miss you more than I could ever describe to you. Already it seems years ago that I last gazed on your sweet loveliness, time is here days even more slowly than it does elsewhere. I am longing to see you again my love longing to hold you close to me and tell you over and over again that I love you and need you more than life itself.

I was ever so thrilled and pleased to read in your letter

Above) Bill's letter to Gladys written on Tuesday, 12th May 1942

118

Mrs Gladys Powell
84a London Road
North Cheam
Surrey

W.F. Powell, T/69083
R.M.P.
The Whim
9 Victoria Drive
Wimbledon, S.W.19

12 May 1942

My own darling beloved sweetheart,

Many thanks for your letter which came as a very welcome surprise on yesterday evening. It was lovely to hear from you and to know you love and miss me darling as I love you with all my heart and soul and miss you more than I could ever describe to you. Already it seems years ago that I last gazed on your sweet loveliness, time in here drags even more slowly than it does elsewhere. I am longing to hold you close to me and tell you over and over again that I love you and need you more than life itself.

I was ever so thrilled and pleased to read in your letter that hearing the 'Anniversary Waltz' played at work reminded you that our anniversary will soon be here and what a happy and perfect year of married life we have spent with each other. It has been my one real ambition and object to make you happy, my darling, to try and make you as happy as I have been with you. It has been the most wonderful year of my life, darling. The happiest, the proudest and the most enjoyable time I have ever had and to know that you too regard it as being perfectly happy makes it even more wonderful. I love you, darling. I wonder sometimes if you will grow tired of hearing me say that, but I know that just as I will never grow tired of saying it, nor will you ever grow tired of hearing me say it to you. I just can't help saying it, darling, as I mean it so very much.

You are my life, darling. I need you and love you now and for always, nothing will ever come between us, my love. We will always be together and will always be rich in our love for each other. Even if we are separated from each other in body, we will be together in spirit. Nothing can stop me dreaming of you, nothing can stop me loving you and nothing will lessen our love for each other. We belong to each other, my darling and nothing will ever part us. You are mine, my precious, and I am yours – till death do us part and even that will only be a temporary parting until we meet again in whatever life it is that follows this one.

I am longing for the day, my sweet, when we will be together for the rest of our lives. No more wars, passes, or sneaking nights with you, but a home of our own and time to do as we please and go where we like. When I can be with you every day and not have to worry about getting caught. Perhaps it will not be too long, darling. Who knows, this little war of ours may end a lot sooner that we all think, or it may last a lot longer.

I was reading a Yankee magazine yesterday called 'Amazing Science Stories' and one of the yarns was about a war starting in Europe in 1940 – and lasting for twenty five years. The magazine was dated October 1935, but it is not too far out on actual happenings – so far. It gives France destroyed by Germany, America over half conquered by the Japs. The rest of Europe and Asia overrun by either Germans or Japanese, but we win by the battle of California (America) in the year 1965. No mention is made of the Soviet Union, but I expect she will upset all the calculations. Anyhow, they also said Paris, London and New York were wiped clean off the map with the first air raids. Quite an interesting story – not only guns, etc., were used but, also death rays, when the ray which is something like a huge torch, is shone on to anything or anybody. Whatever it shines on it melts into dust. Houses, factories, churches, people, animals, trees and everything else, just crumbles into a heap of dust – what a war – but as I said earlier, we won in the end, so why worry.

The nurse has just brought me another letter from you and I have been some time trying to puzzle it out. It is rather funny as I received the letter you wrote in work yesterday afternoon, yet this letter appears to have been written on Sunday and only arrives here on Tuesday. Perhaps it is because of the fact that they were posted in different localities – one in Sutton and one in Epsom. Anyway, it seems as if Epsom is the best place to post them. It certainly is quick moving to post a letter and catch the 12.30 post and it is lovely to hear from you, darling.

I am sorry you did not enjoy the pictures at the Granada cinema a lot on Sunday, perhaps next week I will be able to go with you and we will see if you enjoy it more then. Are there any good films on anywhere this week, don't go to them all, save one so that we can go together in the end part of the week. I am longing to be out of here, darling, so I can see you and hold you again. It seems years and years ago that I saw you last.

I love you, sweetheart, and will always love you. You are my life and I need you and miss you more than anything else in the world. I am very pleased that you like your necklace, I only wish I could have got you something a lot better – something to match your loveliness and charm, but I doubt if any combination of rare metals and precious stones could ever do full justice to you most wondrous beauty and sweetness. You are the loveliest, most charming, sweetest, most beautiful angel on either this side of Heaven or in Heaven itself and I am so proud and happy to know you are my wife, darling. I love you. How I wish I could tell you how much I love you, but I am afraid that our language was never devised for such a passionate love as I hold for you, darling. Try as I might I could never describe how much you mean to me. All I can say is, I would sooner be on a desert island with you than own the whole world and not have you to share it with me. You are more necessary to my happiness than anything else in the world, darling, even more than that, sweetheart, you are my life. I could not live without you, sweetheart, you are my life and I love you and need you so much, darling.

It has been very interesting in here (I don't think). I have not yet got out of bed – all I have been doing is laying here – just laying here. It was not so bad on Sunday. I slept nearly all day, but yesterday the bed felt too hard and every couple of minutes I got either pins and needles or else cramp and had to turn over. I did not feel like reading as I was giddy – at least until about half past eight my headache cleared away and I laid reading until just after nine and then went to sleep. They woke me up again about six this morning – to have my temperature, etc., taken, then I am washed and about 6.30 to 7.00 am breakfast is served. I had some Kellogg's cornflakes this morning and it was the first I have eaten since having some porridge on Saturday morning. Then I started writing this letter to you and was interrupted by the arrival (very welcome arrival) of your Sunday letter. By the time I had read and re-read your letter over and over again, it was time for the M.O. round. So we had to tidy our beds and sit still until after he has gone. He is due at 9.30 am but it is now turned eleven, so I have decided to continue writing until he does eventually arrive.

I don't know if I will be discharged today, but I am feeling a lot better, but still a little giddy. All he said to me yesterday was – "How are you this morning, laddie." I replied: "A lot better, thanks" and that was that, in and out and gone. I don't know if it will be the same today when he does arrive. Probably something like this: "Good morning", "Good morning, sir." "Alright?", "Yes, sir." "Good" and then to the sister: "Discharge." I don't think he likes to say too much, or perhaps he doesn't know very much and is frightened that he will be found out if he talks about it.

I am just about fed up with going to sleep standing up. I might just as well be on guard. At least I could make myself more comfortable. I have four bolsters and three pillows piled one on top of the other, the idea being to keep my head high and thus stop me from coughing – well it works, but it also stops me from sleeping, at least until I am really tired. Instead of being able to sleep all day and sleep all night, I have to be satisfied with sleeping in the night time only.

Last night, darling, I went to sleep with your photo in one hand and a little kitten in the other. You see, there is a mouse somewhere in this room and they left the kitten in the room to catch it. But I thought if I can't have my little girl to cuddle, I'd have to have something, but it was a very poor substitute. I did think of asking one of the nurses to cuddle me, but thought I could just about hang out until tomorrow. I am longing to see you, darling, and tomorrow seems years away, but it is well worth waiting for, to be able to see my own sweetheart, my little girl again. I love you, darling. I believe I have said that before in this letter, but in case I haven't, I will say it again. I love you. I adore you. I worship you. I miss you and need you, beloved.

The M.O. has just been and I am still here, so I will be here to see you tomorrow. He applied his earphones to my chest and said, "Ahum" and that was that. That other fellow who was in the ward when you came on Sunday is being transferred to Putney Hospital for an operation on his stomach. But we have had a new customer arrive today. I don't know anything about him except that he went off to sleep as soon as he got into bed. Well, darling, I don't think there is much more to tell you, except to remind you once again that I love you and will always do so for as long as I live. You are my life, darling, and I am just living to see you again. I can hardly wait until tomorrow as it seems so far away. Don't be late, my love, as I am so much looking forward to seeing you.

Did you get my note I wrote yesterday? I am sorry it was so short, but the paper was going around in circles and I felt pretty queer. As to the writing, well I am afraid this is not a lot better as I didn't know it was so awkward writing in bed. The paper slips and slides about, then my arm starts aching, then it's my behind aching, it's the devil's own job to get comfortable. Still, I suppose it could be worse and anyway it will give me practice for writing to you when I am again in hospital. It will not be long before I am in hospital with my nose lying beside me – or something. I am not looking forward to that very much, as I will be too far away from you for my liking. I believe I did tell you that I will probably have to go to Watford General Hospital for the operation as the hospital I have been attending for treatment at Millbank, Westminster, is only for outpatients. Still, there will be a week or two before I need worry about that and, in any case, I don't expect I will be in there very long (I hope).

I suppose I should utilise all the time I have to spare by catching up on my letter writing, but not sitting in bed, I'm not. If I am allowed to get up tomorrow, I will probably write two or three letters, but if I am still confined to bed, then I will write to my little girl and then call it a day.

All the nurses have asked who is the sweet little face on the photo beside my bed. Naturally I felt very proud when

I told them that it is a photo of my lovely wife. Also, I have told them they will be able to see you for themselves tomorrow, so that they can see what a beautiful girl you are.

You can tell I am feeling a lot better, as I have started smoking again today, but I am not struck with smoking too much in bed. Out of all the cigarettes I bought in here with me, I have only smoked about five and up to now, I have about forty left. Also, I haven't started on my ration card from N.A.A.F.I. [9] yet. Even the nicotine stains are beginning to fade from my fingers and without scrubbing them. I never bit my finger nails for the first two days I was here, but I have made up for that today.

You will have to excuse me for a few minutes, darling, as dinner is served and, boy, am I hungry. Well, that's that – dinner – I was hungry, but not that hungry. Meat, well it would be better for repairing shoes than the majority of leather we are getting nowadays. The greens weren't, they were white and the spuds, black. So now I am waiting for the afters – ah, that was better – raison pudding and some lovely creamy custard. The only trouble was it was ok as a sample, but I am still wondering what's for dinner. Roll on tea time. Who knows, we may have some scrambled eggs and oysters, some sliced bananas and cream with just a few strawberries. Or, it may be bread and margarine and jam – if they've got any jam.

Well, darling, I guess I had better draw to an end now, or else you won't get this letter until after you have been here tomorrow. I know you will be looking forward to hearing from me, as I look forward to hearing from you, darling, and I know you will be very disappointed if you didn't have a letter from your old pot and pan [10].

By the way, darling, will you also bring up with you tomorrow a couple of lumps of rags for my nose as I have just about used up everything I can lay my hands on. Don't forget, also the clean towel and underclothes, etc.

I will now say goodbye, my love, until tomorrow. Hoping and praying that tomorrow won't be too far away. I am longing and living to see you, darling. I love you and need you so much. Remember, darling, you are the only girl in the world for me and I love you more than the rest of the world put together.

Remember me to all at home, darling. Give them all my love and all my love to you, beloved. I am and always will remain your loving and adoring husband,

Bill

xxx

I LOVE YOU ALWAYS MY DARLING

P.S.
I love you, darling
I adore you, darling
I worship you, sweetheart
I miss you, beloved
I need you, dearest
I love you, my wife

[9] N.A.A.F.I. – Naval, Army, Air Force Institutes is an organisation created by the British government in 1921 responsible with selling goods to servicemen.
[10] Pot and pan is a Cockney slang for 'old man' (father or husband).

May – August 1942

Wednesday, 13th May 1942 – Bill is still in the R.M.P. at Wimbledon, the medical officer allowing him to get up for a couple of hours. Gladys visits Bill in the afternoon and *"boy, it was good to see her and longing to be out and with her again."*

Thursday, 14th May 1942 – Bill remains in the R.M.P. at Wimbledon, feeling fine now, but bored to tears. *"It seems all right for a couple of days but doing nothing can be monotonous."*

Friday, 15th May 1942 – Bill, still in the R.M.P. at Wimbledon, amuses himself with jig saw puzzles, reading and playing monopoly and will *"be glad when I am out so I can see my Gladys again."*

Saturday, 16th May 1942 – Bill is *"still here – and even more browned off than ever."* Gladys visits Bill *"nothing could be more welcome"* to make it a lovely afternoon. Bill's parents and sister, Ivy, also visit Bill.

Sunday, 17th May 1942 – Bill is told he will be discharged tomorrow. Gladys visits Bill and they sit outside on the lawn.

Monday, 18th May 1942 – Bill is discharged from the R.M.P. at Wimbledon and he reports to Wandsworth Barracks, London. With a pass in the evening Bill returns home and stays the night with Gladys.

Tuesday, 19th May 1942 – Bill reports to Wandsworth Barracks, London, where he is on fatigues and maintenance duty. In the evening Bill is on picket duty and stays in his barracks reading and writing.

Wednesday, 20th May 1942 – Bill is at Wandsworth Barracks, London, on P.T. and fatigues duties. *"What an exciting life. Thank God I have my lovely wife to go home to in the evenings."* Bill and Gladys see 'Ride 'Em Cowboy' a western/comedy, and 'Maisie Was a Lady', a comedy, at the Rembrandt cinema.

Thursday, 21st May 1942 – Bill reports to Wandsworth Barracks, London. *"Usual day, pretending to be working."* With a pass again in the evening, Bill returns home. However he does not stay the night as he discovers that *"Gilmour is on guard and on the lookout."*

Friday, 22nd May 1942 – Bill has P.T. and a fatigues duty at Wandsworth Barracks, London, then is on picket duty in the evening. Gladys 'phones Bill and it is *"good to hear her even if I can't see her."*

Saturday, 23rd May 1942 – Bill has P.T. and is on his own on his usual fatigues duty at Wandsworth Barracks, London, with everyone else out. Bill later meets Gladys and they walk around Clapham Junction. They later see 'The Four Just Men', a thriller, and 'Nell Gwyn', a historical film, at the Century cinema.

Sunday, 24th May 1942 – Bill reports to Wandsworth Barracks, London. The early detail is just going out so he sleeps all afternoon and is then on guard duty in the evening with Bill Bailey.

Monday, 25th May 1942 – Bill is on fatigues duty at Wandsworth Barracks, London. *"What a way to spend a holiday"*, but he has a pass so he and Gladys go to the Rembrandt cinema to see 'Johnny Eager', a crime film.

Tuesday, 26th May 1942 – Bill reports to his squadron headquarters for fatigues and maintenance duty, a bathing parade then he has a medical inspection. From his B3 category authorised on 24th June 1940, Bill is now classed as an A2 category. He has a pass to return home. Today the Battle of Gazala, one of the fiercest of the Desert War, begins. With a German victory, the British retreat to the defensive position known as the Gazala Line. Churchill places Field Marshall Montgomery, 1st Viscount of Alamein, at the head of the British 8th Army.

Wednesday, 27th May 1942 – Bill reports to his squadron headquarters then the R.M.P. at Wimbledon for a re-grading to an A2 category. All the soldiers in his room at the barracks are on picket duty as a punishment for having a dirty room which they later have to scrub clean.

Thursday, 28th May 1942 – Bill reports to Queen Alexandra's Military Hospital at Millbank, London, and then he is back to his squadron headquarters for fatigues and picket duty in the evening.

Friday, 29th May 1942 – Bill is on fatigues duty and now assigned to lorry no.241531. With an evening pass Bill buys a dinner set as a gift for Gladys at Hardwicks and takes it home to her.

Saturday, 30th May 1942 – Bill reports to his squadron headquarters to take supplies to Dulwich and Norwood, London, and Shirley Park, Surrey. He and Gladys see 'North West Mounted Police', an action film, at the Century cinema.

Sunday, 31st May 1942 – Bill and Gladys visit his parents. It has been a lovely day at home for Bill, but today Japanese submarines attempt to attack Allied warships on Sydney Harbour.

Monday, 1st June 1942 – Bill reports to his squadron headquarters for fatigues and maintenance duty and has a lecture in the evening. He drives a party to the company headquarters to *"hear a lot of junk about Japan."* Mexico declares war on Germany, Italy and Japan after the sinking of their tanker by a German U-boat.

Tuesday, 2nd June 1942 – *"Same old sort of day – bored stiff and fed up."* Bill is on guard duty all night with an air raid warning at 2.30 am; all clear at 3.00 am.

Wednesday, 3rd June 1942 – Bill is on fatigues and maintenance duty feeling tired. He has a late pass in the evening to visit Gladys at home, but returns to his barracks at night.

Thursday, 4th June 1942 – Bill attends Queen Alexandra's Military Hospital at Millbank, London. With an evening pass he returns home to pay his insurance and stays at home.

Friday, 5th June 1942 – Bill reports to his squadron headquarters and is on fatigues duty then goes to an open air swimming pool in the afternoon. With a pass Bill meets Gladys to walk around Carshalton and Sutton, Surrey. America declares war on Bulgaria, Hungary and Romania.

Saturday, 6th June 1942 – Bill reports to his squadron headquarters and is on supplies to Dulwich and Kensington, London. He calls home and takes Gladys in his lorry to Tooting Broadway, London. Bill is on picket duty in the evening.

Sunday, 7th June 1942 – Bill is on maintenance and gate police duty then has a pass to return home. Bill takes Gladys to the Worcester Park Odeon cinema to see 'Busman's Honeymoon', a detective film, and 'Roamin' Wild', a western. He then reports back to his barracks for the night.

Monday, 8th June 1942 – Bill takes supplies to Dulwich, Penge, Putney and Wandsworth in London and later attends another war lecture at the company headquarters.

Tuesday, 9th June 1942 – Bill is on fatigues duty, a bathing parade and on guard duty in the evening with Fred.

Wednesday, 10th June 1942 – Is a *usual day doing usual things – or dodging doing it."* Bill has a late pass to see Gladys, returning to his barracks in the evening.

Thursday, 11th June 1942 – Bill is on fatigues and maintenance duty all day. He has a pass in the evening to return home and to also see Mr. and Mrs. Sawyer. Doll Sawyer is a close friend of Gladys' mother.

Friday, 12th June 1942 – Bill has an interview with his new staff officer regarding a seven day leave and is told he is going into hospital on Monday.   Annoyed Bill now refuses any further army boxing matches.   He reports sick and sees the medical officer.   However, Bill is still on picket duty in the evening.

Saturday, 13th June 1942 – Bill takes supplies to Dulwich, Penge, Wandsworth and Putney in London.   On a 24 hour pass Bill takes Gladys to the Century cinema to see 'Dark Streets of Cairo', a mystery, and 'I Wanted Wings', a drama which Bill and Gladys saw in August the previous year.

Sunday, 14th June 1942 – Bill takes Gladys to see his mother on her 52nd birthday.   With his mother are Bill's Uncle Jack and Aunt Daisy.   That evening Bill reports to his squadron headquarters.

Monday, 15th June 1942 – Bill packs his kit then reports to Queen Alexandra's Military Hospital at Millbank, London. He is taken by ambulance to Watford Hospital, Hertfordshire.   There he writes a letter to Gladys and his mother.

Tuesday, 16th June 1942 – Bill is woken at 5.15 am which *"seems to be the middle of the night."*   He has breakfast at 7.00 am then nothing for lunch with his operation at 2.30 pm to release a nasal obstruction.   Afterwards Bill *"felt pretty sick."*

Wednesday, 17th June 1942 – Bill sleeps most of the day. His nose *"feels like a football and boy, is it sore."*   He sees the medical officer in charge of the troops and is still classed as A2 category.   He manages to eat and writes a letter to Gladys.

Thursday, 18th June 1942 – Bill is *"browned off with being in bed"*, but getting plenty of sleep.   He is looking forward to hearing from Gladys and writes another letter to her.

Friday, 19th June 1942 – Bill is allowed out of bed for two hours.   He receives a letter from his mother, but nothing from Gladys and is getting worried about her.

Saturday, 20th June 1942 – Bill is up for most of the day

and is relieved to receive a letter from Gladys, plus a visit from her in the afternoon.

Sunday, 21st June 1942 – Gladys and his parents visit Bill in the afternoon and they all sit outside to watch a cricket match.

Monday, 22nd June 1942 – *"What a life, looking forward to getting out of here"* and with the news Rommel has taken Tobruk, Libya; *"War news getting worse, still retreating in Libya."*

Tuesday, 23rd June 1942 – Bill spends the day in hospital hoping to leave tomorrow. He writes to Gladys and is *"living to see her again. Love her and miss her more than anything else."*

Wednesday, 24th June 1942 – Bill watches a cricket match in the afternoon and waits all day before he is informed he would not be leaving until tomorrow. He 'phones Gladys and it is *"lovely to hear her sweet voice again."*

Thursday, 25th June 1942 – Bill is eventually discharged from Watford Hospital at 2.30 pm. He has a glass of beer before leaving by train to report to his squadron headquarters at 5.00 pm and stays in all the evening.

Friday, 26th June 1942 – Bill reports sick at the R.M.P. at Wimbledon and is given five days sick leave. Bill leaves his barracks to return home. Fred is promoted to Lance Corporal.

Saturday, 27th June 1942 – Bill meets Gladys from work to travel to Kingston by bus and walk around the shops. After dinner they see 'Reap the Wild Wind', an adventure film, and 'Almost Married' film at the ABC Odeon cinema.

Sunday, 28th June 1942 – Bill and Gladys travel to Chessington Zoo having a *"very nice enjoyable day"* and then they return home.

Monday, 29th June 1942 – Gladys has the day off from work so Bill takes her to Tooting shops and then to the Sutton cinema to see 'The Foreman Went to France', a war film, and 'Wake Up and Dream', a musical.

Tuesday, 30th June 1942 – Bill takes Gladys and his mother to Stratford and Canning Town in London and calls in to see Gladys' Uncle Bob and family before returning home for the last time for a while.

Wednesday, 1st July 1942 – Gladys returns to work so Bill takes his mother and Gladys' brother, Sonny, to the Granada cinema to see 'This Gun for Hire', a crime film, and 'You're in the Army Now', a comedy. After an evening with Gladys, Bill reports to his barracks. Today is the first Battle of El Alamein.

Thursday, 2nd July 1942 – Bill is on fatigues and maintenance duty and *"back to this rotten monotony again – fed up always when I am away from my little wife."* With picket duty in the evening Bill is *"bored stiff."*

Friday, 3rd July 1942 – Bill is *"still fed up and longing to see Gladys again"* with *"nothing to do all day with all day to do it in. Sleep – work – what a life."*

Saturday, 4th July 1942 – Bill first reports to Queen Alexandra's Military Hospital at Millbank, London, and then goes home to collect his suit to go to Den and Beatrice's wedding at Christ Church. Bill meets Gladys and together they attend the wedding reception.

Sunday, 5th July 1942 – Bill attends a discussion on current affairs in the canteen. After his maintenance duty he sleeps all afternoon before going on guard duty at night where he sees Den and Beatrice.

Monday, 6th July 1942 – Bill is on fatigues and maintenance duty then detail duty at 5.00 pm, a *"fine time to start work. I should be home on seven days leave."*

Tuesday, 7th July 1942 – Bill is on maintenance duty all morning. He leaves his barracks at 3.00 pm and takes Gladys to see 'Henry Hall's Guest Night' show with George Doonan at Streatham Hill Theatre, London.

Wednesday, 8th July 1942 – Bill visits his parents and

sister, Ivy, and it is *"good to see them all once more."* Gladys is not well.

Thursday, 9th July 1942 – Gladys is still feeling unwell. However, she joins Bill and her mother to travel to Wrotham, Kent, to see Gladys' grandmother. They have a walk and a drink in the George and Dragon pub and stay the night.

Friday, 10th July 1942 – Bill, Gladys and her mother leave Wrotham, Kent, to return to Canning Town, London, and spend the day with Gladys' Aunt Flo. Gladys is feeling a lot better.

Saturday, 11th July 1942 – Bill and Gladys see 'Captains of the Clouds', a war film and 'A Gentleman after Dark', a crime/drama, at the Strand Dominion cinema. After tea at the Corner House they see Billy Cotton and Dorothy Ward show.

Sunday, 12th July 1942 – Bill's parents and his sister, Ivy, arrive for dinner and then Mr. and Mrs. Prince arrive for tea becoming *"quite a party."* But Bill and Gladys are *"a little niggly – but all's well that ends well."*

Monday, 13th July 1942 – Bill meets Gladys from work and they see 'Saboteur', a thriller, and 'A Night in New Orleans', a crime film, at the Odeon cinema.

Tuesday, 14th July 1942 – Bill packs his kit and takes his mother to see 'The Man Who Came to Dinner', a comedy, and 'The Valley of the Sun', a western. With *"a few last lovely hours with Gladys"* Bill returns to his barracks.

Wednesday, 15th July 1942 – Reporting sick Bill is with the medical officer all morning. He still is on maintenance duty all afternoon and guard duty at night. Bill is informed that as he still refuses to fight again for the army boxing team he will be leaving tomorrow on a motor course at Brighton.

Thursday, 16th July 1942 – Bill packs his kit to travel by train to Brighton, Sussex, and is attached to T.T. (Technical

Training) Group at Preston. He spends the night at Preston Barracks ready to start a motor mechanic fitter course.

Friday, 17th July 1942 – Bill arrives at Caffyns garage, Preston Road, Brighton, Sussex, to start a course and stays at a civilian lodging for a soldier, with Mrs. Jeram (*"smashing"*) at 52 Exeter Street, Brighton. In the evening Bill sees 'Jeanie'; *"A good play, but wish Gladys was with me"* and then writes to Gladys.

Saturday, 18th July 1942 – Bill has a lecture and an examination. Later he walks around town before he stays in to write to Gladys, his mother and Fred, ending with homework and studying.

Sunday, 19th July 1942 – After a roll call parade Bill returns home with *"only a few hours with her* [Gladys]*, but they are perfect hours"* then returns to Brighton.

Monday, 20th July 1942 – Bill *"starts real work today"* with filing and hacksawing. A hacksaw is a fine-tooth hand saw with a blade held under tension in a frame used for cutting materials such as metal and plastics. He stays in at Mrs. Jeram's civvie billet and writes to Gladys.

Tuesday, 21st July 1942 – Bill has more filing, making a pair of callipers, a device with two curved legs used to measure the distance between two opposite sides of an object. The tips of the calliper are adjusted to fit across the points to be measured, the calliper is then removed and the distance read by measuring between the tips with a measuring tool, such as a ruler. It is used for mechanical engineering, metalworking, woodworking, science and medicine. He then makes a pair of dividers, an instrument with two straight legs pivoted to each other at the top with two sharp points, one for the centre, the other for scribing or marking. Bill thinks he is getting on well. In the evening Bill goes with Don to the Theatre Royal to see 'Auld Acquaintance', a play, starring Edith Evans.

135

Wednesday, 22nd July 1942 – Today Bill is soldering, a process in which two or more metal items are joined together by melting and flowing a filler metal (solder) into the joint, and the filler metal having a lower melting point than the work piece. He is given a lot of homework to do which he completes after writing to a letter to Gladys wishing *"hurry up Saturday."*

Thursday, 23rd July 1942 – Today Bill is brazing, a metal-joining process where a filler metal is heated above melting point and distributed between two or more close-fitting parts by capillary action. The filler metal is brought slightly above its melting temperature while protected by a suitable atmosphere, usually a flux. It then flows over the base metal (known as wetting) and is then cooled to join the work pieces together. It is similar to soldering, except the temperatures used to melt the filler metal are higher. Bill then has a flat filing exercise; *"Not a bad job."* In the evening Bill and Don see 'My Wife's Family' and 'Emergency Landing', two comedies, at the Tivoli cinema.

Friday, 24th July 1942 – Bill has his homework and all his practical work checked and the instructor seems pleased with his work; *"I hope it keeps that way."* In the evening Bill goes to the Hippodrome to see 'The Western Brothers' show. Back at his civvie billet Bill writes to Gladys.

Saturday, 25th July 1942 – *"School again"* but Bill leaves early to catch the train from Brighton, Sussex, to return home. Bill and Gladys see 'The Spoilers', a western, and 'Don't Get Personal', a comedy, at the Morden Odeon cinema. They then walk around Wimbledon Common fair.

Sunday, 26th July 1942 – Bill and Gladys see 'Three Men from Texas', a western, and 'The Ware Case', a mystery film, at the Worcester Park Odeon cinema. Gladys accompanies Bill to Sutton Station for his train back to Brighton, Sussex.

Monday, 27th July 1942 – Bill returns to *"school"* with *"more and yet more homework."* He avoids P.T. to clear his homework but still manages to write to Gladys; *"Miss her very much and wish she were here with me."*

Tuesday, 28th July 1942 – Bill has a lecture on tyres and wheels and is given more homework. He later goes with Don to the Academy cinema to see 'Ball of Fire', a comedy, and 'Defeat of the Germans near Moscow', a documentary with the latest news of the war.

Wednesday, 29th July 1942 – Bill has a lecture on hubs and lubrication. After completing his homework Bill writes to Gladys.

Thursday, 30th July 1942 – Bill stays in and writes to Gladys. *"What a war – soldiers at school instead of Libya."*

Friday, 31st July 1942 – Bill has *"lectures and more lectures."* He and Don go for a *"good"* steak but they then see a *"lousy"* show.

Saturday, 1st August 1942 – Bill passes his weekly examination. He meets Gladys at Brighton Station to see Jay Wilbur and his 'High Class Band' show at the Hippodrome and *"a good start to our holiday."*

Sunday, 2nd August 1942 – Bill leaves for his roll call at the garage then walks along the sea front with Gladys. They watch Tigers versus Redwings hockey followed by 'The Gracie Allen Murder Case', a drama which Bill and Gladys saw before in February the previous year.

Monday, 3rd August 1942 – With it a Bank Holiday, Bill and Gladys have a walk around the sea front and listen to the band at the pavilion. Gladys leaves to return home.

Tuesday, 4th August 1942 – After *"more lectures and more swotting"* Bill has a walk in the evening then he returns to Mrs. Jeram's house. With no homework set tonight he writes a letter to Gladys.

Bill is 22 years and 11 months old: Gladys is 20 years and 3 months old.

52 Exeter St
Brighton
Sussex.

August 4. 1942.

My own dearest beloved wife,

A whole day has passed since we said goodbye to each othe at the station yesterday. A day that has been both long and dreary as all days seem when I am away from you my darling. I love you sweetheart and miss you so much, life is so empty and dull unless you are there to share it with me, I often wonder why it is that I love and need you so much, but I am sorry to say I have never been able to answer that question satisfactory. There are hundreds

(Above) Bill's letter to Gladys written on Tuesday, 4th August 1942

Mrs Gladys Powell
84a London Road
North Cheam
Surrey

W.F. Powell, T/69083
52 Exeter Street
Brighton
Sussex

August 4, 1942

My own dearest beloved wife,

A whole day has passed since we said goodbye to each other at the station yesterday, a day that has been both long and dreary as all days seem when I am away from you my daring. I love you sweetheart and miss you so much, life is so empty and dull unless you are there to share it with me, I often wonder why it is that I love and need you so much, but I am sorry to say I have never been able to answer that question satisfactory. There are hundreds of reason why I could have fallen so madly in love with you and no doubt each one did contribute to some extent, but still I can't discover what is the real and basic thing about you that drives me so absolutely and completely crazy. It could be because you are so beautiful and lovely, but even if you were very plain and even gawky I know I would love you just as much. Another reason would be your sweet, lovable and generous nature, but I am sure I would still be crazy about you even were you to lose these qualities. Then again, I could have fallen in love with your understanding and sweetness when I get so passionate, darling, but I loved you long before that ever arose, or again your charm and character could easily have made me your willing and devoted slave for life, but I am also certain that without it I would still love and worship you forever.

It is just one of these things over which we can have no control, the whole matter is entirely out of our hands. I was destined to meet and fall madly in love with you and I was just wonderfully lucky to have such a perfect example of womanhood as you, darling. Nothing or nobody could possibly be as perfect as you, every desirable and lovely quality that was ever possessed by anyone is also possessed by you, you are the combination of all that is finest and best in a woman and I love you and need you for more than I could ever describe. Life without you is something that has to be experienced to be believed, it is dull, monotonous and lifeless. It is not living, it is rather a drab existence that has to be endured, all I live for is to be with you, darling. My life consists of a few all too short hours of heavenly bliss broken by days of almost absolute purgatory. I could not live for long without you, sweetheart. You are my life and I miss you, darling, so much you have taken my heart and soul. My mind is always with you, all I have is the rest of me and how can anyone live without their heart, soul and brain. I love you and will always do so as long as I live, nothing will ever be able to alter that. There is only one person in my life and that person is and always will be you and you alone. I would sooner be with you on a desert island marooned away from every comfort in life, than be able to rule the world without you. I have only one ambition and that is to be able to give you everything you need and to make you happy.

One thing I will never be able to do and that is to give you everything you deserve, there is nothing in the world really good enough for you, darling. I would like to be able to lay the whole world at your feet and then set out to bring you the rest of the universe, but as that is impossible then I can only hope to be able to provide you with all you need to make you really and truly happy and proud of me, my sweetheart. I love you, I adore you and worship you always and will always do so for ever. My darling, I am sometimes afraid that you will get fed up with me saying that to you as I write it and say it so often, but I hope you will forgive me as I cannot help it as I mean it so much. All day long my thoughts are with you. I am wondering what you are doing, if you are alright, if you are missing me the way I miss you, you are always in my thoughts and even at nights I cannot escape your bewitching enchantment for all night long I am dreaming of you. I am longing for Saturday to come, it already seems as if years have gone by since I was with you, darling and Saturday seems so terribly far away, but it will eventually arrive and then, sweetheart, we will be together once again. I have applied for and managed to get a pass and if all goes well I will be home about three o'clock or perhaps a little after and once again I will be able to hold you tight in my arms, to feel your arms about me and experience the wonderful ecstasy of your kisses. I will be able to tell you I love you instead of having to write it and be able to say goodnight to you in person instead of to your photograph. Lovely as your photograph is, it is a very poor substitute for you, darling, believe me there is not a lot of fun in kissing a photo – even if it is a photo of the sweetest and most adorable beautiful and wonderful girl in the world.

How I long for the day when we will be together for always, just you and I, darling – no, not even any children, for much as I love children, I know I would only be very jealous of anybody – even our child if it took any of your love away from me. I know it is not a very nice thing to say, but I love you so much, I just could not bear the thought of you ever loving anybody more than you love me, even if that person be our own child born as a result of that love. Just think, darling, a home of our own, me going out to work to provide you with all the things you desire. It will be my turn then, sweetheart, to try and recompense you in some measure for your wonderful and unfailing generosity and kindness that you have shown to me since I have known you. We will be able to have holidays together, darling, holidays at the seaside that will be even better – far better than this last weekend. That was the first time we have been together at the seaside, but it is by no means the last. We will visit every seaside resort there is – and be able to go on the beach and go swimming as well. It will be wonderful, darling, and I hope it will not be long in coming true.

Of course a lot will depend on how this war ends and when it ends. One thing, it cannot end too soon for my liking, tomorrow will not be quick enough for me. It is now almost three years since I first 'answered the call of my King and country', or at least answered my mobilization papers and donned my khaki suit. It was a novelty then and made a nice change, but with the passing of time my ideas on the subject have altered pretty drastically. I am completely and absolutely fed up with this lousy bloodbath. Although I have seen little or nothing of any real action, I am probably even more anxious to get it all eroded than those lads who are up to their ears in it out in Libya and Russia. I wonder if ever people will eventually realize that they can live together peacefully and happily and that war has no place in a real civilized community. Life is far too short to waste in an attempt to blow other people to smithereens.

Some people declare that there has always been wars and always will be, while such idiocy exists no doubt there will be, but if only they could learn to look a little further than their nose and to use their heads for some other purpose than just balancing a hat on then we could get down to the basic causes of war and begin to eliminate them. Just because there have been wars before is no reason why we should have wars in the future, it is like saying when asked to ride in a motor car, train or airplane that primitive people always walked or even crawled to their destinations. They should also ignore the electric light, electric fire and every other development of our civilization. If the inventors of all these amenities and things, which we now regard as essentials of life, thought that way we would still be living in caves with goat skins as our clothes. But we have progressed in everything beyond all and every expectations, only war remains of all our primitive ways. The reason for this is very obvious, there was profit and fame in radio, motors and all other advances, industry has progressed enormously only because by improvement it can show more profit. But as there is no financial gain to be made out of peace, no one has bothered to try and bring it about permanently. It is only the rotten unfair system under which we subject ourselves to be governed that directly results in war and a large part of that blame must be taken by the working classes themselves, they are in the position of being in the huge majority and thus they have the power to govern themselves as they wish. One of the first things that we all must learn is that we are no better than anybody else, that nationality is only an accident of birth and not anything to be proud of or to despise. We must realize that people have a right to live as they wish and the fact of us being English does not give us any right to dictate to others, Indians, Irish, or anybody else.

We must learn to live together as citizens of the world and not as nationals of some state or other. How can we call ourselves separate and distinct from others when almost any place in the world can be reached by days or even hours? When we can talk by cable and wireless to someone living on the other side of the world. It is obvious that we are far too close to each other now to keep up this idiotic pretence of independent nationalities, we are all occupants of the same globe and there is plenty of everything for everyone. When we realize this fact and stop the divisions into German, Italians, Jews, Russians, British and other such sects and clans then we will be well on the way to peace and plenty. When this will happen, God only knows, but unless we realize it soon we will be in a chaotic state and it may be ages before we ever pull ourselves out again. It is up to us ourselves and the result will be of our own making. After this war – we can either have unemployment and poverty, or peace, plenty and prosperity, the choice is ours – I wonder just what we will do about it. In any case, it will be of no use to blame anybody else – the choice is ours and ours alone, no one else can do it for us, we must act and act solely. Then we will be able to have all the holidays and other benefits of life, there will then be no more worry over the future.

Well, dear, I have finished the first day of the third week of the course. It has been very interesting, but also very, very, complicated. It seems a hell of a lot to learn but I am hoping to manage it somehow (I hope). We have been studying gearboxes and clutches and I can tell you there is some works inside them, but the instructor is pretty good at explaining it all, so I may learn it all. I do hope I manage to pass right through as I am very interested in it all and am learning a lot. One day, with a bit of luck, I will be a motor mechanic and then I will be pretty pleased with myself. The reason I am able to write you a real letter for a change is due to the fact that there is no homework for today, so I have plenty of time to write to you, darling. Although I think that I have done more writing than I would have done if I had had some homework to do. The boys have been saying that I am nuts writing such a letter only a day after seeing you for the weekend. They are quite right, I am nuts, but nuts about you, sweetheart. I love you and need you more than anything else in the whole world.

I hope you enjoyed yourself, darling, down here, as I had such a lovely time with you, especially when we were lying off the cliffs by Black Rock. It was just perfect having you with me and I appreciate your coming down very much and I hope and pray that you enjoyed the change as I have not had many better times. I always enjoy myself when I am with you and I hope you also enjoy my company. I believe you do as I know you look forward so much to seeing me. I also know you love me and also that you miss me a lot. It means so much to me to know that you love me and I love to hear you tell me and write it, darling. I look forward so much to your letter. That is the thing I live for when you are away from me, dear. I love you and adore you and will always do so, my love. I only wish I could tell you how much you really mean to me, darling, but that is something I cannot do. It is not only beyond my power to describe, but I don't think any man could ever manage to express or convey the love I have for you. It is far greater than anything I have ever visualized, sweetheart. I am sure that our love for each other makes other love stories seem so unimpressive and tawdy. Romeo and Juliet [11], Scarlett and Rhett, Nelson and Hamilton and Elizabeth and Essex were mild calf love compared to our love for each other. I love you and need you so much. Without you I am completely lost, it is like the day without any sun, just a black and murky mess. I need you as the flowers need the sun and the rain, I long to be with you and live for the occasion when we are together, darling.

It is now almost a year since we first really belonged to each other. It has been a year of ever increasing happiness and wonder to me. I never thought it was possible for anyone to be so happy, as I have been with you, my darling. Life has been so wonderful and enjoyable. We have been so happy together and believe me, sweetheart, I have never loved anyone or anything so much as I loved you. It is as if on a dark and stormy day and then the love you hold for me came along and drove away the clouds and the glorious sunshine of our love came shining through. I only hope you have been as happy as I have, darling, and also that I have not made you disappointed in me. I know I have not been a model husband, sweetheart, but I have tried to act as well as I could under the circumstances.

I am sorry if at any time I have fallen short of your estimation of me, but I apologise, darling, and hope to try and be better in the future. I love you so much though, darling, that it is very hard to act unpassionately when I love you with a passion that is beyond all explaining. I have tried, darling, to treat you always with the respect that you deserve and I am sure you understand that. Sometimes I feel that perhaps I love you too much, as if I were to love you less then I might not maul you about so, dear.

One thing though, darling, I have always told you and I want you to remember and that is, if at time you have any complaints in my conduct towards you, then please tell me and I will do my best to see that it is altered and put right. I love you far too much to risk losing your love through any reason whatsoever. Don't forget, my love, as if you don't tell me, I may offend you in some way and not know about it. If at any time I have done so, you know that it was unintentional, but unless you tell me I may continue without knowing it. I think of you so much, dear, and long to be with you. I love you miss you and need you and will always do so.

Well, dear, I am beginning to run a bit dry on subject matter, although time permitting I could continue to write about how much I love you for ages. But I would only be continually repeating myself. I have not counted how many times I have written here that I love you and miss you, but it must be quite a good few. But, as that is the dominant feature of my life, I suppose it is excusable. In case I have not said it before, I will repeat it. Also it will help you to remember that I love you, need you and miss you more than I could ever tell you, darling.

I don't know if I will be writing tomorrow. If I have a little homework I will, but if I don't have any I will probably go to the pictures. I don't know how much homework we will get this week, already Monday and Tuesday have gone and we have not had any. I hope the old instructor is not saving us a batch until the end of the week and above all, I hope he is not going to tell us to draw one of his gearboxes. If he does, I can see myself having to stay in every night working on it. All it consists of is a maze of cog wheels and shafts nuts and bolts. It looks like a jumbled mess to look at, let alone to try and draw.

Well, dear, I will draw to a close now as I have been writing for over three hours, with only two short breaks for a smoke. It is now eleven o'clock and I started this letter at half past seven so you can see I have been writing for some time and my wrist is beginning to ache like blazes. All the other boys have been out and Bert [Lord] only went out for about an hour – down to the local, I believe. Don and John have been to the pictures and have just come in and are having their supper. Frank went away today to Portsmouth for his holidays. He has a fortnight, so we won't have him around for a little while. It is a bit awkward to concentrate now as the boys are describing the pictures to me as I am writing, so I will end up and say goodnight, my darling.

How is everyone at home, Dad, Mum, Eileen and Sonny? I hope they are all well and that Mum has quite recovered from her sickness. Give them my love and regards and hope I will be seeing them all on Saturday. I have not heard from my Mum yet this week, but I believe she is on holiday at Southend (if she got through the police barrier). How did you like returning to work? By the time you get this you will have got used to it again.

Somehow I think you had about the best of the weather when you were down here, as it has been raining nearly all day today and now it is really cold. My feet are frozen and I am feeling shivery all over. Of course it is a new experience for me to feel shivery, but usually I am hot at the same time and you are the cause of it. But, for a change it is not you, but the weather that is responsible. What is the weather like down your way? I hope it keeps fine for the weekend as it will be nice to go out for a walk together, that is if I did not wear your legs down too much with the walking we did down here. What did you think of Brighton, it is not a bad place is it? The only trouble is the hills and some of them are hills and all. Have there been any more raids lately on London? I get ever so worried about you, darling. I hate to think of you up there and only hope that Jerry stays away. If anything happened to you, it would kill me, darling. I hope that he does not start any more of his big raids on London, as it will have me worried stiff. He has been over here four times today and for a change twice we actually heard some gunfire. It was like old times, but so much and all over in a few minutes.

I have met a fellow down here who lives opposite the Cheam Barracks and he is calling for me on Saturday and we are coming home together. No doubt I will also arrange to meet him at East Croydon on the way back. It will be company for us both and will make the journey seem a lot quicker. Don't forget to let me know how long it took you to get home and whether your Epsom ticket got you through ok and also whether you had any difficulty in getting the trolley bus and also the 156 bus or not. I was looking to see you wave goodbye from the train, darling, and was quite disappointed when you did not. I would have liked to have caught a last glimpse of you before you went out of sight.

Still, it won't be long before I am with you again for the whole weekend. Only another three and a half days and we will be in each other's arms once more. It will be lovely and I am looking so forward to it. The only trouble is that at the moment three and a half days seems like three and a half years. It is funny how slowly time passes when we are apart and how it flies by when we are together. Minutes seem days, days seems weeks and weeks, years when I am away from you, yet it seems that I no sooner get home than it is time to leave again. I think they must have two sets of time, one when we are together and another for when we are apart.

Well, dearest, as I said once before, I must close now. It is now half past eleven and all the others are in bed and I am feeling dead tired. Also, my wrist feels as if it is on fire. I hope you enjoy this little letter. I know you like me writing long letters to you, but please, darling, don't expect them too often as I am afraid time will not allow it, but I will write one every so often just to remind you that I love you more than anything in the world. I will close by saying goodnight, my darling, write to me soon and don't forget to tell me that you love me and miss me as I do you. Goodnight, beloved, I love you always.

Your loving husband,

Bill

xxx

ALL MY LOVE TO YOU MY DARLING

P.S.
I love you always

[11] Romeo and Juliet (two young lovers), Scarlett and Rhett (Scarlett O'Hara and Rhett Butler in 'Gone with the Wind'), Nelson and Hamilton (Lord Nelson and Emma, Lady Hamilton) and Elizabeth and Essex (Queen Elizabeth I and Robert Devereaux, 2nd Earl of Essex).

August – November 1942

In August 1942 the Allies succeed in preventing a second attack against El Alamein and, at a high cost, manage to deliver desperately needed supplies to the besieged Malta. As many as 400,000 Jews are murdered in occupied Europe during the month. Brazil declares war on Germany and Italy.

Wednesday, 5th August 1942 – Bill has another *"dull day with lecturing and waiting."* He misses Gladys, wishing he is with her.

Thursday, 6th August 1942 – Bill is *"getting on ok at school, be glad when Saturday comes."* With Don he goes to the Gaiety cinema to see 'Sergeant York', a biographical film about Alvin York and the most decorated World War I American soldier. It is *"a good film but wish Gladys was with me."*

Friday, 7th August 1942 – Bill manages to get through his weekend examination. With Don and John Bill goes to the Grand cinema to see 'Love Life and Laughter', a comedy show which Bill thinks is *"lousy."*

Saturday, 8th August 1942 – Bill is at *"school"* all morning before he leaves Brighton to return home and take Gladys to Canning Town, London, to see her Aunt Flo and spends all evening with her and then they return home.

Sunday, 9th August 1942 – Bill and Gladys visit Mrs. Prince then Bill leaves from East Croydon Station, Surrey, to return by train to Brighton, Sussex.

Monday, 10th August 1942 – Bill starts another course on engines with more homework, but still writes to Gladys.

Tuesday, 11th August 1942 – Bill has *"school all day long, getting the hang of it all somehow."* In the evening Bill goes to the Hippodrome to see Caroll Levis, a talent scout, impresario, television and radio personality and *"a pretty good show."*

Wednesday, 12th August 1942 – After *"school again"* Bill goes to the Theatre Royal in the evening with Don to see 'Vintage Cocktail', *"a pretty good play."*

Thursday, 13th August 1942 – Bill is *"still swotting away"* for his examination tomorrow and stays in all evening to try and catch up on his homework and he also writes to Gladys.

Friday, 14th August 1942 – Bill's weekly examination starts and he hopes to pass as *"everything seems alright."* In the evening he and Don see 'Yankee Doodle Dandy', a musical about George M. Cohan, at the Grand cinema.

Saturday, 15th August 1942 – Bill finishes his weekly examination then catches the train from Brighton to return to Gladys and *"lovely to be with Gladys again."* Friends Maggie and Arthur visit for tea.

Sunday, 16th August 1942 – Bill and *"my beautiful wife"* walk around Wimbledon Common, London, before Bill returns to Brighton, Sussex.

Monday, 17th August 1942 – Bill starts another week on an electrical and carbonation course. In the evening Bill goes to the Hippodrome to see Max Miller show which is *"very good."*

Wednesday, 19th August 1942 – Bill has an oral examination.

Friday, 21st August 1942 – Bill has his end of course examination; *"Don't think I did too bad"* and hopes he has passed. With Don he sees 'Paint and Powder', a 1925 silent black and white film, at the Grand cinema.

Saturday, 22nd August 1942 – Bill returns home by train to take Gladys to the Rembrandt cinema to see 'The Courtship of Andy Hardy' and 'Gert and Daisy Clean Up', two comedies.

Sunday, 23rd August 1942 – Bill and Gladys travel to East Ham, London, to visit Gladys' Aunt Elsie, Aunt Maud and her grandmother. Bill leaves Gladys at Clapham Junction Station, London, to return to Brighton, Sussex, by train.

Monday, 24th August 1942 – Bill starts what might be his last week course on motorcycles and how they work. He and Don go to the Grand cinema to see 'Hi Diddle Diddle', a black and white comedy.

Wednesday, 26th August 1942 – Bill's examination results are through: Bill and his friend, Bert Lord pass; but Don and John, his other two friends, fail.

Thursday, 27th August 1942 – Don and John leave to return to their units, Bill wondering who will take their place.

Friday, 28th August 1942 – Bill has his last day's work on the course. He is granted a three day leave so returns home to Gladys.

Saturday, 29th August 1942 – Bill and Gladys go swimming then see 'The Man Who Wouldn't Die', a mystery, and 'Uncensored', a war film.

Sunday, 30th August 1942 – Bill and Gladys visit his parents, but they are out. Instead they visit a friend, Mrs. Dunsdon.

Monday, 31st August 1942 – Bill takes Gladys to Leicester Square, London, to see 'No Orchids for Miss Blandish', a thriller, at the Prince of Wales cinema. Bill later leaves Gladys at Victoria Station to return to Brighton, Sussex, by train.

Tuesday, 1st September 1942 – Bill begins another course, but is *"not so good."* He later sees 'White Cargo', a war film, at the Royal cinema.

Wednesday, 2nd September 1942 – Bill has nothing much to do.

Thursday, 3rd September 1942 – *"Still working?"* Bill has a walk in the evening.

Friday, 4th September 1942 – Bill has his weekly examination and finishes third. He completes his homework in the evening.

Saturday, 5th September 1942 – Bill reports in sick and catches the train back home to Gladys. They see 'The New Adventures of Tarzan', an action film, and 'Old Mother Riley', a comedy, at the Rembrandt cinema.

Sunday, 6th September 1942 – A year ago Bill and Gladys were married. Bill and Gladys return to St. Phillips Church to relive their wedding. They have a party in the evening and Bill *"got pretty merry and had a wonderful time."* To Bill his time with Gladys has been *"one whole year of married life, a year of heaven with a real angel for a wife."*

Monday, 7th September 1942 – Bill is up at 3.45 am not feeling too good but the walk to Sutton Station sobers him. Catching a bus to Croydon Station, Surrey, Bill returns by train to Brighton Station, Sussex.

Tuesday, 8th September 1942 – Back at *"school all day"* Bill has a course on basic filing. In the evening he goes to the Royal cinema to see 'Young Woodley' and *"quite a good play and a darn good seat."*

Wednesday, 9th September 1942 – Bill is *"fed up with filing and hack sawing."* In the evening he writes to Gladys.

Thursday, 10th September 1942 – *"Same as usual, but not a lot to do."* In the evening Bill sees 'Forsythe, Seamon and Farrell' show at the Imperial cinema. Bill goes on the stage and has a sketch done by an artist.

Friday, 11th September 1942 – Bill has an examination, not doing so well, but hopes to make up for it later. He goes into the Labour Club for a drink.

Saturday, 12th September 1942 – Doing little all morning Bill meets Gladys at Brighton Station, Sussex, to walk around town then they see 'Flying Fortress', a war film, and 'Kid Glove Killer', a crime film, at the Savoy cinema.

Sunday, 13th September 1942 – Bill's 23rd birthday. He attends his roll call then has a walk with Gladys. They see another hockey match: Tigers versus Ramblers before

Gladys return home.

Monday, 14th September 1942 – Bill starts a fresh week's course on engines. He goes to the Grand cinema to see 'Take It Easy' film. He is *"not too impressed, fed up and bored stiff."*

Tuesday, 15th September 1942 – Bill seems to be *"getting on okay"* and after *"school"* goes swimming. In the evening Bill goes to the Imperial Theatre to see various shows.

Wednesday, 16th September 1942 – Bill is *"completely fed up and browned off."* He misses Gladys so much living at Brighton, he leaves to return home at 7.15 pm where it is *"lovely to see my Gladys again."*

Thursday, 17th September 1942 – Bill is up at 3.45 am to walk to Waddon, Surrey, and takes a bus to Croydon Station, Surrey, and a train to Brighton, Sussex, arriving at 7.00 am for his course. Tired, he is in bed at 7.00 pm.

Friday, 18th September 1942 – After his course Bill sees 'Troise and his Mandoliers' at the Hippodrome, *"A damn good show."*

Saturday, 19th September 1942 – Bill meets Gladys at Liverpool Street, London, and takes her to Romford, Essex, to see her friends, the Kaufman family. They then go to a dance at the school hall in the evening.

Sunday, 20th September 1942 – Bill and Gladys visit Lily and Laurie, Gladys' friends, then have a walk around Romford, Essex. *"A very good weekend."*

Monday, 21st September 1942 – Bill again leaves Gladys at 3.30 am, catches the 4.48 am bus to Croydon Station, Surrey, then the train to Brighton, Sussex, arriving at 7.15 am. He starts *"a new week at school"* learning about the gearbox and clutch. In the evening Bill goes to the Curzon cinema to see 'Dangerous Moonlight', a war film, and 'Four Mothers', a drama/romance he saw before with Gladys in July the previous year.

Tuesday, 22nd September 1942 – Today there is *"not much doing, pretty boring."* Bill stays in at his billet all evening with Mrs. Jeram and other guests.

Wednesday, 23rd September 1942 – After work Bill returns home to spend the night with Gladys.

Thursday, 24th September 1942 – Bill catches the 5.48 am train back to Brighton, Sussex, to continue his course.

Saturday, 26th September 1942 – Bill returns home and takes Gladys and her mother to the Rembrandt cinema to see 'Gone with the Wind' epic.

Sunday, 27th September 1942 – Bill takes Gladys to the Palais de Dance at Hammersmith, London, and then visits his parents.

Monday, 28th September 1942 – Bill again leaves Gladys to catch the 5.45 am train back to Brighton, Sussex.

Wednesday, 30th September 1942 – After work Bill returns home and *"it's lovely to be with Gladys once again."* He leaves *"in the middle of the night"* to return to Brighton, Sussex, the following day.

Saturday, 3rd October 1942 – Bill leaves work at Brighton, Sussex, and returns home to Gladys in North Cheam, Surrey.

Monday, 5th October 1942 – Bill catches the 5.45 am train to return to Brighton, Sussex; *"Back to school again."* In the evening he watches the Inter Services boxing: Navy versus R.A.F. at the Theatre Royal.

Tuesday, 6th October 1942 – *"Still swotting away, or something."* Bill then spends the evening indoors.

Wednesday, 7th October 1942 – Bill leaves *"school"* early to return home to Gladys where *"it's wonderful to be with my little girl once again."*

Friday, 9th October 1942 – After Bill finishes his work he does his homework then has a drink and a game of billiards with Bert.

Saturday, 10th October 1942 – After Bill finishes work he leaves Brighton to meet Gladys and his mother and travel to Canning Town, London, for Gladys' Aunt Flo's birthday party and stays the night.

Sunday, 11th October 1942 – Bill and Gladys spend the day with Aunt Flo then they later return home for the evening.

Monday, 12th October 1942 – Bill is up at 3.30 am to catch the 5.45 am train from East Croydon Station, Surrey, to Brighton, Sussex; *"Tired out."*

Tuesday, 13th October 1942 – After work Bill reports to Preston Barracks, Sussex, for a change of clothing.

Wednesday, 14th October 1942 – Bill is *"still busy swotting"* but later leaves to return home to Gladys.

Thursday, 15th October 1942 – Bill is up at 3.30 am to return to Brighton, Sussex. Although he is tired, Bill goes to the Academy cinema to see 'Jungle Book', an adventure film, and 'Man with Two Lives', a thriller.

Saturday, 17th October 1942 – Bill stays for work in the morning before he leaves to catch the train home. Bill and Gladys see 'Pardon My Sarong', a musical/comedy, at the Rembrandt cinema.

Sunday, 18th October 1942 – Bill and Gladys go to Hammersmith Palais to see 'Kenway and Young' show then visit his parents where it is *"good to see them again."* Bill is up at 3.30 am next day to return to Brighton, Sussex.

Wednesday, 21st October 1942 – Bill has his last day at Brighton, Sussex. He packs and then the results of the examination are announced: Bill comes first. He joins everyone to go to the Imperial theatre to see actor/comedian Issy Bonn.

Thursday, 22nd October 1942 – Bill spends the morning in his barracks then returns home. He meets Gladys from work to see 'Tarzan's New York Adventure', an adventure film, and 'The Mississippi Gambler' at the Rembrandt cinema.

Friday, 23rd October 1942 – Bill and Gladys walk around Kingston then see 'Harry Roy and his Band' show at the

Kingston Empire.

Saturday, 24th October 1942 – Bill and Gladys see Max Miller at Wimbledon Winter Garden. Bill has previously seen Max Miller on Monday, 17th August 1942.

Monday, 26th October 1942 – It is pouring with rain. Bill takes his mother to the Rembrandt cinema to see 'Invisible Agent', a war/sci-fi film.

Tuesday, 27th October 1942 – Bill travels to Willesden, London, to meet his mother then they go to Kensington, London, and home for tea.

Wednesday, 28th October 1942 – Bill travels to the Haymarket to see 'Du Barry Was a Lady', a musical.

Thursday, 29th October 1942 – Bill, Gladys and his mother see 'Belle of New York', a musical, at the Coliseum, Strand in London. They then go to a dance at Canning Town, London.

Friday, 30th October 1942 – Bill and Gladys visit her Aunt Flo and also see her Aunt Maud and grandmother. Bill later moves his mother away from London to live in Southend, Essex, which he hopes will help improve her ailing health.

Saturday, 31st October 1942 – Bill packs his kit to report to the company headquarters and has a pass to return home to Gladys.

It is the beginning of the end of the war in Africa after the Battle of El Alamein. Winston Churchill says: "Before Alamein we never had a victory – after Alamein we never had a defeat", sensing this is a turning point in World War II.

Sunday, 1st November 1942 – Bill has a pass in the afternoon so takes Gladys to visit his mother in Southend, Essex.

Monday, 2nd November 1942 – Bill is posted back to 'B' section. He returns home to see Gladys then reports to his barracks.

Tuesday, 3rd November 1942 – Bill works as a section driver mechanical transport and instructor and is on night picket duty. The second Battle of El Alamein forces a German retreat.

Wednesday, 4th November 1942 – Bill is still *"wrecking"* lorries. There is a darts match in the evening followed by an army film at the Curzon cinema.

Friday, 6th November 1942 – Bill reports to Wandsworth Barracks, London, for a few inspections, pay parade, a medical inspection then is on picket duty.

Saturday, 7th November 1942 – After working on the lorries all morning Bill and Gladys see 'The Glass Key', a crime film, and 'Whispering Ghosts', a comedy, at the Epsom Odeon cinema. Bill stays at home with Gladys.

Sunday, 8th November 1942 – From his squadron headquarters Bill is posted to the company headquarters. He later takes Gladys to see 'Angles Wash Their Faces', a drama, at Cheam cinema.

Monday, 9th November 1942 – Reporting to the company headquarters Bill catches the 11.55 am from Liverpool Street Station, London, to Newmarket, Suffolk. There Bill is posted to 15 Tank Transport Company at 6.00 pm, where it is *"right out in the wilds, but leaving very soon."*

Tuesday, 10th November 1942 – Bill has an inspection by the medical officer and an interview with the commanding officer.

Friday, 13th November 1942 – The British 8th Army captures Tobruk, Libya, Montgomery quoting: "We have completely smashed the German and Italian armies."

Tuesday, 17th November 1942 – The British 8th Army moves westward in Tunisia and recaptures Derna and British paratroops engage German troops with the first conflict arising between the newly landed American and German forces.

Wednesday, 18th November 1942 – With the eventual

prospect of Bill leaving England to fight in the war, Gladys takes three days off work from Whatcliffe Works without permission to stay with her husband.

Sunday, 22nd November 1942 – Bill writes Gladys a short farewell letter as she leaves Bill at Newmarket, Suffolk, to return home. Although Bill is now to leave and fight in the war, he still remembers to enclose Christmas cards for the family.

Bill is 23 years and 2 months old: Gladys is 20 years and 6 months old.

1942

Same address
for another how.

Sunday 22 Nov.

My own darling beloved wife,

Heres hoping you managed to git home alight, and that you found Mums place O.K. I am enclosing Xmas Cards for you to dispose of as I will not be able to post anything else. I have written one out for you, the rest go between us to whoever you like.

I love you darling, and will always do so, I am living only to be home with you once more. Look after yourself and don't worry over me. Give my love to all at home, I am looking forward to seeing

(Above) Bill's letter to Gladys written on Sunday, 22nd November 1942

161

Mrs Gladys Powell
92 St. Clair Drive
Worcester Park
Surrey

W.F. Powell, T/69083
Same address
for another hour.

Sunday 22 Nov.

My own darling beloved wife,
　　Here's hoping you managed to get home alright, and that you found Mums place o.k.   I am enclosing Xmas cards for you to dispose of as I will not be able to post anything else. I have written one out for you, the rest go between us to whoever you like.
　　I love you darling, and will always do so, I am living only to be home with you once more.   Look after yourself and don't worry over me.   Give my love to all at home, I am looking forward to seeing them all again soon.   Please excuse short letter, but we are moving at one pm and I have still a few more bits to get ready.   Cheerio, darling. Thanks for coming down on Wednesday, it has made me a lot happier about going, longing to be home with you again soon.   I am now and will always be your loving husband,
　　　　　　　　　　　　　　Bill

xxxxxx

I love you, adore you,
worship you, need you,
miss you, cherish you
with all my heart and soul

(Above) Bill, aged 23, in North Africa, January 1943

November 1942 – April 1943

Bill is embodied from the U.K. on Monday, 23rd November 1942. He leaves England by boat on Wednesday, 25th November 1942 from Liverpool. He again sails on Friday, 27th November. On Tuesday, 8th December Bill docks, but re-sails the same day. He also docks and sails on the following day, then docks on Thursday, 10th December and is disembodied at North Africa.

On arrival in Libya, North Africa, Bill is attached to 15 Tank Transporter Company with the Royal Army Service Corps (R.A.S.C.) under the Commanding Officer Major V.H. Austin. A tank transporter is a specialized road vehicle for the transport of tanks to and from the battlefield. Transporters are merely for the carriage of tanks. They are necessary to limit the mileage of the tracked vehicles (as the tracks have a limited lifetime) and also to reduce wear on road surfaces which can easily be damaged by such heavy vehicles. Tank transporters also use less fuel than tracked vehicles and may have a higher road speed if provided with a good road network. They may also be used for wheeled armoured cars or for unarmoured tracked vehicles, though the advantages of using transporters are usually less substantial in these cases. It is not their function to recover a damaged, broken down or bogged down tank. Specialist armoured recovery vehicles are used for this which may have powerful winches or even cranes. Tanks are usually deployed in groups with groups of transporters to support them. Recovery vehicles are more complex and more expensive to build than transporters so a handful of recovery vehicles need be supplied to support a troop of transporters. For similar reasons tank transporters are rarely armoured to recover tanks under fire, although tracked recovery vehicles frequently are.

Military tanks first appeared in World War I, but their potential was not fully exploited until World War II with modern armoured fighting vehicle tactics. All tanks share the same three basic characteristics: they are covered with armour for protection, they can move and they can fire weapons. There are different types of armour, including modern modular, composite and explosive reactive armour. Other changes in tank design have been made to increase the safety of the tank crew. Improvements to engines and suspensions enable tanks to move faster over rough terrain. Tank armament is constantly being upgraded; tank weapons have ranged from machine guns to missile launchers.

A 'heavy' armoured tank is slower and less agile than a tank with 'lighter' armour. However, the crew of a more 'light' armoured tank is at greater risk of being injured from a direct hit. Sometimes the focus on one characteristic can be taken to extremes. Nazi Germany's Maus Super 'heavy' tank (which never got past the prototype stage) was so 'heavy' that it couldn't move off of level ground by itself or cross an unreinforced bridge.

Friday, 18th December 1942 – Bill's 15 T.T. Company send 15 light tanks to Ajdabiya, the capital of the Al Wahat District in northeast Libya. The area was the scene of heavy fighting during the war. During Operation Compass in December 1941, British forces forced Erwin Rommel's Afrika Korps to retreat through Ajdabiya, Libya, but they lost control of it again on Thursday, 2nd April 1942 when a reinforced Rommel counter-attacked. The town finally reverted to Allied control on Monday, 23rd November 1942 when it was recaptured by the British 7th Armoured Division.

Saturday, 19th December 1942 – Six light and seven heavy tanks from Bill's 15 T.T. Company return to Ajdabiya,

Libya.

Sunday, 20th December 1942 – Two light tanks from Bill's 15 T.T. Company proceed to Derna, a port city in eastern Libya. Derna had originally been captured by the Australian troops on Thursday, 30th January 1941 from the Italians in the North African Campaign. On Sunday, 6th April 1941 the Germans took back control from the British, but on Sunday, 15th November 1942, the British forces recaptured Derna.

Monday, 21st December 1942 – One heavy and seven light tanks from Bill's 15 T.T. Company return to Ajdabiya, Libya.

Friday, 25th December 1942 – Christmas Day and two thirds of Bill's 15 T.T. Company are fortunate to be stationed in the army camp. N.A.A.F.I. orders purchased have arrived safely which included pork, poultry, Christmas puddings, cakes, beer and cigarettes. Major V.H. Austin reported that 'since the company have returned from a refit in September, no tyre replacements for 30 ton trailers have been received. The tyre situation is acute and all methods of reducing tyre wear are impressed on all tanks.' He also reports that 'some very useful repairs to tyres have been performed by the company': this is part of Bill's work.

Sunday, 27th December 1942 – 12 light and 18 heavy tanks from Bill's 15 T.T. Company are included in a convoy of 104 transporters under Major V.H. Austin. They load tanks at Tmimi, a small village in Libya about 75 km east of Derna and 100 km west of Tobruk, Libya. They then proceed to Nofaliya, a town in the desert in the Sirte District of Libya, the site of a brief battle in late 1942 when some of Erwin Rommel's retreating forces ran out of fuel. At the time Nofaliya is home to a small fort and a few Italian buildings in addition to a mosque, some shops and a school.

Tuesday, 29th December 1942 – Two heavy and three

light tanks from Bill's 15 T.T. Company are sent to Belhamed, an area of hills near Tobruk, Libya, where fierce fighting took place in late November 1941.

Wednesday, 30th December 1942 – Two light tanks from Bill's 15 T.T. Company are sent to Benghazi. Benghazi is the second largest city in Libya, the capital of the Cyrenaica region (or ex-Province) and the former provisional capital of the National Transitional Council. The port city is located on the Mediterranean Sea. During the actions of Operation Compass, Benghazi was captured by the Australian 6th Division on 6th February 1941. It was recaptured by the Axis Powers, led by General Erwin Rommel of the German Afrika Korps, on Friday, 4th April 1941. It was taken again during Operation Crusader by the British on Wednesday, 24th December, only to change hands again on Thursday, 29th January 1942 in the Afrika Korps push to Egypt and the fateful Battle of El Alamein, 66 miles (106 km) from Alexandria, Egypt, in which British troops led by Field Marshall Bernard Montgomery defeated the Afrika Korps in the decisive battle of the North African portion of World War II. The Africa Korps make a long steady retreat across Libya passing through Benghazi for the final time. On Friday, 20th November 1942 Benghazi was captured by the British 8th Army.

Friday, 1st January 1943 – The New Year begins as Bill's 15 T.T. Company commences to move from Bomba, a village in eastern Libya on the Gulf of Bomba, located 38 miles (61 km) south of Derna to Marble Arch. Marble Arch, formerly known in Libya as 'El Gaus' ('The Arch'), is a monument in Libya built during the days of Italian colonization. The arch marked the border between Italian Tripolitania and Cyrenaica and located on the Libyan Coastal Highway. It was unveiled on 16th March 1937 in a lavish night ceremony attended by Benito Mussolini. 'Marble Arch' became the code name given to a 'Harbour

Area' which is a term used by the military to describe a 'gathering' point for troops, transport, armour, artillery, logistics, etc., prior to an 'operation', 'exercise', 'deployment' or 'onward move'. Only trailers with six tyres make the move. All fit transporters remain at the rear headquarters to ferry work from Belhamed, Libya.

Wednesday, 6th January 1943 – Bill's 15 T.T. Company are established from Marble Arch to Nofaliya Road.

Thursday, 7th January 1943 – Bill's 15 T.T. Company, led by Major V.H. Austin, return to their location.

Saturday, 9th January 1943 – 11 medium and 15 heavy tanks and transporters are detailed for 22 armoured brigades. Considerable repairs have to be completed to provide these transporters to roadworthy condition.

Saturday, 16th January 1943 – Iraq declares war on the Axis Powers.

Sunday, 17th January 1943 – Bill is remustered as a motor mechanic, group B, class 3 driver. Bill's 15 T.T. Company commences moving from Marble Arch, south Benghazi, Libya. The wireless communication is maintained with the company headquarters at Sirte and rear at Bomba, Libya.

Monday, 18th January 1943 – Bill's 15 T.T. Company headquarters and workshop is established. A fuel dump of 10,000 gallons commences.

Tuesday, 19th January 1943 – Transporters from Bill's 15 T.T. Company return from the forward area under Captain Nichol, D.S.O. (Distinguished Service Order). They refuel and are checked in the workshop during the night.

Wednesday, 20th January 1943 – 20 medium and 24 heavy tanks under Captain Nichol, D.S.O., in Bill's 15 T.T. Company proceed to Bomba, Libya.

Saturday, 23rd January 1943 – News has come that the British forces have captured Tripoli from the Italians. Tripoli, the capital city of Libya, is located in the northwest on the edge of the desert on a point of rocky land projecting into the Mediterranean and forming a bay. Gladys wonders if Bill is now stationed in Libya, North Africa.

When Gladys returned to Whatcliffe Works in Epsom on Monday, 23rd November 1942 having left Bill at Newmarket, Suffolk, she was given the sack for taking three days' leave without permission. Although the firm later relents and offers her job back, Gladys refuses to return on principle. Instead, she starts work for Accurate Recording Company along Garth Road, nearby to her new home. Here she soon becomes good friends with Hilda Brighton. Hilda's son, Frank, is friends with Gladys' younger brother, Sonny, both in their early teens. Gladys is finding the time apart from Bill very lonely, spending times as well as she could under the circumstances, living from day to day.

Confirming where Bill is stationed, Bill has sent Gladys three lemons from Africa in a wooden box. Gladys takes the lemons to work to raffle and is able to raise £3 10s 0d [£134.99p in 2013] and arranges several more raffles for the Merchant Navy, something Gladys was keen to organise.

Once Gladys is aware that Bill is stationed in Libya, North Africa, she writes to Bill informing him that Fred is also in Africa and would probably see him. Bill replies, comparing how big Africa is to England to give Gladys an example on how unlikely that meeting would be. After posting his letter, Bill unexpectedly comes across the regiment Gladys has told him Fred is in. He walks over to some soldiers to ask if, by chance, there was a "Fred Stagg here." Hearing, a man appears: it is his friend – Fred Stagg!

As Bill leaves Fred's camp to walk towards his tank transporter, an army truck is deliberately driven towards him. Quickly Bill manages to jump on to his tank trailer to avoid being hit and loudly calls out at the driver, a black American, who stops and reverses back to Bill and then he says apologetically: "Sorry, limey. I thought you were one of those f**king yanks"!

Wednesday, 27th January 1943 – Under the command of Lieutenant Cripps reinforcements arrive at Bill's 15 T.T. Company from Bomba, Libya.

Saturday, 30th January 1943 – The training detail transportation returns to Bomba, Libya, to move 10 Corps on completion of their duty.

Monday, 1st February 1943 – The light aid detachment under the command of Captain H. McHolmes in Bill's 15 T.T. Company proceeds to Barca to establish a location in the station yard where they are to remain until the 10 Corps move is complete. Barca (or Barce, now called Marj) is a city on the coast northeast of Libya and the capital of the British occupied Cyrenaica from 1942-1943.

Tuesday, 2nd February 1943 – One reinforced driver arrives from the Royal Army Service Corps Base Depot. Rommel retreats further into Tunisia, establishing his troops at the Mareth Line. The Mareth Line was a system of fortifications built by the French between the towns of Medenine and Gabès in southern Tunisia. It was designed to defend against attacks from the Italians in Libya, but following the fall of France and Operation Torch (the British/American invasion of French North Africa in November 1942) it fell into Axis hands and used by the Italians and Germans to defend against the British instead. Within two days Allied troops move into Tunisia for the first time and Rommel retreats.

Wednesday, 3rd February 1943 – One driver from Bill's 15 T.T. Company is admitted into hospital.

Thursday, 4th February 1943 – Instructions to Bill's 15 T.T. Company are received from the main column to prepare a platoon of A.E.C. Matadors, a World War II British heavy transport vehicle with a 5.5 inch gun, for handling over to R.E.M.E. (Royal Electrical and Mechanical Engineers) and the R.E. (Royal Engineers) to be replaced by articulated

170

Federal Transporters carrying 19 ton 100 lbs, classed as light transportation.

Friday, 5th February 1943 – The Allies now have all the area of Libya under their control.

Sunday, 7th February 1943 – Bill's 15 T.T. Company hands over the prepared platoon of A.E.C. Matador vehicles and they leave Bomba, Libya, loaded with 16 Crusader tanks of the field force column. Crusader tanks are one of the primary British cruiser tanks of the early part of World War II and perhaps the most important British tank of the North African Campaign. The Crusader's mobility made it a favourite of British tank crews.

Monday, 8th February 1943 – A convoy from Bill's 15 T.T. Company is on the road to Bomba and Benghazi, Libya. The U.S. 6th Corps arrives in North Africa.

Tuesday, 9th February 1943 – Bill's 15 T.T. Company arrives at their location.

Wednesday, 10th February 1943 – 10 Corps are contacted in the area for the off-loading of field force column with Bill's 15 T.T. Company. The British 8th Army sweeps through North Africa to Tunisia.

Thursday, 11th February 1943 – The Crusader tanks are delivered to the Benina area, near Benghazi in Libya.

Friday, 12th February 1943 – A demonstration is given by staff to Bill's 15 T.T. Company on maintenance, etc., of Federal transporters for all drivers taking over these vehicles. Federal transporters are used to salvage crashed or broken down vehicles and perform general towing.

Saturday, 13th February 1943 – Rommel launches a counter-attack against the Americans in western Tunisia; he takes Sidi Bouzid and Gafsa. The Battle of Kasserine Pass begins, a series of battles fought around Kasserine Pass, a two mile (3.2 km) wide gap in the Grand Dorsal chain of the Atlas Mountains in west central Tunisia. The Axis forces involved, led by Field Marshall Erwin Rommel, were primarily from the Afrika Korps Assault Group, elements of the Italian Centauro Armoured Division and two Panzer divisions detached from the 5th Panzer Army. The Allied forces involved came from the U.S. Army's 2nd Corps commanded by Major General Lloyd Fredendall, and the British 6th Armoured Division commanded by Major General Charles Keightley, which were part of the British 1st Army commanded by Lieutenant General Kenneth Anderson. Inexperienced American troops are soon forced to retreat and results in America's first major battle defeat of the war.

Sunday, 14th February 1943 – A German offensive breaks through de Faid Pass, Tunisia. American troops suffer heavy casualties and are pushed back over 50 miles (80 km) from their positions west of Faid Pass in the initial days of the Battle of Kasserine Pass. Despite early defeats, elements of the U.S. 2nd Corps, reinforced by British reserves, rally and hold the exits through mountain passes in western Tunisia, defeating the Axis offensive plans.

Wednesday, 17th February 1943 – The handing over of the A.E.C. Matadors is completed after they have been checked in the workshop.

Thursday, 18th February 1943 – 15 Federals with loaded Crusaders of the field force column at Benina proceed west to Tripoli.

Saturday, 20th February 1943 – Captain Nichol, DSO, with two platoons of heavy tanks loaded with the 10 Corps armour leaves Bomba, Libya, for the destination west of Tripoli. Allied troops occupy the Kasserine Pass in Tunisia.

Monday, 22nd February 1943 – Nine A.E.C. Matador transporters from Bill's 15 T.T. Company leave Bomba loaded with the 10 Corps armour for the destination west of Tripoli. This is changed to the British 8th Army time (Zone 'A' Time). Arrangements are made for the transporters to tow the armoured cars behind the trailers; the tow bars made by training. Bill has an 'accidental injury of a trivial nature that is not likely to interfere with his future efficiency as a soldier'.

Wednesday, 24th February 1943 – It is noted three Federals reported for transportation to Benghazi are to load guns for delivery to 557 Army Ordinance Department in Tripoli, Libya.

Friday, 26th February 1943 – A light aid detachment rejoins Bill's 15 T.T. Company headquarters at their area in Benghazi, Libya. Rommel retreats northward from the Mareth Line to Tunisia.

Saturday, 27th February 1943 – Bill's 15 T.T. Company receives instructions from company headquarters to move to an area west of Tripoli, Libya.

Sunday, 28th February 1943 – Bill's 15 T.T. Company leaves their Benghazi area and arrives at Ajdabiya, Libya, for night fall.

Monday, 1st March 1943 – Bill's 15 T.T. Company headquarters leaves Ajdabiya at first light and arrives 40 km from Nofaliya, Libya, by night fall. The company workshop leaves the Benghazi area.

Tuesday 2nd March 1943 – Bill's 15 T.T. Company leaves their position 40 km from Nofaliya to Buerat, a village in western Libya 90 km west of Sirte. Rommel intends to withdraw further into Tunis, but under pressure from his superiors, he establishes a new defensive line at Buerat.

Wednesday, 3rd March 1943 – Bill's 15 T.T. Company arrives at an area of Hun by night fall. Hun is an oasis town in the southwest of Libya, halfway between Sabha and the Mediterranean coast in the Sahara desert. The natural landscape around Hun mainly consists of a black basalt volcanic rock from the rapid cooling mountains with extensive sand dunes and date palm trees. In London 173 people are killed in a crush while trying to enter an air raid shelter at Bethnal Green tube station.

Thursday, 4th March 1943 – Bill's 15 T.T. Company arrives at their location at Tripoli, Libya.

Saturday, 6th March 1943 – Bill's 15 T.T. Company headquarters arrive at their location. The Battle of Medenine, also known as Operation Capri, takes place. Medenine is a major town in southeast Tunisia 48 miles (77 km) south of the port of Gabès and the island of Djerba on the main route to Libya where a German attack started with the intention to disrupt and delay the 8th Army's attack on the Mareth Line. This failed to make much impression and abandoned at dusk and German forces withdrew northward. The attack has been beaten with the loss of 52 German tanks. The Luftwaffe attempts to support the attack are ineffectual. The Battle of Medenine is General Erwin Rommel's last engagement in Africa. Adolf Hitler replaces Rommel with General Hans-Jürgen Bernhard Theodor von Amin. Amin was captured by the British Indian Army's 4th Infantry Division two months later on 12th May 1943. When captured, Amin expected to be met by Dwight D. Eisenhower. The American general refused; he would not meet with any German officers until the final surrender. Instead von Amin was brought to the British 1st Army commander-in-chief, General Kenneth Anderson to obtain as much information as possible. Amin served the rest of the war as a British prisoner of war interned along with 24 other German general officers at Camp Clinton, Mississippi, America, and was released on 1st July 1947. He returned to Germany where the estates he had held before the war had been taken and divided by the Soviet occupation authorities as part of a process of land reform. Amin died in 1962, aged 73, in Hesse, Germany.

Sunday, 7th March 1943 – Bill's 15 T.T. Company headquarters receive an invitation to join the main body area at Ben Gardane. Ben Gardane is a commune and coastal town close to the border of Libya in southeast Tunisia.

Monday, 8th March 1943 – Bill's 15 T.T. Company headquarters leave the Tripoli area while the company workshop remains and assists in the repairs of transporters still in the area.

Tuesday, 9th March 1943 – Bill's 15 T.T. Company headquarters arrive in their location at Ben Gardane, Tunisia.

Wednesday, 10th March 1943 – 27 transporters of 'A' and 'B' Platoon leave the location of Bill's 15 T.T. Company for Medenine, Tunisia. The convoy, under the command of Captain Nichol, D.S.O., is to lift Scorpion tanks. Scorpions are variant tanks that had a Matilda chassis with a mine flail mounted on it. The mine flail is a device that deliberately detonated mines in front of the vehicle that carried it, in order to make a safe path through a mine field. One Bedford M.W. truck and one Matchless motorcycle went down from the ten vehicle company.

Thursday, 11th March 1943 – 21 transporters of 'A' and 'B' Platoon are off loaded and return to the company location.

Friday, 12th March 1943 – At Bill's 15 T.T. Company, Matadors with 45 ton Rogers trailers are used for aerodromes. During World War II Rogers built 70 45 ton tank retrievers a week for the armed forces.

Sunday, 14th March 1943 – One Matador, five Federals and 20 D.T.s leave Bill's 15 T.T. Company location at 9:00 hour under the command of Major Austin. D.T.s is the Diamond 'T' 980 heavy tank transporter, used in World War II designed as a heavy prime mover for tank transporting and a product of the Diamond T Company in Chicago. In 1940 the British Purchasing Commission, looking to equip the British Army with a vehicle capable of transporting larger and heavier tanks, approached a number of American truck manufacturers to assess their models. The

Diamond T Company had a long history of building rugged, military vehicles for the U.S. Army Quartermaster Corps and, with a few slight modifications, met British requirements and an initial order for 200 is very quickly filled. The result was the Diamond T 980, a 12 ton hard-cab 6x4 vehicle which proved to be one of the most successful and memorable in its class. The tank is intended mainly for hauling damaged tanks aboard trailers mounted behind the cab. Armour is lifted from Medenine to a destination south of Foum Tataouine. Tataouine is a city located in southern Tunisia with below ground 'cave dwellings' of the native Berber population, designed for coolness and protection. From 1892 to 1951, Tataouine is the garrison town of the French penal military unit known as the Battalion of Light Infantry of Africa.

Monday, 15th March 1943 – Bill's 15 T.T. Company moves out at dusk to proceed east of Foum Tataouine, Tunisia.

Tuesday, 16th March 1943 – Four Federals of 'C' Platoon from Bill's 15 T.T. Company picks up loads at field training detachments and lifts to the east of Medenine.

Wednesday, 17th March 1943 – Seven Federals of 'C' Platoon under the command of Lieutenant H. Kemp picks up loads at field training detachments to lift to the east of Medenine, Tunisia. They return to the location the same night. One section of the company workshop arrives at Bill's 15 T.T. Company location from the Tripoli area. Three Matadors are handed over to R.E.M.E. One A.E.C. Matador is despatched to Tripoli, Libya.

Thursday, 18th March 1943 – Four Matadors and Rogers 30 ton trailers at Bill's 15 T.T. Company prepare for handing over to D.C.G. roads. D.C.G. could mean Deputy Commanding General (Roads), an official acronym associated with a component command, in this case roads. It could also mean Disaster Control Group or Defence Control Group. The tyre situation for the trailers is now acute. The main body of the workshop arrives at Ben Gardane location from Tripoli. General George S. Patton leads his tanks of 2nd Corps into Gafsa, Tunisia.

Friday, 19th March 1943 – Major Austin's convoy returns empty: the detail complete. Six A.E.C. Matadors, under the command of C.S.M. Watson, arrive at the company location from a detail of advanced aerodromes. Ten Federals under the command of Lieutenant H. Kemp leave the company location to pick up aerodrome construction apparatus for advanced airfields.

Saturday, 20th March 1943 – Seven A.E.C. Matadors are handed over to R.E.M.E.; 13 Federals are handed over by 'D' Platoon from 175 Company. Field Marshall Bernard Montgomery's forces begin a breakthrough in Tunisia striking at the Mareth Line.

Sunday, 21st March 1943 – The British Army opens an assault on the Mareth Line, a system of fortifications between the towns of Medenine and Gabès in southern Tunisia. This is designed to defend against attacks from the Italians in Libya but, following the fall of France and Operation Torch on 8th November 1942 when a force of over 70,000 British and American soldiers went ashore on the coast of Vichy French northwest Africa, a period of close Anglo/American co-operation began. The Mareth Line fell into Axis hands and used by the Italians and Germans to defend against the British instead.

Monday, 22nd March 1943 – While Bill is at his 15 T.T. Company camp, a petrol primus cooker that has been causing trouble is being repaired in the workshop during the evening and tested with a biscuit tin fire protector around it. When a peculiar flame came from the top, the officer commanding the 15 T.T. Company grabbed the petrol primus cooker and protector and deposited them outside. A number of soldiers from the surrounding tents arrive and Bill tries to extinguish the fire. The commanding officer left the scene to return to his tent. Before he is able to release the air valve, the cooker explodes shattering the contents over Bill's face, neck, chest and arms inflicting severe burns over him. Three other soldiers nearby are also badly injured while endeavouring to put the flame out. Bill is admitted to 8 Casualty Clearing Station.

Tuesday, 23rd March 1943 – American tanks defeat the Germans at El Guettar, a town in the centre of Tunisia.

Wednesday, 24th March 1943 – Bill is transferred to 72nd General Hospital in order to have his severe burns treated. His face is completely bandaged. When the bandage is removed, to his relief, Bill is able to see again. However, one soldier next to him does not regain his sight. Also today, 76 Allied P.O.W.s escape from Stalag Luft III in Sagan, a town on the Bobr River in western Poland. This becomes known as the Great Escape, a subject for the 1963 film. The number of prisoners attempting the escape was 200, of whom 80 managed to leave the camp; 73 are caught, and 50 executed on Hitler's orders and 23 are sent back to prison camps. Just three successfully escaped: one to Gibraltar, and two to Sweden.

Thursday, 25th March 1943 – A convoy of 20 D.T.s and eight Federals leave the location under the command of Major Austin to pick up loads west of Medenine, Tunisia, on the 23rd March return; the head of column entering the company location at 10:00 hour.

Friday, 26th March 1943 – The British break through the Mareth Line in southern Tunisia, threatening the German army who retreat north.

Saturday, 27th March 1943 – 'B' Platoon comprising of 17 D.T.s with Lieutenant Cripps, the officer in charge, returns from the Tripoli area to work from Sea-Head, a term to describe a military marine embarkation/disembarkation point, to field training detachments.

Monday, 29th March 1943 – Lieutenant Cripps leaves the company location with the 'B' Platoon for the Tripoli area to Sea-Head.

Tuesday, 30th March 1943 – Bill's 15 T.T. Company moves to an area in Medenine, Tunisia.

Thursday, 1st April 1943 – The Allies continue to squeeze the Germans into the corner of Tunisia.

Friday, 2nd April 1943 – Bill is transferred to 95th General Hospital. Since his serious accident, Bill has a lot to be thankful for and has taken an unusual interest in religion. He has been busy relearning the Ten Commandments, the Creed and the Lord's Prayer.

Tuesday, 6th April 1943 – The British and U.S. Army link up in Africa.

Wednesday, 7th April 1943 – Allied forces; the Americans from the west, and the British 8th Army from the east, link up near Gafsa in Tunisia.

Sunday, 11th April 1943 – Bill is confirmed and attends his first confirmation. While he is in the 95 General Hospital, British North African Forces, Bill writes a letter to Gladys. Letters are now numbered in order to keep a record of the ones each receives. This letter is number '2'.

Bill is 23 years and 7 months old: Gladys is 20 years and 11 months old.

(Above) Bill aged 24, (left) with Fred Stagg, 1943

(Above) June Alston, Bill's foster sister, 1943

PTE. POWELL. T/64083.
1S. T. T. COY. R.A.S.
95. G. HOSPITAL.
B. N. A. F.

3/

Sunday 11 April 1943.

My own darling beloved wife,

Hello sweetheart, I hope this
letter finds you in the best of
health and that you are not
worrying about me. I am getting
on O.K. and hope to be out
of here soon, another week will
probably see me quite well once
more. I won't be sorry to leave
as it is very boring in here,
nothing to do and all day to do
it in, and it makes the time
pass so very slowly. It seems as
if I have been in here for
years already. The rest was very
welcome at first, but now the
effect is beginning to wane and
I am looking forward to rejoini

(Above) Bill's letter to Gladys written on Sunday, 11th April 1943

181

Mrs Gladys Powell
84a London Road
North Cheam
Surrey
England

(2)
PTE. POWELL T/69083
15 T.T. COY., R.A.S.C.
95 G. HOSPITAL
B.N.A.F.

Sunday 11 April 1943

My own darling beloved wife,

Hello sweetheart, I hope this letter finds you in the best of health and that you are not worrying about me. I am getting on ok and hope to be out of here soon, another week will probably see me quite well once more. I won't be sorry to leave as it is very boring in here, nothing to do and all day to do it in and it makes the time pass so very slowly. It seems as if I have been in here for years already. The rest was very welcome at first, but now the effect is beginning to wane and I am looking forward to rejoining the boys again.

From the news it seems as if I will have to hurry or the war will be over out here before I am back in it again. Like most people at home now, our main topic of conversation is "where next." Well, your guess is as good as mine. Rumour tells us that we are going to invade here, there or somewhere else, that we are going to stay here and that we are coming home, each new rumour reputed to have come from some official source, so you can take your choice. Probably the best one is that we are going to give Canada to the Italians to save the trouble of taking them home after the war. The number of prisoners we have taken must mean there are more Eyeties [12] in Canada than in Italy.

I have something to tell you that will probably surprise you a lot. I have spent most of my time since I have been up with the Padre and this morning I went through a confirmation and attended communion. For this last week I have been busy relearning the Ten Commandments, the Creed [13] and the Lord's Prayer. I expect you will think it is a great change for me, but I have not altered a lot, except in thinking I have a lot to be thankful for and also believing that Christianity is compatible with socialism. Fundamentally they are the same and together they can create an entirely new world. Although I do not even now agree completely with the church or the way it works, but I do believe in the ethics of teaching as was taught by Christ.

I am eagerly waiting the day when I will be returning home to you, darling. I love you and miss you with all my heart and soul. I only wish I was able to put into words just how I feel, my beloved, you have given me a happiness that I could never recapture without you. Life to me, to be life at all, must have you to share it with me. I live only to be with you once more, you are everything in the world to me and I love you so very much, darling.

When I look back on the great times we have had together in the past, how happy we have been, how wonderful our love for each other, it makes the future for us seem very bright. Always when I have been with you I have been very happy, no matter where we have been or what we have been doing. The mere fact of you being with me has meant that I have lived in an ecstasy that had to be experienced to be believed. I only hope that I have in some small measure given you the happiness that you have given me.

My only regret about our life together is that I have been unable to give you all that you have given me. All that I have been able to give you, darling, has been my love, but I have given you that with all my heart, no one else has or could take that away from you. I love you, miss you and need you, sweetheart, with all my heart and soul and I pray that very soon I will be reunited with you, darling. It is very hard to be separated from the person you love, but I know you feel the same and that helps a lot. The fact that I have you waiting to welcome me when I return makes this enforced separation bearable, darling. Don't ever change, as you mean such a lot to me. I could not live without you, you are my life. I am the luckiest fellow alive as I have the sweetest, loveliest, most unselfish and most charming girl in the world as my wife.

I hope that soon I will be able to hold you again in my arms and tell you how much I love you and how much I have missed you, darling, but even then I could never fully describe just what you mean to me. Look after yourself, my beloved, and let's hope that in the very near future we will be together again.

As I walk round the grounds in the hospital, I am reminded of some of the great times we have had in the past, of the hospital at Watford when you were with me on visiting days, how I used to live for those few hours each week when I would see your sweet ever welcoming smile again. Of the walks through Nonsuch Park and the sun glinting on your hair making you look even more like a vision from heaven than usual. I see your beauty reflected in the flowers and sunshine, my sweet, their fragrance, beauty, softness and freshness all serve to remind me of you.

Then those great times we had at Brighton, the leaves together and odd days and evenings we spent with each other, of the days at Evercreech when your love, sweetness and understanding made me so cheap and childish by comparison. I will never forget that, beloved, even now I feel ashamed of myself and terribly grateful to you.

Our first trip to Evercreech also stands out in my memory, for it was then that I tried so very hard to ask you to marry me, but I just didn't have the courage and I had to wait until a week or so later before I had the courage to ask you. Then at Syd's when I asked your Ma and Pa for their consent, your Mum was sewing at the machine, Dad was reading. I went over what I was going to say in my mind a hundred times and when at last I did say it, it was deathly hush that settled in the room.

Then the preparations and at long last the great day arrived, how beautiful you looked. Even the photographs, good as they were, could not recapture that wondrous beauty that was yours. Yes, my darling, I have many lovely memories and I have a lot to be thankful about, but despite the happiness we have had in the past, I am sure that the future will be even better. It will be up to us, darling. I know we will make our married life a real success.

All other great loves of the past [14] – Romeo and Juliet, Darby and Joan, Napoleon and Josephine, they will all fade into insignificance beside our love. We will be the envy of all our friends, because our love for each other will be unsurpassed. We were meant for each other and for each other we will live, nothing can alter that, nothing can or will come between us. Let us hope that the day will soon dawn when we will be able to enjoy life together in the new world we have helped to create in which poverty, unemployment and hunger will have no place, a world in which each and everyone will have a fair chance of enjoying a real life.

The Beveridge Report [15] was a great step forward, a step towards that brave new world. The big business and other forces of reaction in conjunction with the short sighted policy of our so called Labour leaders have carved it about beyond recognition. They hope that we will return to the

185

muddle and chaos that existed before the war, the same muddle and chaos that will lay the foundations of the next war.

I am afraid they are due for a big shock, the people have already sat up, once over the Hoare-Laval Pact [16] and once over the kick out of Chamberlain [17] and I think they can do it again over the Beveridge Report.

If those at home don't, well, they will soon find that we can fight fascism and reaction at home just as hard as we can fight it abroad. We know what we are fighting for and we will see that we are not twisted out of it. If the Government are sincere in wishing to create a fair, just and decent order after the war then their adoption of the 'whole' Beveridge Report will help to convince everyone of their sincerity, until then we must look on their so called post-war aims an eyewash. We remember that our fathers were told of a country "fit for our heroes to live in" [18]. Also we know what sort of land they got. I, for one, don't intend to sell matches after this lot is over and there are a lot like me. A little less talk about the new land they are going to create and a bit more action in starting to build it now.

We expect the Conservatives to attempt to preserve the status quo, but I am disgusted with the Labour Party, at least something better was expected from them. There seems to be hardly any difference between either party now and I don't think people will look to them for a lead, it will be a golden chance either the C.P. [19] or else a non party alliance of all the really progressive elements throughout the country.

Whatever the party that leads the way, we will make sure that we have not fought in vain, this time we will not be put off by any nice sounding, but empty promises. I hate fascism and would willingly die to smash it, but that goes not only for German and Italian fascism, but also for any attempt to introduce it in Britain. Churchill has done a great deal towards leading us to victory, perhaps he will see that the victory will be well worth winning and the full adoption of the Beveridge Report in its entirety now will show how that can be done. We have told all the oppressed people of the world that Britain now stands for justice and decency. We have told the U.S.S.R. and U.S.A. the same, yet we have missed a golden opportunity to prove that we mean what we say. Surely, the people will not be side tracked by the story that we can't afford it. If so, then how have we paid for the war, the total cost of the report is less than a day or so of the war. It is up to us, the future is in our hands and we will see that future is worth having.

Well, I guess that is enough of that. If I write anymore I am afraid the censor will get a nasty headache and perhaps even what I have written will be one long blue pencil, so I had better change the subject.

The weather now is glorious, just like a June day at home, sun shining and a lovely blue sky. I expect the weather at home now is pretty good and with the double summer time in force, the days are nice and long. Also by now, spring is well on the way and the trees and flowers beginning to blossom. To me out here, the words of Robert Browning's poem hold a special meaning, 'Oh to be in England now that April's there', [20] is a sentiment I heartily endorse, but England at any time is a very welcome place and with you there waiting for me, it is almost a Utopia. May God grant that I will soon be home with you, darling.

How is Lily [21] getting on now, I expect her baby is growing up now. Remember me to her when you see her again. Also, to the others at Romford and any others of our mutual friends and relations you see. Give my love to all at home. I hope they are well. How are you getting on at work, you have been there about four months now, so I expect you are well used to it by now.

Well, dear, I will draw to a close. All my love to you,

darling, look after yourself and don't worry about me. I love you now and always and am proud to be your loving husband,

Bill

xxx

I AM LIVING TO BE WITH YOU

[12] Eyeties is a World War II-era nickname for Italian soldiers.

[13] The Creed is a statement of belief that describes the beliefs shared by a religious community.

[14] Romeo and Juliet (two young lovers), (John) Darby and Joan (an elderly married couple), Napoleon and Josephine (Napoleon Bonaparte (Napoleon I) and his first wife, widow, Josephine de Beauharnais).

[15] The British government asked Sir William Beveridge to write a report on the best ways of helping people on low incomes. In December 1942 Beveridgepublished a report that proposed that all people of working age should pay a weekly contribution. In return, benefits would be paid to people who were sick, unemployed, retired or widowed. Beveridge argued that this system would provide a minimum standard of living 'below which no one should be allowed to fall'. These measures were eventually introduced by the Labour Government when elected in 1945.

[16] The Hoare-Laval Pact was a proposal made in December 1935 by British Foreign Secretary, Samuel Hoare, and French Prime Minister, Pierre Laval, for ending the Second Italo/Abyssinian War. Italy had wanted to take Abyssinia as part of its empire and have an empire like the Romans had and also to avenge

previous defeats in the region. The Pact offered to partition Abyssinia (as Ethiopia was then called) and thus achieve Italian dictator Benito Mussolini's goal of making the independent nation of Abyssinia into an Italian colony.

[17] Neville Chamberlain was Prime Minister of Great Britain in September 1939 as Europe descended into World War II. Chamberlain paid a political price for the failure of Britain in Norway in the spring of 1940 and resigned as Prime Minister to be succeeded by Winston Churchill. Chamberlain died shortly afterwards.

[18] David Lloyd George was a British Liberal politician and Prime Minister of the U.K. leading the Wartime Coalition Government between 1916-1922. After the armistice on 23rd November 1918 he promised the returning troops from World War I comprehensive reforms to deal with poor education, housing, health and transport: "What is our task? To make Britain a country fit for our heroes to live in." Lloyd George's post-war government raised the school leaving age to 14 and a total of 170,000 homes were built, a landmark measure. Although re-elected he remained dependent upon the coalition with the Conservatives, who had little intention of delivering such radical reforms. In place of this utopia they found a land blighted by unemployment and shortages. Inspired by the end of the war and the victory of the Russian workers and peasants, the spectre of revolution was taking on across the continent and Britain was no exception. In 1918 strikes had already cost six million working days. This exploded to almost 35 million in 1919, with a daily average of 100,000 workers on strike. In the face of such a crisis the ruling class split into two main camps: those who wanted an all-out assault against

the working class, like Winston Churchill, soon to be Secretary of State for War. Alongside the struggle of the workers in industry, the armed forces and the police were to then take action. After years in the bloodbath of filthy foreign trenches, Churchill now expected British soldiers to fight a new war against the young workers state in Russia. This was unacceptable and the troops revolted. Christopher Addison became the first Minister of Health in June 1919. Addison was responsible for the first Housing and Town Planning Act under which the state built 213,000 low-rent home (council houses) for the working class. He also presided over large increases in public spending until he was removed from Ministry of Health in April 1921 for his extravagance and it was then decided to halt the housing construction scheme.

[19] C.P. – Conservative Party.

[20] 'Oh, to be in England now that April's there' is from Robert Browning's poem, 'Home Thoughts, From Abroad'.

[21] Lily is Gladys' best friend. They have been friends since Gladys' mother, Hilda, and Lily's mother, Maggie Kaufman, were neighbours and also close friends. Most of Gladys' time was spent with Lily and her sister, Doreen Kaufman and was practically brought up by their mother and thought to be lucky with having two mothers, her own and also Mrs. Kaufman. Gladys was also friends with Doris who married Lily's brother, Reg Kaufman. Lily married Laurie Shrubsole and Doreen married Jack Braiden. Lily and Laurie had a baby girl, Pamela Doreen, born in February 1943.

April – May 1943

While Bill has been in 95 General Hospital, Adolf Hitler and Benito Mussolini meet at Salzburg, Austria, to boost Mussolini's declining morale. Bolivia has declared war on Germany, Italy and Japan. Finland officially rejects Russia's terms for peace. The British 8th Army has entered Sfax, Tunisia.

Sunday, 18th April 1943 – On what is to be called the Palm Sunday Massacre, a large number of German troop transport aircraft on their way to pick up isolated German troops are shot down before they reach Tunisia. Leaders from Great Britain and America meet in Hamilton, Bermuda, for a conference to discuss the plight of the European Jews.

Friday, 23rd April 1943 – (Good Friday) Bill's burns are now healing enough for him to be transferred from 95th General Hospital to 9 Convalescent Depot.

Monday, 26th April 1943 – The British finally take Longstop Hill in Tunisia, a key position on the breakout road to Tunis.

Saturday, 1st May 1943 – Since November 1942 Benghazi in Libya has been held by the British until over 250,000 German soldiers and their Italian Allies in North Africa surrender in May 1943. After being hemmed into the Tunisian port cities of Tunis and Bizerte by the British advancing from the east and an Anglo/American army advancing from the west, this effectively ended Axis operations in the North African portion of World War II.

Sunday, 2nd May 1943 – From his convalescent depot, Bill writes a letter to Gladys. This letter is number '9'.

Bill is 23 years and 8 months old: Gladys is 21 years old today.

9/

Sunday May 2. 1943.

T/69083.
PTE POWELL.
15. T.T. COY. R.A.S.C.
9. CON. DEPOT.
B.N.A.F.

My own darling beloved wife,

Many happy returns of the day darling, I hope that you have a very nice time for your birthday and that we will be with each other for your next one. I have had a day out myself to celebrate the occasion, I have just returned from town, where I saw Brian Donlevy in 'Wake Island' and then remembering last year when we went to the Wimbledon Theatre together (Harry Parry if you remember) I then went to a french theatre and saw a variety show. I believe the comedian must have been good as everyone was roaring with laughter, but I could not make head or tail of him, but one of the singers sang a couple of songs in English, can you guess what one of them was, it was about the best song she could have sung as far as I was concerned, it was 'All the

(Above) Bill's letter to Gladys written on Sunday, 2nd May 1943

192

Mrs Gladys Powell
84a London Road
North Cheam
Surrey
England

(9)
PTE. POWELL T/69083
15 T.T. COY., R.A.S.C.
9 CON. DEPOT
B.N.A.F.

Sunday May 2, 1943

My own darling beloved wife,
    Many happy returns of the day darling, I hope that you have a very nice time for your birthday and that we will be with each other for your next one.   I have had a day out myself to celebrate the occasion.   I have just returned from town, where I saw Brian Donlevy in 'Wake Island' [22] and then remembering last year when we went to the Wimbledon Theatre together (Harry Parry, if you remember).   I then went to a French theatre and saw a variety show.   I believe the comedian must have been good as everyone was roaring with laughter, but I could not make head or tail of him, but one of the singers sang a couple of songs in English.   Can you guess what one of them was, it was about the best song she could have sung as far as I was concerned, it was 'All The Things You Are' and you can bet I was thinking of you all the time, darling.   The only other thing in the show that I could understand was a lightening artist, a conjurer and the chorus girls.   I have heard a lot about the French chorus girls, how good they are, how little they wear and also their dancing ability, but my impression

is they would not yet get a job at any third rate music hall at home. They were somewhere round an average age of 35-40 and looked it and I even believe I could dance as good, if not better than any of them.

On the whole though, I had a good time until I started to come home, then it poured with rain and you have to see the rain here before you would believe it possible. It comes down in a deluge and can keep it up for days at a stretch. I got soaked through getting home and it is still raining like blazes now. If it doesn't ease up we will have to turn out to dig some more channels for it to run away, or else we will be flooded out. This must be the world's worst climate, rain, sun, cold, no two days seem to be alike, tropical kit one day, overcoat the next and then they say the English climate is very unorthodox and unreliable, but compared to this, it is heaven.

One of the funniest sights I have seen was the trams in the town. They are single decks, narrower and shorter than at home, but usually three or four linked together like a train, each tram having its own conductor, but only the front one has a driver and that tows the rest. They are never full up, as no matter how many are already on, they can always pack on some more. Even the driver's platform is packed full, so that it is impossible for him to move. The people hang on the step, the sides and the back, looking like a lot of flies round a jam pot. In fact, you can hardly see the tram for people hanging on the outside. Hardly ever is the fare collected as the conductors are jammed in and unable to move. Yet, each time the tram stops, more people seem to get on or hang on each time. I have never seen anyone ever left at a stop unable to get on.

We went to town by bus. It was also a single decker and, according to the notice on board, it held 28 people, but when we got on it was already full and quite a few standing. Nevertheless, over thirty of us also piled on and

I had a lovely ride. There was somebody standing on my feet all the way down, elbows digging in me and I could hardly breathe and see because of tobacco smoke. Actually, smoking is not allowed in buses, trams, cinemas, theatres or shops, but nobody seems to take any notice of the fact. The words 'Defence de Fumer' or 'No Smoking' appear almost everywhere, but maybe the people can't read, or else they follow the example of the British troops. By the way, don't ever talk about the behaviour of the Canadians any more. Some of our fellows and a good few too, put the Canadians in the shade. Sometimes I am ashamed of being English when one sees how they act. The Yanks are far better mannered and better behaved than we are out here and also they are a lot more popular. It is a pity though, that a bunch of hooligans and rowdies by their behaviour give a bad name to the rest, but I suppose that wherever large numbers of men are gathered there will always be some who get the rest a bad name by their actions.

How is everything at home? I am very sorry to say that except for that one air mail (no.10) that arrived about ten days ago it is nearly seven weeks since I heard from you, so I am well behind with the news. I hope everything both at home and at work is alright and that you and all at home are in the best of health. Up to the time I caught my packet I had been receiving your mail as regularly as I could wish. I had had all your letters from one to fifty-one except number 29, also your first six air mails and nine airgraphs by ordinary mail and one airmail and one airgraph by the air route. Also, I had twenty letters from Mum and Ivy and eight from your Mum. Since then, though, only one airmail and a parcel have reached me and it was three weeks before I came in hospital that I last received a letter from anyone else except you. What I can't make out is how the parcel got through and yet the letters haven't. I know you are writing and also Mum (yours and mine) but where the letters are going to, God only knows, but they don't seem to find me. I don't mind the war, the hardship or even the separation from you, but not even to hear from you is above a joke. To say I am fed up with it would be to put it very mildly. I am living to be home with you again so that mail will no longer interest me. I might as well not be out here as far as the post office is concerned. Perhaps they are having a sit down strike with me as they think I have been receiving too many letters from you. Still, I suppose one of these days everything will be ok and I will once again begin to get your letters through regularly. The sooner the better, as I am longing to hear from you. I wonder how you are getting my mail, I usually write about three airgraphs and a couple of letters each week. I hope you receive them and that they don't take too long to reach you. I know what it is like to wait each day for the post and only get disappointment. I know you live for my letters as much as I live only for yours, so I hope that you are receiving them alright and that very soon I will begin to receive all yours once more.

Did you receive the increase in the allowance, darling, and also I hope if you have, that you also kept the back pay for yourself for your birthday. I was hoping to be able to increase it further to £3 [115.71p in 2013] a week, but this holiday has put a damper on that. I had been told by our platoon officer that I was next on the list for a first class fitters pay and that is seven shillings [£13.50p in 2013] a day, an increase in pay of 1/6d [£2.89p in 2013] a day, which I intended to make over to you. Another 10/6d [£20.25p in 2013] a week would have made my allotment exactly three pounds a week [£115.71p in 2013], but this had to happen and now I have lost the opportunity. Even if I go back to my old company, I will have to wait for another vacancy and as most of the fighting will probably be over out here by then, that vacancy may not occur. Instead, someone has no doubt filled my place and I will go to some other company and there I will have to content myself until some more fun starts and vacancies occur.

Still, even now we should have a little to help to build our home when all this is over, but don't forget, darling, that the allowance is yours, if you need it at all, use it. It is my responsibility to keep you, (that's the idea of having a husband) and if because you are working you can do without the allowance, it is your savings and yours to do as you wish with. All I want is for you to be happy, that is my main concern. As long as you are happy, then I am satisfied. I love you, sweetheart. I have told you that many times before, but no matter how often I say it, I can never manage to tell you how much I love you. My entire life is bound up with you and I am always thinking of you, living for the day when we will be together once again. God alone knows how much you mean to me, I live for you alone, my beloved, and need you more than I could ever describe. I long to see your sweet face again, with that beautiful smile and shining eyes, those ruby lips pressed against mine and to hear you tell me that you love me as I love you. May God grant that in the very near future, darling, we are reunited, as I miss you so much.

Life without you to share it with me is meaningless and empty. You are everything in the world to me and it will always be that way. It is over twenty three weeks now, my darling, since I last saw you, one hundred and sixty two days to be exact. It has been like a lifetime. Time drags very slowly away from you, yet whenever we were together the days, weeks and months seemed to fly by. I wonder how long it will be before all this is over and I come home to you again. How long it will be before I am sitting in the armchair with you on my lap, telling you that I love you and our life with each other begins again. If only I could hold you in my arms again, to feel you close to me and experience the wonderful feeling of complete happiness that I always have when I am with you. I hope and pray that before very long those dreams will become reality and then I will once again begin to live, sweetheart. All day I am thinking of you and each night you are with me in my dreams, my idea of heaven and Utopia now, is just to be with you. I love you with all my heart and soul, no matter how long I am away from you nothing will alter that and always I will be true to you, for you are the only person in the world for me. No one else could ever hold any attraction for me, for you are the sweetest, the most beautiful, unselfish and charming girl in the world and there is not anyone to compare with you.

All I wish is to come home to you at the earliest possible moment and settle down to a lifetime of happiness and contentment with you by my side. With you, sweetheart, I will always be very happy. I only hope that I can make you as happy as you have made me. I will do my best, darling, as you have done for me, although I can never repay your kindness and sweetness, or never hope to equal your unselfish character, but you can depend, darling, that I will do all I can to make you happy and to give you all you need. Your happiness is all that matters to me, as long as I know you are happy then I am satisfied. But as long as I live, I could never give you the things you deserve because there is nothing good enough for you, dearest. Nothing that could ever be too good for you and even the best of everything would only amount to a small fraction of the things you should have. You are perfect, sweetheart, and I thank God that I am lucky enough to be your husband and to have you love me as you do.

Take care of yourself, sweetheart, and let's hope that very soon we will be together once again. Just think, no more war, passes, separations or barracks, just a lifetime together, a lifetime of ecstasy and fulfilment. It will be heaven, just to be home with you again. I love you and miss you and only hope that very soon I will be coming home to find you waiting for me, a vision of loveliness, as you always are and then to take you into my arms and tell you over and over again how much I have missed you and how much I love you. That is the day I am living for, beloved, and may it dawn very soon, the day of our reunion.

Well, darling, I must draw to a close now as it is getting very late. Everyone else in the tent has been sound asleep for some time, but I had to write to you on your birthday. Give my love to Mum, Bill, Eileen and Sonny. I hope they are all well and that everything is ok with them. Tell them I am looking forward to being with them again and in the near future.

Look after yourself, darling, and don't worry over me as I am well and safe.

All my fondest love to you, sweetheart. Keep smiling and enjoy yourself as much as you can. Don't upset yourself about the letters not reaching me, I know you are writing and that you are doing all you can.

Goodbye, beloved, may we soon be together again. I am always your loving husband,

Bill

xxx

MIZPAH [23]

[22] 'Wake Island' was a 1942 film starring Brian Donlevy.
[23] MIZPAH means 'May the Lord watch between me and thee when we are absent from another' taken from Genesis 31:49 of the Bible – an emotional bond in separation (either when a loved one left for action or after death).

[This letter also includes a poem, 'Fidelity', Bill wrote for Gladys.]

'FIDELITY'

I will be forever faithful
And forever true,
Less than all my heart and soul
I could not offer you.

Love like ours is based on truth
On loyalty and trust,
Far too beautiful a thing
To drag into the dust.

False delights and stolen joys
For me no pleasure hold,
Little infidelities
That tarnish loves pure gold.

I am more than satisfied
With your sweet memory,
Counting myself fortunate
That you should care for me.

May 1943

Eventually the war in North Africa is over after nearly three years when 300,000 Germans and Italians driven into the extreme northwest corner of Tunisia have no option but to surrender with no possibility of a German 'Dunkirk'. The commanding British Field Marshal, Sir Harold Alexander, sends word to British Prime Minister Winston Churchill: "It is my duty to report that the Tunis campaign is over. All enemy resistance has ceased." Having captured Tunisia, the Allies begin the bombing of the Italian island of Pantelleria, 100 miles from Tunis.

Wednesday, 12th May 1943 – Winston Churchill and Franklin D. Roosevelt meet for The Trident Conference to discuss their future strategy.

Saturday, 15th May 1943 – The French Resistance Movement is formed.

Sunday, 16th May 1943 – The Dambuster Raids are carried out by no.617 Squadron, R.A.F. on two German dams, Mohne and Eder. The Ruhr war industries lose electrical power. The Warsaw Ghetto Uprising ends with about 14,000 Jews killed and about another 40,000 sent to Treblinka death camp.

Wednesday, 19th May 1943 – Winston Churchill praises the partnership of the two Allies when he addresses a joint session of the U.S. Congress.

Saturday, 22nd May 1943 – The Allies bomb Sicily and Sardinia, both of which are to be possible landing sites.

Monday, 24th May 1943 – Bill has now left 9 Convalescent Depot where he arrived on Friday, 23rd April and is now transferred to Algiers, the north central of Algeria on the Mediterranean Sea. Bill writes another letter to Gladys.

Bill is 23 years and 8 months old: Gladys is 21 years old.

[This letter starts from page 4. Either the first three pages are censored, or lost. There is no date but, judging by the letter numbers Bill has received and that he is still in hospital and has received Gladys' letter posted on 29th April, this letter suggests it would probably be the next one Gladys would receive from him.]

4.

but Jerry must have spotted it as he kept a barrage of machine gun fire on the spot. But our fellows had realized that something had gone wrong and a patrol brought us all safely back and so to hospital. So now you know the full story of how I came to have this holiday.

It is a holiday as well as I am having a really nice time, although I am afraid it will not last very much longer. I am almost as fit as I can be now, and fully expect to be discharged at the end of the week. You can guess that I am pretty fit as yesterday I swam a mile and my arm stood it very well. I go to the beach every day and amuse myself swimming all the afternoon, the exercise has done my arms the

(Above) Unknown date of letter that starts on page 4

202

Mrs. Gladys Powell
84a London Road
North Cheam
Surrey
England

4/.

.......but Jerry must have spotted it as he kept a barrage of machine gun fire on the spot.   But our fellows had realized that something had gone wrong and a patrol bought us all safely back and so to hospital.   So, now you know the full story of how I came to have this holiday.

It is a holiday as well, as I am having a really nice time, although I am afraid it will not last very much longer.   I am almost as fit as I can be now and fully expect to be discharged at the end of the week.   You can guess that I am pretty fit, as yesterday I swam a mile and my arm stood it very well.   I go to the beach every day and amuse myself swimming all the afternoon, the exercise has done my arms the world of good and now, except for the scars, they are as right as rain.   Even the scars will gradually fade away, even now they are not nearly so pronounced as they were, but it may take more than a year before they disappear altogether.   Not only do we have the swimming, sunbathing and physical training, but on Tuesday evenings there is a camp concert and we have a good amount of local talent.   The concerts have been very good up to now and pass a very interesting evening.

Yesterday I again went into Algiers and spent a few hours in a cinema where I saw Jimmy Cagney in 'Yankee Doodle Dandy' [24], quite a good film and also a recent issue.   Most films out here are very old, for example, the cinema that I went to is showing next week Spencer Tracy and Mickey Rooney in 'Men In Boys Town' and other films on show are 'Parachute Battalion', 'Nurse Edith Cavell', 'Dr.

Jekyll and Mr. Hyde', 'Fantasia', 'Coastal Command' and all these are in English, also there are many cinemas showing films in French. Then, there are one or two theatres and a couple of boxing shows, so I do alright for entertainment when I am in town. The worst of it is that the last bus to our camp leaves very early and is always full, usually I have to hitchhike or walk back and it is almost fifteen miles, but I always get a lift for part of the way, at least. I will be sorry to have to leave here, as it is a real holiday after the do in Tunisia. I don't know where I will go to after I leave here, but doubt very much if I will return to my old company. I wonder what they will do with us all now the war is over out here. Wherever it is, I hope it will be very soon so that we can get it over and come back home again.

I miss you so very much, darling, and live for the day when I will be home with you once more. I often wonder what our reunion will be like. I picture it in my mind and imagine whether you will laugh or cry, whether I will seem the same to you and if you will be disappointed with me. I love you with all my heart and soul, you are the only girl in the world for me and I am living only to hold you in my arms once again.

I received your number 20 airgraph yesterday and, as it was posted on April 29, it only took three weeks to reach me, also a parcel of newspapers (Pictorial and News of the World dated Feb 14) and they only took just over three months to arrive. Up to date I have received letters 1-65 except no.29, airmails 1-10 except no.9, airgraphs 1-24 except no.21 and no.22; also nine parcels, ten lots of newspapers and two parcels of cigarettes. The end of April is the latest date on any of the letters I have received, so the mail seems to be getting slower than ever. At one time an airmail took less than ten days and only just over two weeks for an ordinary letter. I did receive a letter (airmail) from Ivy during the week which only took seven days, but somehow all the others are taking three weeks to arrive here. Still, who knows, it may speed up soon. I hope so anyway, as it is bad enough being away from you and not to hear from you is beyond a joke. I hope you are still getting my letters through alright and also that you received the postcards I sent. I hope to be able to have my photograph taken next week and I will send you one as soon as I can. I can't promise as I may not be able to make it, but I will do my best.

The weather is simply grand here now, a clear blue sky and brilliant sunshine every day and it is ideal for lounging about, but I will not be looking forward to starting to work again as it is too hot for that. I would love to stay here until the day came for us to come home again. It is easily the finest place I have been to since I first came to this country, although I am sure there are many better places in England. Wherever a person may be, that place can never compare with home and you can bet that I am living for the day when I will be home with you again. Even this country would be heaven if you were with me. I would be happy anywhere in the world as long as you are beside me. I love you, sweetheart, and live only to hold you only in my arms and tell you how much I have missed you. God knows that you are the only thing I live for, darling. No matter how I try, I can never tell you how much you mean to me. Let's hope that very soon we will be together again able to resume our lives with each other and once again to know that ecstatic happiness that I always have when I am with you.

On the way back from Algiers yesterday I got into conversation with a French soldier who had just arrived from England and had been billeted [25] in London. He knew about as much English as I knew French and our conversation was typical of most of our efforts at conversing with a French man. It went something like this. I started the conversation with "Comment allez vous?" ["How are you?"] and he replied "OK" and said he had been in England and London. So far so good, but I tried to ask if there was any raids on London now and what they were like, then the trouble started. "Boche [26] aviation, whee – boom, bang", he said. "Ah, oui ["Ah, yes"], oui." "Boche aviation whee – bang – da-da-da – London, oui." "No, no, Boche pas bon" ["No, no, 'Germans' not good"]. Then a lot of hand waving and he carried on like this, "Macaronis [27] Boche, whee – bang." All this was repeated about a dozen times which I de-coded to mean that spitfires were knocking the hell out of Jerry and Eyetie. The next thing he wanted to know was how I got my scars on my face and arms. I tried to explain like this, "Tunisia, la guerre, Boche, la feu, comprendre?" ["Tunisia, the war, 'Germans', the fire, understand?"]. "No comprendre" [No understand]. "Stove, burn, tea, comprendre?" "Comprendre, tea. No comprendre, stove." "Eh, tea, water, boil, comprendre?" "No comprendre." "Tea, la feu" ["Tea, the fire"]. "Ah, oui, comprendre" [Ah, yes, understand]. "Comprendre, explosion?" "No, no." "Eh, bang, whoosh, comprendre?" and so it went on for all the journey back and the final result was that I discovered he had been in London and I believe he discovered that somehow I was burnt. All of which goes to show how difficult it is to talk to the people out here. Still, I get along by pointing to what I want, then saying "combien?" ["how much?"] and leaving it at that.

I hope that Mum, Bill, Eileen and Sonny are all in the best of health and that everything at home is quite ok. Give them all my love and tell them I am looking forward to seeing them all again soon. Also, convey my best wishes to Lily and her baby and here's hoping that they are both well, also that Laurie is able to get home frequently to see them [28]. Remember me to all at Romford, Canning Town and to all our other mutual friends and relations who you may meet. I am looking forward to the day when I will be seeing them all again. By the way, I hope you are not wearing out my armchair too much as I hope to be sitting on it again soon and with you on my lap, of course.

Well, darling, I must close now as I have not got any more to say, except to remind you that I love you always with all my heart and soul and will do so as long as I live. Goodbye, my beloved. Look after yourself, my darling, and don't worry about me, sweetheart.

I am always you ever loving husband,

Bill

xxx

LOVE TO YOU MY BELOVED

[24] Bill had previously seen 'Yankee Doodle Dandy' film with Don on Friday, 14th August 1942 when he was at his motor mechanic fitter course in Brighton.
[25] Billeted is lodging for a soldier to sleep.
[26] Boche is a World War II-era derogatory French word referring to the Germans.
[27] Macaronis is an Italian fighter plane.
[28] Lily's husband, Laurie Shrubsole, is also fighting in the war in the navy.

June 1943

With the Allied invasion of Italy imminent, Pope Pius XII sends an appeal to American President Roosevelt asking that American bombers spare the destruction of Rome, noting that the "many treasured shrines of religion and art" are "the precious heritage, not of one people, but of all human and Christian civilization."

Monday, 31st May 1943 – While Bill is still in the convalescent depot American B-17s bomb Naples.

Friday, 4th June 1943 – General Henri Giraud becomes Commander of the Free French forces in North Africa.

Friday, 11th June 1943 – Without opposition the British forces invade the islands of Pantelleria and Lampedusa situated between Tunisia and Sicily. Pantelleria would now serve as a base for attacks on the larger Italian island of Sicily, 60 miles away.

Wednesday, 16th June 1943 – Bill has now left Algiers and makes his way east to Tunis, the capital of Tunisia.

Thursday, 17th June 1943 – To prevent a predicted invasion the Allies bomb Sicily and the Italian mainland.

Friday, 18th June 1943 – Bill arrives at Tunis, Tunisia. From his 15 Trade Training Company, Bill is stationed at the Royal Army Service Corps, 2 Section, 5th Company, 6th Battalion (the driver training battalion) with the British North Africa Forces. He is still part of the British 8th Army under Montgomery until Rommel is defeated. Two days later Bill writes a letter to Gladys on Sunday, 20th June. This letter is number '26'.

Bill is 23 years and 9 months old: Gladys is 21 years and 1 month old.

26.

PTE. POWELL. T/69083.
R.A.S.C.
2 SEC. 5 COY. 6. BATT.
1. G.R.T.D.
B.N.A.F.

Sunday 20 June 1943.

My own darling beloved wife,

I hardly know how to begin this letter sweetheart, and having once begun it, then it is, ever harder to find something to write about. There is still no mail arrived yet for me, so I have no letters I can answer. I am three months behind with the news, as the only letters I have got dated since march are three airmails and about half a dozen airgraphs, and those tell me that you love me and miss me but do not tell me how, what, why, where, and when of the news from home. As a matter of fact the only item of news I have had at all was that Lis

(Above) Bill's letter to Gladys written on Sunday, 20th June 1943

Mrs. Gladys Powell
84a London Road
North Cheam
Surrey
England

(26)
PTE. POWELL T/69083
R.A.S.C.
2 SEC. 5 COY. 6 BATT.
1. G.R.T.D.
B.N.A.F.

Sunday 20 June 1943

My own darling beloved wife,

I hardly know how to begin this letter sweetheart, and having once begun it, then it is, ever harder to find something to write about.   There is still no mail arrived yet for me, so I have no letters I can answer.   I am three months behind with the news, as the only letters I have got dated since March are three airmails and about half a dozen airgraphs and those tell me that you love me and miss me but do not tell me how, what, why, where and when of the news from home.   As a matter of fact the only item of news I have had at all was that Lin *[29]* has had her teeth attended to and that your Mum invited Fred's wife down for a day and that was in a letter from your Mum and is now almost history.   I have given up going for the mail now and almost given up hope of any ever reaching me.   Up to a few days ago I used to go every day for the post and, except on one day a week, I would not think of going out until it had been. Then, as disappointment followed disappointment, I gave it up as a bad job.   Perhaps one day some letters will reach me.

I am longing to hear from you, darling, as I love you and

miss you so very much. I know, beloved, that you are writing to me regularly so please don't imagine for a minute that I am blaming you for the lack of mail. I know, sweetheart, that in you I have the truest, finest and most wonderful, charming and beautiful girl in the world for my wife. I could not wish for anyone better. And I know that you love and miss me as much (or almost) as much as I do you. We belong to each other, darling, our lives are bound up in each other, intertwined in a manner that makes us each essential for the others happiness. I need you so very much, beloved, and pray for the day to come when we will be together again.

Did you like the poem I sent you? I hope you did and here is another one for you, which helps me to tell you just how much you mean to me.

> 'Long is the distance
> That keeps us apart,
> But strong is the love
> That is locked in the heart.
> And the smile on your face
> That I always knew,
> Is more than a memory,
> Steadfast and true.
> Each thought of you, prayer for you,
> Whispered each night,
> Shall give me new courage
> And strengthen my fight.
> For wherever I go
> I never will find
> A dear wife as sweet
> Or as loving and kind.'

Does that in some small manner tell you how much you mean to me, darling. I only wish I could really put my love into writing, but I could never do that. It would be harder for me to describe my love for you, than it would be for a man who was blind and dumb to explain the beauty of a summer sunset or a field of flowers.

Often, darling, when I write to you, I wonder if you ever become bored reading these letters. I know each one is almost the same as the last and even my rather puny attempts at poetry are much of a muchness. I do hope that even if you are rather bored with reading the same things over and over again, you will bear with me and remember that I have absolutely nothing of interest to tell you about this country, other than little things that I have told you of at odd times. The one thing that takes up most of my time is thinking of you, therefore most of my letters are about you and I feel it beyond my limited capabilities to tell you exactly how I feel. I can only plod along as I have been doing and trust that the continued repetition does not bore you, darling.

One rather big item of interest did occur last week and I expect you have read about it all now in the papers. Last Sunday as usual I was at the beach swimming and making the most of my last few days at the convalescent camp. Then just as I was coming out of the water to dress for tea, the King came on to the beach. There was one mad scramble around him and they all sang 'God Save The King' then as he came down towards us they broke into 'For He's A Jolly Good Fellow'. What struck me most from the whole performance was the spontaneousness of the cheering and singing [30].

You know my feelings and ideas about the King [31] and our system of government, but I was very much impressed by the wholehearted admiration of the King's visit. If it was Hitler, Mussolini, or any other of the Axis [32] chiefs visiting their troops, there would have been armoured cars, armed soldiers guarding the entire route and a big parade complete with cheer leaders to direct the cheering and singing in the appropriate places. Here though, while we had been told that a general may come to see us, we knew nothing about his visit until he arrived. Then, as one man, everyone broke into 'God Save The King' and one huge uproar of cheering and the King replied by standing to attention and saluting.

Then, as he made his way towards us, everyone started singing 'For He's A Jolly Good Fellow' and then the King asked quite a lot of fellows how and when they were wounded [33] and then, wishing us all the best of luck, he departed. Since I was in the command depot I have seen a lot of celebrities including Winston Churchill, the King, Anthony Eden, General Alexander, General Eisenhower, Field Marshall Montgomery, Admiral Cunningham, General Anderson, Air Marshall Tedder and many other military and political big shots, some visiting us and others being in Algiers when I have been there.

Now, for a word or two about the place where I am now residing, it will only be a word or two as the less said about it, the better. I spent one night at a transit camp, then one night beside the sea in another camp, leaving com depot on Wednesday and arriving here Friday. I am sleeping in tents called biviacs, or known more popularly as pup tents as they are about the size of a dog kennel. About seven feet long, four foot six inches wide and standing about two foot six inches high, they are meant to house two persons. The only way to get in is to either make your bed, get into it and between the two of you erect the tent afterwards around you, or else crawl in one at a time and make your bed down, throwing all kit out as you do so, then crawl out again to enable the other fellow to put his bed down, then crawl in again and so to bed.

We are camped on sand and lately a strong wind has been blowing, the result being each day you have to dig your way out of bed then dig your way out of the tent. You sleep, eat, drink and breathe sand, you wash (after a fashion) but before you can dry yourself, sand has stuck to your wet body and you are as dirty as ever. Then the site of the camp is on the road to nowhere, the nearest village being three miles away and boasting of one café and the prices at that café took my breath away. I used up the last of my soap washing all my clothes and kit, hung them up to dry, the few articles that were not blown off the line into the sand had sand blown all over them and all were worse than before I washed them.

Meal times – well, this is the day here. Reveille is 6.30 am, line up to wash, when you eventually reach the water and wash it is 7.30 am and time to line up for breakfast, then after about an hour in the queue you get what passes for breakfast, it looks a lot but three parts of it is sand. Then it is time to parade and you line up again. By the time that's over, it's almost time to queue up for dinner. That uses up your two hours for dinner, so you line up for the afternoon parade. After that you may have time to line up for the use of the latrines [34], or even line up for a drink of water or to do some of your washing. Then we line up for tea, line up to wash, line up for mail, (I miss that queue), once a week line up for rations – line up for pay, line up for the N.A.A.F.I. and so to bed. I am not worrying, though, since I have been out here I have got used to most things and life could be a lot worse. For instance, I have not been paid for two weeks.

The week before last I did not bother as I was out in Algiers and thought I would have enough to last me until this week, but this week I arrived here on Friday and they pay out on Thursdays, so I was unlucky. The result being I have about the equivalent of a shilling [£1.93p in 2013], but as there is nowhere to spend even the shilling, unless I want a six mile walk for a glass of wine, I am still well off. If I had been in a town and broke, I would have been very annoyed. As it is, well, the cash is of no use again. But, as for the lining up all day, I have often thought that after we die, do we have to queue up at the Pearly Gates to await admission to heaven. All we can get here without a queue is sand and, believe me, there's plenty of that.

When I am not thinking of you, darling, my thoughts are on other subjects about home. Can you guess what they are, well food and drink mostly. How often I sit and imagine a real dinner again, such as roast beef or lamb, peas, greens, baked potatoes and Kellogg's or Shredded Wheat and plenty of milk, scrambled eggs on toast and a real cup, or rather many cups, of tea made in a tea pot. Mind you, we get enough to eat out here and the food is fairly good, but no matter how good, there is always that difference. No army food – even if they open the same tin as at home – can taste as good as food cooked in small portions, served out on china plates and eaten on a table. Also, at home if I was not hungry, then I need not eat. If I was hungry, then I could eat until I felt full again. But here, I may not feel hungry at dinner, so I leave half of it, but at tea time I am extra hungry, but I only have one tea and I feel rather peckish for the rest of the day. So, whether you feel hungry or not, you just eat each meal as it comes.

Still, one day this war will be over then I will be home with you again and able to make up for all the time we have missed through this long separation. What a day that will be, darling. I need hardly say how much I am looking forward to it. I love you, miss you and need you with all my heart and soul and will always do so.

You are the only girl in the world for me, darling, you and you alone I am living for. Look after yourself, my beloved, you mean so much to me. Give my love to all at home and all my love to you, sweetheart. Remember I love you always and will do so as long as I live. Here's hoping that we will be reunited very soon.

I am forever and always your loving husband,

Bill

xxx

LIVING FOR YOU ALONE DARLING

[29] Lin is Bill's affectionate nickname for Eileen, Gladys' younger sister, who Bill always had a soft spot for. Eileen is still living with her Aunt Elsie and Uncle Syd nearby at Worcester Park.

[30] After the victory at El Alamein, King George visited North Africa. From Pathé (1896-1976) Review of the Year – June 1943: Several shots of a great Allied army parade which marked occupation of Tunis. Generals Eisenhower, Giraud, Alexander and Anderson are standing at dais. There were various shots of King George VI chatting with troops during his visit to North Africa. The King is seen driving in an open car with troops cheering from both sides of the road.

[31] Although Bill was prepared to fight for 'King and Country', he is not a royalist. However, in his later years he was always the first to stand for the national anthem and passionately sing the words.

[32] Axis is an alignment of great powers that fought World War II against the Allies.

[33] When the King approached Bill he thought he is from India as Bill is so dark brown from the sun. The King stopped to speak to Bill and told him how pleased he is to see the Indian contribution to the war effort. Bill looked the King straight in the eye and replied in his broad Cockney accent: "Actually, mate, I'm from Battersea." (Cockney refers to people born within the sound of the Bow Bells, a church of St. Mary-le-Bow in the City of London, ringing at an estimated six miles to the east, five miles to the north, three miles to the south and four miles to the west. Geographically and

216

culturally, it is often used to refer to working class Londoners, particularly those in the East End. Linguistically, it can refer to the accent and form of English spoken by this group. The sound of the bells of St Mary's is credited with having persuaded Dick Whittington to turn back from Highgate and remain in London to become Lord Mayor. The church is also immortalised in the nursery rhyme, 'Oranges and Lemons' – "I do not know, says the great bell of Bow." The association with Cockney and the East End in the public imagination may be due to many people assuming that Bow Bells are to be found in the district of Bow, rather than the lesser known St Mary-le-Bow church. Thus while all East Enders are Cockneys, not all Cockneys are East Enders. Bill was born in the sound of the Bow bells; therefore classed as a true Cockney.)

[34] Latrine is a pit toilet.

(Above) Bill, aged 23, July 1943

July – September 1943

The Allies invade Sicily in a major air, land and naval combat which take six weeks from 9th July 1943. Bill is now on his way to Sicily.

Saturday, 10th July 1943 – Operation Husky is launched. The Allies invade Sicily and the start to liberate Europe begins.

Sunday, 11th July 1943 – The 15th Army Group is formed by the British and American H.Q. troops for the invasion of Sicily and then on to the invasion of Italy. The 15th Army Group commands the British 8th Army and the U.S. 7th Army (8th + 7th = 15th).

Monday, 19th July 1943 – Rome is bombed by the Allies for the first time in the war. Rome is later declared an open city by the Italian government with Italy offering to demilitarize the capital in return for an Allied agreement not to bomb the city further.

Saturday, 24th July 1943 – Bill is now transferred to the General Headquarters Car Company in the 15th Army Group and then in August he leaves North Africa and arrives in Sicily.

Sunday, 25th July 1943 – Italian dictator Benito Mussolini, the fascist Prime Minister since 1925, is summoned by the king, Victor Emmanuel III. He is relieved of his duties and arrested after the Grand Council of Fascism withdrew its support. Mussolini is replaced by Marshall Pietro Badoglio to form a new government.

Tuesday, 3rd August 1943 – Is the first of two 'slapping incidents' when Lieutenant General George S. Patton, who is supporting Field Marshall Montgomery's British 8th Army during the Sicily Campaign, did not believe that two soldiers from his 7th U.S. Army had a medical condition.

Compelled to apologise for his actions, Patton was later sidelined from combat command for almost a year. General Dwight Eisenhower is later to use Patton as a decoy as the commander for the invasion of Europe.

Friday, 6th August 1943 – German troops arrive to take over Italy's defences.

Wednesday, 11th August 1943 – German and Italian forces evacuate Sicily.

Tuesday, 17th August 1943 – The Allied invasion of Sicily, codenamed Operation Husky, is complete when the Allies drive the Axis from their air, land and naval forces on the island. The Mediterranean Sea lanes are now open ready for the Allies' invasion of Italy. The Sicily campaign has cost the Allies nearly 25,000 casualties. Italian dictator Benito Mussolini is toppled from power. The British 8th Army suffers 11,843 casualties (2,062 killed or missing, 7,137 wounded and 2,644 captured). The U.S. 7th Army lost 8,781 men (2,237 killed or missing, 5,946 wounded and 598 captured). The Royal Navy lost 314 killed or missing, 411 wounded and 4 captured. The U.S Navy lost 546 killed or missing and 484 wounded. The U.S. Air Force reported 28 killed, 88 missing and 41 wounded. The Canadian forces have suffered 2,310 casualties, including 562 killed, 1,664 wounded and 84 captured.)

Thursday, 19th August 1943 – In a joint agreement between Great Britain and America, Winston Churchill and Franklin D. Roosevelt sign the Quebec Agreement during the Quebec Conference. The Quebec Agreement is a document by the Anglo/Canadian/America outlining the terms of development relating to nuclear energy; and, specifically weapons that employ nuclear energy.

Friday, 3rd September 1943 – The forces of the British 8th Army under Field Marshall Montgomery invade the 'toe' of mainland Italy for the first time in the war at Reggio di Calabria. An Italian Armistice is signed and Italy surrenders. In Berlin, Germany, the evacuation of civilians begins.

Saturday, 4th September 1943 – Russia declares war on Bulgaria.

Monday, 6th September 1943 – From his W/S Platoon Bill writes to Gladys on their second wedding anniversary. Bill's letters are now posted in a light Active Service brown envelope at the Base Army Post Office signed by W.F. Powell and censored with a stamp. W/S could be 'wounded and sick' platoon. Units were made up by: 12 men in a Section; 3 Sections in a Platoon (36 men – Sections were normally numbered 1, 2 or 3 Section); 4 Platoons in a Company or Squadron (144 men – Platoons could be numbered or lettered); 5 Companies or Squadrons to a Battalion (700+ men – Companies can be numbered, lettered or named i.e.: Inkermann Company). Many battalions make Corps or Regiments; all the different Regiments form a Brigade; 3 Brigades made a Division and Divisions made Armies (i.e.: 8th Army). He is based in the Central Mediterranean Forces. This letter is number '11'.

Bill is soon to be 24 years old: Gladys is 21 years and 4 months old.

PTE. POWELL 769083
W/S PLATOON
G.H.Q. CAR COY. R.A.S.C.
H.Q 15 ARMY GROUP
C.M.F.

Monday September 6 1943.

My own darling beloved wife,

Today beloved is the second anniversary of our wedding, two years of married life darling. I only hope that you agree with me in saying "No regrets", the day I took you for my lawful wedded wife was indeed the most eventful and happiest day of my life. It was the realization of all my dreams. You know sweetheart that I fell madly in love with you almost as soon as I met you. Our first meeting something strange seemed to occur inside me, you were so

(Above) Bill's letter to Gladys written on Monday, 6th September 1943

222

Mrs. Gladys Powell
84a London Road
North Cheam
Surrey
England

(11)
PTE. POWELL T/69083
W/S PLATOON
G.H.Q. CAR COY. R.A.S.C.
H.Q. 15 ARMY GROUP
C.M.F.

Monday September 6 1943

My own darling beloved wife,

Today beloved is the second anniversary of our wedding, two years of married life darling. I only hope that you agree with me in saying 'No regrets', the day I took you for my lawful wedded wife was indeed the most eventful and happiest day of my life. It was the realization of all my dreams. You know sweetheart that I fell madly in love with you almost as soon as I met you. Our first meeting something strange seemed to occur inside me, you were so different and so lovely and in a few days I knew I was head over heels in love with you.

It was hard for me in those days, darling, being so close to you and needing you so much. I rather think you know how I felt but, believe me, sweetheart, I loved you, even then, very, very, much. Then two years ago today came our wedding day and we were man and wife, each belonging absolutely to each other. You know what happened then, our honeymoon.

Then, for over a year I enjoyed a perfect celestial happiness with you, beloved, a happiness that I never believed existed. I loved you so terribly that it was heaven

223

just to sit with my arms around you and as you know my idea of a perfect time was to be as close to you as possible. Every night I would lie with my arms around you and I was still in the same position in the morning. I knew that you loved me almost as much as I love you. That meant far more to me than you could ever realize, to love a person with all your heart and soul and to know that person was equally in love with you.

All I ask now, sweetheart, is to be home with you again and to hold you in my arms once more. Just thank your lucky stars, darling, that you weren't as hot natured as me, because quite often this separation has been almost unbearable for me. The first month was an almost continual agony, but thank God I have got over the worst if it now and I only experience that agony very occasionally now. Times, darling, when I lie in bed longing to be with you so much, that tears run down my face. Much as you love me and miss me, I don't think you ever experience the agony of separation that I have, darling. Sometimes – in fact, very often, I dream of you, having you beside me once again. I live again all those moments of ecstasy that I knew before our separation. I feel you in my arms and hear your heart pounding as I press you tight to me. I kiss you over and over again, reliving all the exquisite and wondrous happiness as my lips meet yours. Those red ruby lips of yours that were created only to be kissed and to see your eyes, bright and happy, shining like stars and reflecting all the love you have for me.

You need never tell me you love me – anyway, it was not very often you did unless I asked you, but it was very plain to see that I meant a great deal to you. Your smile so radiant and joyful which lit up your beautiful face as I came in, your look of perfect happiness and contentment whenever I was with you and the way you tolerated all my little peculiarities and my fits of bad tempered sulks.

These things all told me, far more than words ever could, that you loved me very much. Words could be lies, but those little actions proved conclusively that I was the only person in the world to you. You may wonder how and why I love you so much. I can't answer that in full, but I can give you a rough idea. You are the finest and loveliest person in the world, far more beautiful than any creation of nature. The only thing I have ever seen that in any way rivals your beauty is a sunset on a summer's day. Often, when I watch the sun going down on the Mediterranean tingling the blue sea with a hue of unbelievable colour and the sky showing many different shades of red, silhouetting the faint wispy clouds into phantom-like wraiths and making the mountains around the coast look like great grey sentinels guarding the sea. Then, as I look upon this exotic beauty, I am reminded of you, beloved, and that beauty of yours that equals if not excels this masterpiece of nature. But it is not your beauty alone that makes me worship you as I do. No, it goes far deeper than that. Your character is easily the sweetest I have ever known, completely unselfish and generous, thinking always of me and never acting unkindly to anyone. Beauty is fairly common, character is a lot rarer, but a combination is a very rare and priceless treasure. Can you wonder that I fell in love with you now?

Let's examine this beauty of yours a little deeper. I have to rely on memory now, sweetheart, but your image is indelibly printed in my mind – and in my heart. They say that hair is a woman's crowning glory. The person who said that must have had you in mind. Your hair is indeed glorious, soft and luxurious, so natural yet so lovely. How I used to love to feel it against my face as I held you in my arms and what a wonderful vision you made when the sun glinted on it, sending cascades of gold dancing across it. Then, darling, your eyes. Never have eyes shone so brightly, making even stars look dim and dull in comparison – your rosy cheeks and exquisite lips, lips so full and red and a smile that turned darkness into light, a complexion so fresh and natural, one that did not come off in the wash. All set upon a head that many artists would give their right arm to model, a head such as is only seen in pictures of a Grecian Goddess.

Then, to make a complete picture, a mind that is both clean and intelligent, a mind that is pure and a body that is also pure, clean and a envious figure of womanhood. I can't go much further, darling, or else I will be set for another sleepless night, but I will sum up by saying that you are the perfect creation of loveliness and the essence of perfection personified. I love you with all my heart and soul now and always. I miss you far more than you ever dream and need you so very much. When I dream of you, as I often do, I am happy and live again, but then when I awake – my dissolution you are gone and then I can almost cry. Have no fear, darling, that I will never be unfaithful to you, you are my life, you and only you matter to me. I live just to be with you again and to try and tell you in words what I can't tell you in writing, that I love you and only you and how much you mean to me. I hope that very soon I will be holding you in my arms again and putting my kisses on your lips instead of on paper. Well, darling, I think I have said enough to convince you that after two years of married life I love you as much if not more than ever, so now I will go on to other topics.

On Saturday I received your telegram, it was a wonderful surprise to me and very much appreciated. I wish I could have reciprocated, but I could not. It came on our anniversary day, so was very apt. Then today, on our anniversary date, I received five parcels, no.10, no.11, two others one from April and one May and also your birthday parcel in very good condition, so I have had a piece of your birthday cake and drop of your port wine to celebrate our wedding.   Also, on Saturday I received no.118, no.122, no.123 and no.29 airmail and 18 parcels from you, also letters from my mother and Charlie Dunsdon [Bill's friend]. Sunday was a blank day, but today brought me the five parcels I mentioned and letters no.120 and no.26 airmail. The no.26 airmail was badly burnt and almost unreadable, but nevertheless, it arrived.   Thanks for them all, darling. I am more than grateful for all the things you have sent me and I appreciate it very much.   I only hope that in the near future I will be able to repay you in some way for your kindness.

As no doubt you have heard, we are on the move again, on to Italy and then on to Germany.   You can believe me when I say the morale and spirits of our troops are excellent. Not only are we absolutely confident of final victory, but we are sure of our ability to achieve it quickly.   We know now that we are more than a match for the German soldiers and we are certain that we will drive him out of Europe or wipe out his entire army for him.   As for the Eyeties, well, the biggest trouble is to house all the prisoners we take.   I could, if I were allowed, tell you some almost unbelievable stories of the Italian fighting – or rather, lack of fighting. The Messina Straights, only about a mile or so wide which separate Sicily from Italy, is like an English river and our boats ran up and down it as if it were miles from any action. Our air force completely dominates the sky.   All day long they are roaring overhead and the much vaunted Luftwaffe confines itself to a very occasional tip and run raid at night. With both air force and navy in full command of the air and sea and our armies knocking hell out of the Axis – when we get them to stand and fight, can you wonder that we have complete confidence in winning this war in the near future. Of course, I have no idea what is in the minds of our generals, but we all have complete confidence in their leading us forward to find victory – and very soon.   We have great leaders in Monty [35] and Alex [36] and Eisenhower [37] and believe me they will lead us right through to Berlin and then God help the Japanese, for then we will give them a taste of real war. It will not be long before I am home once more, but much as I want to come home to you, my darling, you know that I must see this job through now.

Then, having played my part in the fight against fascism and slavery, I hope to also play my part in making the dream of a socialist Britain a reality. I sincerely wish that the Soviet Union will play a big part in the peace settlement after the war. I think they will then if we, the United States and the U.S.S.R. unite together, perhaps war will be a thing of the past. I certainly don't want any of my children – sorry our children – if we have any – to undergo the same horrors as I have had to put up with and I have not had nearly so much as a lot of people. There is no such thing as the glory of war – it is one long sequence of filth and horror, but if necessary I will willingly continue for any length of time, knowing that the full and complete defeat of the Nazi barbarians is essential to the building of a real decent civilization, a civilization that will give us a land fit for heroes to live in and not a land that needs heroes to be able to live in it. There is no doubt, beloved, that we have a lot to look forward to when this war is over. We will have our own home, just to ourselves, unless of course you prefer to increase our numbers. That is entirely up to you. I will be, as always, your obedient servant. By the way, you have never mentioned what your intentions or wishes are regarding children. I would like to know just what you think, whether you want a child as soon as you can, or whether you would prefer a few years of freedom with just the two of us together, or if you would rather have no children at all. Let me know your views, sweetheart, and don't be afraid to tell me what you really think, as I don't mind anyway, all I want is to see you happy. Your happiness is all that matters to me. I live only to see you happy and contented. If in some small way I succeed in making you happy then I will have realized my biggest ambition.

Well, darling, I will say cheerio for now. I am looking forward to seeing you soon. Very shortly I will be coming home to you again, so get a good stock of Shredded Wheat and Kellogg's for me and don't bother to send me a Christmas card as I hope to be home to receive it. All my love and fondest regards, I am always your ever loving husband,

Bill

xxx

HERE'S TO A SPEEDY REUNION

P.S.

What the betting on who reaches Berlin first – us or the Russians [38]. Talk about confidence. Our boys are arguing what they will do with the money they get for pawning their uniforms at Uncles [a pawnbroker] in a short time.

[35] Monty is the nickname of Field Marshall Bernard Montgomery.

[36] Alex is the nickname of Harold Rupert Leofric George Alexander, 1st Earl Alexander of Tunis. He was a British military commander and field marshal who served with distinction in both world wars.

[37] General Dwight 'Ike' Eisenhower is a five-star general in the U.S. army during World War II who serves as Supreme Commander of the Allied Forces in Europe and is responsible for the planning and supervising of

the invasion of North Africa in Operation Torch in 1942-43 and later for the successful invasion of France and Germany in 1944-45 from the Western Front. He became the first supreme commander of N.A.T.O. in 1951 and from 1953-1961 became the 34th President of the United States of America following the simple but effective slogan, 'I Like Ike'.

[38] The 'Race to Berlin' refers mainly to the competition between two soviet Marshals to be the first to enter Berlin during the final months of World War II. On Wednesday, 2nd May 1945, with the war in Europe coming to an obvious conclusion, Soviet leader Joseph Stalin purposely set his two Marshalls, Georgy Zhukov and Ivan Konev, in a race to capture Berlin. Their separately commanded two armies competed against one another, ensuring that they would drive their men as fast and as far as possible to a quick victory. This led to a climax in the bloody Battle of Berlin. The Soviet advance and ultimate capture of the German capital was virtually unopposed by their allies. In an effort to avoid a diplomatic issue, Allied General of the Army Dwight Eisenhower had ordered his forces into the south of Germany to cut off and wipe out other pieces of the Wehrmacht, a unified armed forces of Germany from 1935-1945. It consisted of the 'Heer' (army), 'Kriegsmariner' (Navy) and the Luftwaffe (air force). The decision to leave eastern Germany and the city of Berlin to the Red Army eventually had serious repercussions as the Cold War emerged and expanded in the post-war era, but in doing so, the western Allies were also honouring agreements they made with the Soviet Union at Yalta.

(Above) Gladys, aged 21, 1943

September – October 1943

Wednesday, 8th September 1943 – the King Victor Emanuel III and Prime Minister Pietro Badoglio agree to an armistice with the Allies, signed at a conference of generals from both sides in an Allied military camp at the recently captured Cassibile in Sicily. This signalled a total surrender of Italy. However, Italy is now plunged into a civil war with some joining forces with the Allies while others remain supportive to Benito Mussolini and the Axis.

Thursday, 9th September 1943 – Following Italy's surrender, Germany attacks the Italia battleship on its way to Malta. This battleship was the Littorio renamed after the fall of the fascist government. Germany also attacks and sinks the Roma battleship, going down with 1,253 people, including the ship's captain still on board. On the same day the British, American and French troops land in Salerno on the western coast, known as Operation Avalanche.

Friday, 10th September 1943 – The British 8th Army occupies Taranto, a coastal city in southern 'heel' of Italy. German troops occupy Rome and take over the protection of Vatican City now that Italy has surrendered to the Allies. The Italian fleet surrenders at Malta and at other Mediterranean ports.

Saturday, 11th September 1943 – The Allied forces conquer Salerno followed by the Free French landing at Corsica.

Sunday, 12th September 1943 – Adolf Hitler orders the rescue of Benito Mussolini who is being held prisoner by the Italian government at Gran Sasso (Great Stone) by the Waffen-SS commandos.

Monday, 13th September 1943 – Bill's 24th birthday. He

spends it in jeopardy on the beachhead of Salerno, Italy, as the German counter-attacks increase.

Wednesday, 15th September 1943 – The British and American troops link up near the Salerno beachhead. In Italy Benito Mussolini forms a rival fascist government, the Italian Social Republic and the anti-fascism opposition begins in Naples, northwest of Italy.

Thursday, 16th September 1943 – A mutiny takes place with men from the British X Corps. About 600 refuse assignments to new units as replacements during the Allied invasion of Italy after many have sailed from Tripoli believing they would join the rest of their units based in Sicily. Once aboard ship, they are told that they are instead to go to Salerno, southwest of Italy. Having been misled and finding a total lack of organisation when they reach Salerno, many refuse their postings despite the warnings of mutiny in wartime. With this, many reluctantly follow orders, leaving 192 to face mutiny under the Army Act, the largest number of men accused at any one time in all of British military history. The accused are shipped to Algeria. Also today British forces land on various Italian-held Greek islands in the Aegean Sea beginning the Dodecanese Campaign, an attempt mainly by the British to capture the islands following the surrender of Italy.

Monday, 20th September 1943 – Allied forces approach Naples.

Tuesday, 21st September 1943 – Bill passes as a T.T. (Tank Transporter) motor mechanic in group B, class 2 and is upgraded. Also that day Bill is awarded the Africa Star medal.

Tuesday, 28th September 1943 – The people of Naples, sensing the approach of the Allies, rise up against the German occupiers with many civilian deaths.

Friday, 1st October 1943 – The Allied forces capture Naples after the German military occupation.

Sunday, 3rd October 1943 – The British 8th Army lands at Termoli, east Italy, followed by the Free French capturing Corsica.

Tuesday, 5th October 1943 – The Allies cross Italy's Volturno Line, the southernmost German defensive position.

Wednesday, 13th October 1943 – Italy declares war on former Axis partner Germany.

Saturday, 16th October 1943 – There is an anti-Jewish riot in Rome. A Jewish quarter is surrounded and they are sent to Auschwitz, the first transport out of Rome reaching Birkenau concentration camp on Saturday, 23rd October.

Bill has left Sicily and has arrived in Italy. He writes a letter to Gladys on Saturday, 23rd October 1943 from his headquarters. Bill is still stationed with the 15th Army Group at the W/S Platoon, General Headquarters Car Company in the Royal Army Service Corps based in the Central Mediterranean Forces. This letter is number '16'.

Bill is 24 years and one month old: Gladys is 21 years and 5 months old.

Pte Powell T/69083.
W/S Platoon.
G.H.Q. Car Coy. R.A.S.C.
H.Q. 15 Army Group.
C.M.F.

Saturday 23 October 1943.

My own darling beloved wife

Hello sweetheart, I hardly know how to begin this letter as yesterday and today have been real mail days for me, on Friday I recieved fourteen letters in the morning and two letters and a parcel in the evening, today I have had five letters. Out of all these fourteen letters and the parcel were from you, and the numbers were – sea letters 110, 130, 131, 132, 146, 148, 149, 150, 151, 152, 153, 154, 156, 157 and parcel No 32. thanks a lot darling and now I will endeavor to answer them. Before I do though I must admit I was a trifle disappointed in recieving such a large batch of mail – every letter from 148 to 157 — except no 155 and

(Above) Bill's letter to Gladys written on Saturday, 23rd October 1943

Mrs. Gladys Powell
84a London Road
North Cheam
Surrey
England

(16)
PTE. POWELL T/69083
W/S PLATOON
G.H.Q. CAR COY. R.A.S.C.
H.Q. 15 ARMY GROUP
C.M.F.

Saturday 23 October 1943

My own darling beloved wife,

Hello sweetheart, I hardly know how to begin this letter as yesterday and today have been real mail days for me, on Friday I received fourteen letters in the morning and two letters and a parcel in the evening, today I have had five letters. Out of all these fourteen letters and the parcel were from you and the numbers were – sea letters 110, 130, 131, 132, 146, 148, 149, 150, 151, 152, 153, 154, 156, 157 and parcel no.32, thanks a lot darling and now I will endeavour to answer them. Before I do though I must admit I was a trifle disappointed in receiving such a large batch of mail – every letter from 148 to 157 – except no.155 and of course that is the letter I have been looking forward to for a long time, the letter containing your photograph. Of all the letters that had to be delayed it has to be that one. However, the poly photos compensated me and I hope no.155 will soon arrive.

Now, I will attempt to answer your letters in some sort or order. Letter no.110 describes all your doing during Whitsun, but as that is rather ancient history, I will not deal with that. Letter no.130 just tells me how much you love me and miss me and I will tell you how I feel about you later in this letter.

In your letter no.131 you ask what I meant about saying 'I was over two months without any mail except an occasional air mail and airgraph from you' and you seem to worry about me implying that you weren't writing to me. What I meant, darling, was that through no fault of yours or mine, I had to wait two months for a sea letter. So if your mail is delayed in reaching you, don't blame me, blame the war, the navy, post office or anybody, but even after two or more months it will still turn up in the end. As a classic example of that, you will remember how your no.29 letter posted last January arrived only a few weeks ago. I never at any time imagined that any long period awaiting mail was in any way due to you, darling. I know only too well that you write and think of me far more than I could ever expect you to, my only complaint on that score is that you write so often that I can't see how you get any time to yourself and that you spend too much in sending me so many parcels and, as for me 'thinking too bad of you' as you put it, I hardly think I need say anything about that except to remind you once again that I love you. I love you. I love you and God alone knows how much you mean to me. I live for you alone always. Also, you tell me how hot it is in England now, but as you wrote that in July and it is now October it will be the end of November by the time this letter reaches you. I don't think I need answer that, as from what I remember of an English November, it will be far from hot.

In letter no.132 you say how pleased you are with my poems and wonder how I write them. That's easy to answer as I am always thinking of you, darling, and just try to put those thoughts into rhyme. I only wish I could find time to write some more, but most of those I wrote before were written either in hospital, convalescent camp or

G.R.T.D. *[39]* and that was about all I had to do all day. Now, however, it is all I can do to find time to write my mail, as we don't finish work until 5 pm, tea is at half past, back to the billet just after six, then a wash, shave, clean my boots and rifle and it is seven o'clock, down to the mess room at half past seven and by the time I return it is eight o'clock, then I can get down to writing, but lights go out at nine thirty, so it means only an hour and a half is available at night and you can guess it does not give me a lot of time to think up any poems, but one day I will write you another one, sweetheart. You also question the fact that I was sunburnt all over and say 'bet it's not all over' well, you're wrong, darling, it is – or rather, was all over – not one little bit missing or neglected. Notice I said was – as by now I have reverted almost to a normal colour again, as I can't run about here in the raw – too many people and too damn cold, anyway. You say that you will 'wait on me hand and foot' but I will never let you do that, darling, rather I will try to repay in some way for all you have done for me.

In letter no.146 you remind me of the bed and photo frames you have bought and ask what I think about it. Well, darling, I think you are very sensible to get all you can, as we will need it all very soon. We won't have a lot of money to spare and everybody will want stuff after the war and the more we have now, the better it will be. Don't, however, get too good furniture, as we will only need enough to last for a year or so until the prices of new stuff drop. Anyway, darling, you have my complete confidence and trust in using the money sensibly, you know all about what things are worth and if you think a thing is cheap and we will need it – then get it by all means. You also say you have a good idea where I am now – well, now you know for certain, I am at the time of writing in Italy. I can't tell you as soon as I get into a place where I am, for reasons of security, we have to wait some few weeks before we are allowed to divulge the country where we are, but the change in my series of letter numbers will indicate that I have moved to other lands, but what land will have to remain a secret until permission is given to divulge where we are.

Whilst on the topic of Italy, I might mention the terrific reputation we received when we landed, crowds lined the docks cheering, clapping, blowing us kisses, throwing fruit and flowers and giving us the V sign with great enthusiasm, so when you see that sort of thing on the cinema or in the paper, you can take it for the truth. Whatever stories Jerry tries to tell to the contrary, the British and American troops are really welcomed by the Italians and I wonder if Jerry dare walk through any town in his occupied countries without arms of any sort as we do here. As a matter of fact, even before Italy came on our side, the situation here was very funny. Every Italian soldier walking about the towns or villages carried rifles or revolvers, but I have never seen an Allied soldier, except the Redcaps [40] at all. The only time we use our rifles is once a week for inspection, does that sound like a 'British reign of terror'.

You people in England however can thank God that the powers that be imposed rationing as they did. Never grumble at the amount of food you get. Some of the folks in the countries I have been to were prepared to pay any price for food and the Italians could tell you what hunger is like. We are at least feeding them now and even if that is nothing like what you have in England it is ten times as good as they got from the German thugs. As for the Italian girls, they are pretty, but some of the men are even prettier. No wonder they couldn't fight. They spend so much time having their hair curled and face massaged and also manicures that they couldn't find time for anything else. The cockney slang has some words that I needn't mention that describe them aptly. Enough to say that I had to wait over an hour in a barbers for a haircut whilst the Eyetie, who was in the chair when I arrived, was being dolled up and he was still there when I left as the smell of the junk they were pouring over him made me feel sick.

Your no.148 letter asks about the Italian girls – I have answered that above. No.149 you tell me about your teeth. I am very glad that you have had them seen to and hope that you feel a lot better for it, darling. Also, you mention the birthday cake you sent me, up to now I have not received it. I don't know why all the important things are always delayed, first your birthday cake which arrived months after you sent it on our wedding anniversary, then my birthday cake which, like letter no.155 with the photos, is still to reach me.

In letter no.150 you thank me for the photo I sent from Sicily. I hope that you received them ok and that you like them. As you can see, my Italian photo is enclosed with this letter. I know it is very bad but I have sent it in any case, but hope to get another taken soon. It's no wonder the camera packed up last time, I look a wreck on the photo, but really I am no worse than I was before I left you.

Letter no.151 and no.152 again remind me how much you love me and I am more than 'pleased' to know that and, as I have said before, I will tell how much I love you later on.

Now I come to the masterpiece, fourteen lovely pages. Letter no.153, thanks so much for it, sweetheart. I am very glad to know you had a nice time at the Palladium and I only wish I could have been with you. It is lovely to read such a wonderful letter from you, darling, and as most of it is once again telling me how much you love and miss me (I can never grow tired of hearing it) I will leave answering the rest until later.

In letter no.154 you try to make me jealous because you 'are eating a lovely red, luscious English apple', sorry pal, but we can buy and eat as many apples as we like – and at 2d [32p in 2013] a pound, the only reason I don't get many is because grapes are only three half pence (1½d) [24p in 2013] a pound and I prefer them. Try again with something else. The only thing I am jealous of, darling, is you because you have the pleasure of your company always. How I wish I could be with you again, sweetheart. I miss you so very much.

Well, next on my list is letter no.156 in which you say what a nice time you had at the firms dance and also that you danced every dance with Irene. I am glad you enjoyed yourself, darling, but why dance with a girl all the time. I trust you always, beloved, and if you go to a dance in the future, let a few of the fellows have the pleasure of dancing with you. I certainly won't mind, I know you love me and me alone and that no one else could ever take my place with you. All I wish is that you make the most of any opportunities you get to enjoy yourself as much as possible. When I know that you are happy then I too am happy, for your happiness is all that matters to me.

Last, but not least, in the batch of mail I received is letter no.157 and in it, you made the crack about my being 'happy and reasonably contented' and suggest that it is a slight improvement on being 'merry' when I should say 'drunk'. However, that is not the case. Even when I go into a café for a drink I very seldom exceed three wines and the most I have had since leaving Africa is six in a day and that is not very much. The phrase I used was more in accordance with the fact that I had passed an enjoyable day out and I was quite pleased with myself. I will admit, however, that was the day in which I had the six wines. I don't think you will ever have cause to worry about me drinking too much, either now or after the war. Each week we get a pint bottle of beer from N.A.A.F.I., but I always sell mine, this week's issue, which I got last Wednesday is still at the back of my bed – untouched. Even when I go out with a crowd of fellows, I very seldom have more than a couple of glasses of wine and in any case wine, like beer, makes me sick before I can get drunk. Don't think I am choking you off, by the way. I know you were only joking, but I may really celebrate when I get both feet on good old English soil once again. (But, I'll only get merry.) In any case, a person is not drunk until he can't stand up and doesn't know where he lives. While he's on his feet, he's just tight. If he can walk and talk, he's merry and if he's still able to walk straight, read or write, then he's 'happy and reasonably contented', are you quite clear now.

Well, darling, that ends my resume of your letters, so on to a subject that I like even better. Before I change the subject, however, I will give you the latest list of the total mail I have received up to date. Sea letters – nos.1-90; no.92; nos.94-96; no.99; nos.106-140; no.143; no.146; nos.148-154; and no.156 and no.157, still quite a few to arrive yet and a large batch from no.99-106. Airgraphs – everyone from nos.1-36. Airmails – everyone from nos.1-41. Parcels – numbered ones only no.1-6; no.8; no.10-14; no.16; nos.18-29; and no.32 (sorry, no.25 still to arrive) quite a few of these missing but living in hope they are on the way and only delayed from some reason. Also I have received six lots of cigarettes, five some time ago and 200 Woodbines arrived just over a week ago. So, out of the 157 letters you have written up to 15th Sept, I have received no.141 and out of the airmails and airgraphs every one has been received. Of the parcels, out of 32 I have received 24, the latest dated Aug 23, no.32.

(Continued Sunday)

Darling, I have had some more mail arrive, letters no.141 and 144, parcels no.40 and 41, also the birthday cards – one from Lin and one from Rene [41]. Still no sign, however, of the birthday cake or letter no.155.

Letter no.141 describes the weekend you had in the West End – at the Coliseum, the Canadian show, Odeon and Petticoat Lane. Getting around a bit, eh? Still, sweetheart, I am really pleased to know that you are enjoying yourself as much as you can. It is a great weight off of my mind to know that you are keeping happy and cheerful. I only hope that the day will soon dawn when I will be home with you, then we will both enjoy real happiness at last.

Letter no.144 tells me of the day you spent with my mother at Southend and about Florrie's visit to you at Cheam. How I wish I could have been with you at Southend. The last time I was there was at the end of 1941 when I took a convoy down there. The last time I was at the seaside with you was, of course, at Brighton on my last birthday, or I should have said last but one birthday. Still, when I come home we will go away together for another honeymoon, to my mother's at Southend, if you have no objection. It will be like getting married all over again, a celebration party and also a honeymoon. I only hope it will be very soon.

I am glad that you like Florrie, as I expect you will see her quite often after the war, as Fred and I will want to see each other as you know what pals we are. I expect we will visit his home and he visit *ours* quite frequently. What a day, darling, when every day will be our own, also our own home, able to go out or invite people home and no worry of passes, getting back to barracks or anything else that used to annoy us like that. The rest of our lives our own entirely, just you and I together, darling, always.

I don't know what was the matter with parcels no.40 and 41, they certainly arrived very quickly. They were only posted on the 15th Sept and the latest sea letter I have received (no.157) was posted on the 14th Sept. They were addressed direct to my C.M.F. [42] address, but so were all the letters from 146 onwards and they only arrived

243

yesterday and they were posted at dates between August 25th and September 14th, so the two parcels have taken less time to reach me than any of the sea letters except no.157 and that only took a day less. I guess the whole lot had to wait for the same convoy and all came over together. I am hoping that the other letters and parcels were with them, but have not all been completely sorted out yet. I suppose you think I am very greedy, after all the mail I have received during the past three days. I still hope for more, well you know I can't have too many letters from you, darling, and besides I want that piece of cake – and that photo.

I have had a very good week this week, what with the arrival of all that mail, (another moon however – no airletters for over a week – have to complain to the air force, as they usually arrive every two or three days) and, besides the mail, I have also seen a couple of picture programmes. There is a cinema in the village where we are, but unfortunately it is closed, but last Wednesday a mobile cinema gave a show there for us and if all goes well they hope to utilise the cinema every Wednesday evening and give us a film show. The film that was shown this week was called 'Above Suspicion' with Fred McMurray, Conrad Veidt and Joan Crawford. It was quite a good show and made a very welcome show and break for me. It is the first film I have seen since leaving Africa and I enjoyed it immensely. A week before, as I believe I told you, I saw 'Wee Georgie Wood' in his usually mother and son show, that being the first entertainment of any sort, except an amateur show in Sicily, that I have been able to see since I left Tunis.

Yesterday (Saturday) I had a half day off duty and again went into town and as usual had quite an orgy of ice cream eating. Of course, as I have said before, we are not allowed to eat it [43], but that only makes it taste all the better – sort of stolen fruit always being the best. Also there is a cinema open now for British and Allied troops (including the Eyeties – only really speaking, they aren't Allies – only co-belligerents) anyway, we went in and saw the Marx Brothers in 'The Marx Brothers Go West' and, boy, did I laugh, they kept me in fits right through the film and I really enjoyed the show. On coming out of there I went to collect my photos and was very disappointed with them and was in two minds whether to send them to you, or not. I still don't know why I decided to post them on to you, as they are not worth sending.

After picking them up from the photographs, however I – as usual started to look for something to eat and after last week's fiasco I did not intend to go to the same restaurant, but after much searching, we found a very nice looking place with a notice outside in English which read 'Chicken Dinner', so you can bet we went in for a 'basin' of fowl and boy, that fowl was foul. First of all we had some stuff called soup which was as bad as the tack we had last week, so we 'had it', then came the big event, the chicken arrived, one little piece about 1½" long and as thick as a matchstick. I did not know whether I was supposed to eat it all at once, or ask for some paper and take it back with me. However, I decided to eat it on the spot, so very gingerly I placed the slice of chicken on a slice of bread and took a nice bite. I tasted only bread – so looked again and found that I hadn't reached the chicken as it was in the middle of the slice, so took another bite, ate that and still tasted no chicken, looked again and found I had a piece of bread only left and I still don't know if I ate the chicken or if it fell off my bread without my noticing it. Yet another lesson bought in hard school of experience. On the whole I spent a pleasant day and it made a nice change from the continual round of work.

Since I have been writing this another two parcels have arrived, nos.36 and 37, thanks a lot, darling. I think I had better begin to close this letter, because if they keep on interrupting me with mail I will never finish it. I love you so very much, beloved and live only to be with you once again, you are my entire life and I cannot live without you. To say I love you is a gross understatement. I idolise and worship you. You mean more to me than anything else in the world. I long for the great day when I can hold you in my arms again and feel the soft touch of your flesh against mine. I live to hear you tell me how much you love me, how much you have missed me, to feel that ecstatic agony as those lovely ruby lips of yours press against mine and to feel you tight against my chest and to hear and feel the pounding of your heart as I hold you, darling. I can always see those eyes shining like stars with love and that wonderful smile you always welcome me with. I hope, darling, that dream will soon be realized as I need you so very much. Look after yourself, beloved, and keep smiling. Here's hoping that we will be together very soon.

Give my love to all at home and thank Lin and Rene for their cards. Cheerio, darling. Remember I love you with all my heart and soul and am proud and happy to be your ever loving husband,

Bill

xxx

YOU ALWAYS ARE IN MY HEART.
I AM YOURS ALONE FOREVER

[39] G.R.T.D. could refer to the General Re-enforcement Training Depot. This is a special unit where injured soldiers slowly recovered and eventually recuperated enough to be discharged back to their units and back into the war. There is one depot 20 miles outside of

Algiers, plus several elsewhere and in the U.K.

[40] Redcaps are the Military Police section of the allied Assortment who wore red caps.

[41] Rene is Gladys' friend, Irene.

[42] C.M.F. – Central Mediterranean Forces.

[43] Benito Mussolini banned the sale of ice cream throughout Italy, the land that claims to have given birth to the ice cream. Mussolini would later complain that the people of Italy were a "mediocre race of good-for-nothings only capable of singing and eating ice cream."

October – December 1943

In London, on Friday, 29th October 1943, troops are replacing dockworkers who are on strike.

Sunday, 31st October 1943 – The Allied advance south to Rome has been hindered by heavy rain in Italy.

Tuesday, 2nd November 1943 – British troops in Italy reach the Garigliano River, the confluence of the rivers Gari and Liri. This river stood at the centre of a system of German defensive lines (the most famous of which is the Gustav Line) around which the Battle of Monte Cassino took place in 1943-1944. It was stated that the waters of the river ran red in the Cassino area during the famous battle, because of the blood of the many corpses of soldiers.

Friday, 5th November 1943 – The Italians bomb the Vatican in a failed attempt to knock out the Vatican radio.

Tuesday, 9th November 1943 – The Allies take Castiglione in Rieti, Lazio, Italy. General de Gaulle becomes president of the French Committee of National Liberation.

Monday, 15th November 1943 – The Allied Expeditionary Force for the invasion of Europe is officially formed.

Tuesday, 16th November 1943 – The anti-German resistance in Italy increases. There are explosions in Milan. The Battle of Leros on the Greek island ends with the surrender of the British and Italian forces to the Germans: one of their last victories and criticised as another Gallipoli-like disaster; the blame is laid at Churchill. The story formed the basis for the 1957 novel The Guns of Navarone and the successful film of the same name.

Saturday, 20th November 1943 – The British troops under Field Marshall Montgomery continue their slow advances on the eastern side of Italy.

Sunday, 21st November 1943 – Gladys writes to Bill: "*My*

own darling Bill, Living only for you and your return. Praying we may soon be together this time for always. I'm now and always your ever loving wife, sweetheart, being more than proud to be. I love and miss you with all my heart and soul. God bless you always, Gladys."

Monday, 22nd November 1943 – British Prime Minister Winston Churchill, American President Franklin D. Roosevelt and Chinese leader Chiang Kai-Shek meet in Cairo, Egypt, for the Cairo Conference to discuss ways to defeat Japan. The Cairo Declaration issued on Saturday, 27th November 1943 follows with the outcome. The R.A.F. begins air bombings on Berlin, Germany.

Sunday, 28th November 1943 – Churchill, Roosevelt and Russian leader Joseph Stalin meet in Teheran, Iran, to discuss war strategy codenamed Operation Overlord, the code name for the Battle of Normandy (D-Day), with the planned invasion of German occupied Western Europe by Allied forces. The meeting ends on Wednesday, 1st December 1943.

Thursday, 2nd December 1943 – The Germans conduct a successful air raid on Bari, Italy. One bomb hits an Allied cargo ship carrying mustard gas, releasing the chemical killing 83 Allied soldiers. Over 1000 other soldiers die in the raid.

Tuesday, 7th December 1943 – In Trent, northern Italy, Chiara Lubich, a, Italian Catholic activist and leader, establish the religious Focolare Movement and work with people in the poorest bombed areas and bomb shelters.

Sunday, 12th December 1943 – Rommel is appointed head of Fortress Europa (Festung Europa) against the expected Allies, a military propaganda term from World War II which referred to the areas of Continental Europe occupied by Nazi Germany, as opposed to the free United Kingdom across the Channel.

Saturday, 20th December 1943 – Bill is admitted to hospital [no reason recorded].

Tuesday, 21st December 1943 – Bill leaves hospital to return to army duties.

Thursday, 23rd December 1943 – Field Marshall Montgomery is appointed Commandant for Operation Overlord, the D-Day invasion of Normandy.

Friday, 24th December 1943 – American President Franklin D. Roosevelt appoints General Dwight D. Eisenhower as the Supreme Allied Commander in Europe. Three days later he is officially named as the overall commander of Operation Overlord.

Bill's next letter is number '42', written on Friday, 24th December 1943: Christmas Eve. This is Bill and Gladys' second Christmas apart since their wedding in September 1941. Bill is still with the 15th Army Group at the W/S Platoon, General Headquarters Car Company in the Royal Army Service Corps based in the Central Mediterranean Forces.

Bill is 24 years and 3 months old: Gladys is 21 years and 7 months old.

42.

Pte. Powell T/169083.
w/s Platoon.
G.H.Q. Car Coy. R.A.S.C
H.Q. 15 Army Group
C.M.F.

Friday 24 December. 1943.

My own darling beloved wife,

Hello my sweetheart, here I am once again, hoping that you are in the very best of health and that all at home is OK. Glad to say that I am in the pink, although as you may guess I am feeling terribly homesick, especially as tonight is Christmas Eve. Darling I miss you so very much, God alone knows how much you mean to me as I can not live without to share my life with me, I love you darling, love you with all my heart and soul and need you far more than I

(Above) Bill's letter to Gladys written on Friday, 24th December 1943

251

Mrs. Gladys Powell
84a London Road
North Cheam
Surrey
England

(42)
PTE. POWELL T/69083
W/S PLATOON
G.H.Q. CAR COY. R.A.S.C.
H.Q. 15 ARMY GROUP
C.M.F.

Friday 24 December 1943

My own darling beloved wife,

Hello my sweetheart, here I am once again, hoping that you are in the very best of health and that all at home is ok. Glad to say that I am in the pink, although as you may guess I am feeling terribly homesick, especially as tonight is Christmas Eve. Darling, I miss you so very much, God alone knows how much you mean to me as I cannot live without [you] to share my life with me. I love you, darling, love you with all my heart and soul and need you far more than I could ever put into words. You are my entire life and I live only for that great day when I will be with you again.

Believe me, beloved, when I tell you that at the time of writing I am almost crying. I can hardly describe the feeling within me, as this, the second Christmas since I left you, dawns. You may think that it is only women who sentimentalise at times like these, but all I have been thinking of lately is our last Christmas together. It seems so long ago and yet at the same time it is crystal clear in my memory, every detail standing out as if it were only yesterday. I do miss you so very much, dearest, and times like these accentuate that feeling to such a degree as to make it almost unbearable.

It is even hard to write this letter, as even while I am busy writing, incidents flash through my mind. Little things we did together, places we went to and the happiness we had with each other. Then I stop writing and my mind is miles away, right home with you, sweetheart, and I dream of the things we would be doing if we were together now. Suddenly, with a start, I am brought back to life and the business of writing to you. So if this letter seems a little crazy or disjointed, darling, you must blame it on to the occasion, as believe me my thoughts are very disjointed now. Every few seconds my mind is rambling from the task in hand and travels back to you once again.

In the billet where I am, there are four fellows including little me. (There were five, but one has gone into hospital.) One of the fellows is Alec who I told you used to live only a few doors from me at Battersea, another is also an old Battersea boy, but he now lives in Ewell, just by the Spring Hotel (name of Charlie Clayton). The third fellow is the only foreigner amongst us, his name is Bill Samuelson and he comes from Sunderland. Actually Alec's name is William Alec, but to avoid complications when Bill is wanted, he is called Alec. Bill Samuelson is called Sammy and I am still just Bill. The reason I am telling you all this is because the four of us, Charlie, Alec, Sammy and myself, always go about together and I expect I will often mention their names in my letters. Charlie is the daddy of the party as he is almost thirty eight years old, then comes myself [24], then Alec who is twenty three and Sammy is the baby being just under twenty two and the only single man in the room. At the moment Charlie is busy making some cocoa, Sammy is reading, whilst Alec and I are both writing and sighing in turns.

We have been playing yo-yo [44]. It has been quite

funny, but the old craze for yo-yo has caught on in our workshops. It started with one of the boys being sent a yo-yo in a parcel as a joke. Well, we all had a go of it, then Alec started to make himself one on the lathe, then I made myself one and now well over a dozen of the fellows have them and Alec is utilising all his spare time (at work) making yo-yo's. Do you remember how quickly the craze swept through England about ten years ago? Nearly everybody had one. Yo-yo competitions were held in clubs, schools, dances and concerts. In a small way it is staging a comeback in our company now.

We spend quite a bit of time making little things for our comfort or enjoyment. You remember me telling you about the monopoly board (we still play a couple of nights a week – we had a game last night, but I was soon out) well, since making that, we have made a table and four chairs, all fold up flat when not in use. I have made a proper camp bed for myself. Also, we have fitted up electric lights in our room, made decent draught and blackout curtains, made ourselves boxes and cabinets to keep our things in and many other little things such as coat hangers, calendars, kettles and other cooking utensils. Of course, I am not saying they are equivalent to shop made articles, but they don't look bad and they serve a purpose. We are lucky in that we have a good representation of trades in the room. Charlie is a coppersmith and is technical adviser to making the kettles, etc. Sammy is a carpenter and upholsterer and takes charge of the woodwork, curtains, etc. Alec is a turner and utilises his lathe to make all the fittings we require and yours truly takes charge of fitting and mending such things as lights, door locks, stoves. Also I have to make anything that requires metal and can't be done on the lathe. Between us we have turned a dirty dark hovel [45] of a room into a really comfortable billet. It's surprising what can be made from a few empty petrol cans, some wood, a few nails, some canvas and a length of wire. With these articles, a little ingenuity and a coat of paint, we can make almost all the things we need for comfort.

We have started to do guards again now as we have moved a couple of miles from the company and they are no longer able to guard shops for us. We still live at the same place, but have moved the workshops to a new location and consequently we have to supply a guard for it now. Up to now I have not been on yet, but Alec, Sammy and myself are all on guard tomorrow. It will not be a nice way to spend Christmas night, but I don't really mind, as one day is much the same as any other out here. We have got the day off tomorrow and also the dinner will be quite like an old time Christmas dinner, but except for that, everything will be the same as usual. Anyway, I will be able to enjoy myself up to five o'clock then I will be on guard. I think it is the best day to be on, as everyone will be too busy celebrating to worry much about the guard and, as I don't care a lot for the beer and wine, I won't miss much. I might even gain by it, as the guard always gets a supper and we may get some pork left over from dinner and also an easy guard as well. It will be very strange to me to be on guard again as the last time I did a guard was way back in March. Nine months without doing anything in the way of guard routine and then, bang – I get caught for Christmas day – boy, wouldn't I be raising hell if I was back in England and that happened.

We have been out this evening and bought some fruit and nuts for tomorrow. I bet this will make your mouth water, we have eleven pounds of apples, eleven pounds of oranges, five pounds of walnuts, two pounds of almonds, two pounds of Spanish nuts (cob nuts), two pounds of chestnuts, twelve packets of figs, eight packets of dates and four bottles of wine, that is our own Christmas fare between us four in our billet. So, I don't think we will do too badly and, besides this, on the company menu for tomorrow is breakfast – egg and bacon. Dinner – pork, baked potatoes, cauliflower, peas, turkey and sage stuffing, with pudding custard for sweet. Also, a pint of beer and fifty fags (Vs) to finish off with. So, things could be a lot worse. I don't even mind the V cigarettes *[46]* as yesterday I received the 200 Senior Service *[47]* from Mrs. Prince (at last). They took a very long time to get here, but arrived at an opportune moment. I will have plenty of decent cigarettes over the Christmas period.

Talking of cigarettes arriving, I have received a heck of a lot of stuff this week, although only the one lot of cigarettes, I have also had no fewer than twelve parcels in just over a week, also, fifteen letters and two airgraphs in the same period. They arrived as follows – Monday 13th December, sea letter 180 – Tuesday no.65 and no.68, parcels – Wednesday no.34 and no.70 parcels – Thursday no.181 and no.182 letters and one from your mother and one containing a Christmas card from Mrs. Jeram *[48]* who asks to be remembered to you and hopes you are well. Friday I had your no.56 airmail and also a letter from Fred. Saturday I got no.61, no.74 and no.75 parcels from you and also a parcel from my mother posted in May. I did not know who it was from at first as I could not find any letter or note inside. I naturally took it to be one of the old parcels from you as it was sent to my old mob and was posted in the days when you did not number your parcels. However, the day before yesterday I took a book out to read and a letter from my mother fell out, so I realised she must have sent it to me. Also, on the same day I had your no.183 and no.193 sea letters and enclosed in no.183 was your photograph. I will say more about that later when I come to answering all your letters. Sunday I received three airmails – no.57 and no.58 from you and one from Charlie Dunsdon [Bill's friend]. Monday – letter no.187, Tuesday –

76 parcel, Wednesday – letters no.188, 189, one from your mother, parcels no.67 and 71, Thursday (yesterday) I got letter no.184 and 200 Senior Service cigarettes and finally today I received letter no.186 and also a Christmas airgraph from you and one from your mother.

By the way, in Wednesday's letter from your Mum I had a photograph of her enclosed. It is very good of her and I am very pleased with it. I expect I will be writing tomorrow to thank her for it and to answer her letters. Up to the present I have received no fewer than 175 sea letters, 58 airmails, 37 airgraphs, 34 parcels without numbers and 52 parcels with numbers and seven parcels of cigarettes since I have been out here and all from you and it's not counting those letters addressed to Newmarket as I have no check on those. It's a darn good show for one year, beloved, and I can't thank you enough for them all. It is really wonderful of you, beloved, to do so much for me and I appreciate it far more than I could ever tell you. Thanks again and I hope that one day I will be able to repay you for your generosity. Besides all the letters, etc. from you, I have had 170 other letters from different people and six parcels. So, I have had a grand total of 440 letters and 102 parcels in twelve months. I don't think I have been quite forgotten – do you?

I have told you in my airmail about my sojourn in the camp sick bay. I came out on Tuesday, whilst I was in there I wrote you two letters, but as I did not have my diary with me I could not number them. I expect they will arrive round about the same time as this letter, so I will give you the numbers now. The one written on Saturday, 18 December, should be no.39 and the one written on Monday, 20 December, no.40. They are both written in pencil and both rather brief as it is hellishly awkward trying to write whilst lying down in bed. However, as I told you in that letter, I would try and make up for it by writing a long letter when I come out, so here's hoping that this will make up for the briefness of the other two. I could not do so before as my last letter was an airmail and although I have written long letters on an airmail on a couple of occasions, it is real hard work as in order to get two thousand or more words on each page has to be carefully divided and every word carefully written so that it will be very small and yet quite clear. It took me four hours to write the airmail of a fortnight ago, as on that one I tried to get 2500 words, but despite all my trying, finished up by being two hundred words short.

Well, darling, now I will get down to answering your letters. No, on second thoughts, I think I will get down to bed as it is almost eleven o'clock and lights out is supposed to be at quarter part ten. All the others are asleep now, except Sammy who is just putting his book away. While he was reading I could carry on writing, as I wasn't keeping the light on. Now as he is getting down to it I suppose I had better ring off myself or else I will get a choking off (or something). Goodnight, darling, a very happy and enjoyable Christmas and tomorrow I will continue by answering all your wonderful letters. Goodnight, sweet dreams and all my love.

(Saturday 25 December – Xmas Day, 1943)

Good morning, my sweet, here we are again and it is the second Christmas day I have spent away from you. Although it is midwinter, the sun is shining here and it is quite hot. I think it is easily the hottest Christmas I have ever experienced. I bet it is pretty cold where you are now, but up to a few days ago it was cold here, but now it is real spring weather. After I went to bed last night, I was just dozing off to sleep when there was a hell of a noise outside the billet. Strains of 'Good King Wenceslas', 'While Shepherd's Watched Their Flock By Night', 'Noel', 'Once In Royal David's City' and other carols could be heard, all very much off key and sounding like a cross between an air raid and a chorus of cats. Then, into the billet came our two staff sergeants and our two sergeants yelling "Merry Christmas" and hugging a nice bottle of whiskey. It was five past twelve and as they said: "It is now Christmas Day and we've come to wish you a merry Christmas and give you a drink." Despite the fact that we were half asleep, we soon made a mess of their bottle of whiskey. After that we all had a bout of carol singing and the sergeants, etc. departed – without the whiskey – to continue to serenade the other billets. Right until I fell off to sleep I could hear their voices carolling in the Christmas. So, despite the fact that I went to bed without a drink, I was feeling quite merry when I fell off to sleep.

This morning the good work was continued as about seven o'clock I was awakened by someone again wishing me a merry Christmas. Yes, it was our sergeants again. This time, however, they had a cup of tea each for us instead of the whiskey. You can bet that went down very well, talk about luxury, whiskey brought round to us in bed at night and tea first thing in the morning. It's a pity that Christmas is only one day a year. At eight o'clock we tumbled out of bed and walked over for our breakfast. (No wash – just a wipe round with a flannel.) What a breakfast, two fried eggs and a really good lashing of pork, a slice of fried bread, two slices of bread and butter, marmalade, porridge and tea. After filling myself with eats I returned to my billet, put some water on the oil stove and had a wash and shave in hot water. Alec and Charlie both got back into bed, Sammy also had a wash and shave and then recommenced reading again. After I had made myself presentable, well, here I am writing again. It is now getting on for ten o'clock and Alec is just getting up and Charlie is lighting the stove to make a cup of tea. Maybe later on we may go for a walk – or we may even go to church.

Now, to get on with answering your letters, first of all in your no.183 letter in which you enclosed your photo, you ask me to tell you what I think of it. Honestly, darling, it is good, the second best photo I have from you. Of course, it is not as good as the one you had taken at the Regal Studios in Epsom in February. The one with you sitting on a chair with your arms folded. That is the best of the whole lot and the photo by which all others are judged. It will have to be good to beat that, but don't give up, keep on trying, send them out and I will pass judgement on them. You know I could never have too many photos of you, darling. If I can't have you in person then the next best thing is to have your letters and photos near me, sweetheart. In the same letter you talk some tripe about being a cad and kicking yourself for not treating me fairly when I was home with you. God alone knows what gave you that silly idea. I have had my happiest period in my life when I was home with you, darling. You treated me with the loving kindness and understanding that has always been a major part of your character. I could wish for no more. I am far more than satisfied with all you did for me and I could never thank you enough for it. Just because I had to get up early was no reason why you should, darling. I have never been a person to get up before I had to. If I had to be up early then I had to, but if there was nothing to get up for, then I stayed in bed. Even now it is the same, I never get up until I have to whether the time be four – or twelve o'clock. There was never any reason for you to get up for me and there never will be, darling.

About the furniture and other things you have bought for our home, darling. I am really sorry if I have hurt you in any way by seeming unappreciative about them. I do appreciate all that you have done and are doing to build a home for us. I am sorry I have not emphasised it more, but

I do thank you for everything. I realize what a lot of work you have to do in shopping, buying and planning for our future, working and living to help to create our own home and I know you will continue to do so. All I can say is that I am terribly sorry that I have not shown the amount of appreciation that you deserve. The only thing I can say in mitigation of my neglect is that, as most of your lovely letters are telling me how much you love me and miss me, I am so enthralled by reading that, that I have been apt to skip through the rest without realising what it meant to you. You may realize what I mean when I say that loving you and missing you as I do, I read in your letters that you love me, need me and miss me, that you bought a new chair and that you are living for the day when I return. I spend so long day dreaming about the way you care for me, that I overlook the rest of the letters. It won't happen again, my sweet, and I apologise for my inconsiderate conduct.

In your no.187 letter you remind me of those last few days at Newmarket. I expect the memory of those days is as vivid in your mind as they are in mine. I will never forget that last night as long as I live, how you clung to me, holding me so tightly and loving me so much. I can honestly say that was the last time I had with any girl, darling. I love you so much that it would make me feel sick to even think of being unfaithful to you. You are my entire life, nobody else matters to me. I belong to you only and, as long as I live, no other girl can or will interest me. I love you with all my heart and soul and need you far more than I could ever tell you. You will never know how much you mean to me and even if I could manage to convey my feelings and thoughts to you, I am afraid you would never believe it, as my love for you is so great and I want you so terribly much, darling. It is heart-rending to be away from you, darling. I live only for the day when we will be together once again and I hope and pray that day will soon dawn. I cannot live without you, it is only the thoughts of you waiting for me when I return that keeps me going, sweetheart. I worship you, love you, adore you and will always do so, darling. It is now over thirteen long months since I last experienced the heaven being in your arms. How I have endured our separation for so long is beyond me. It has been very hard and at times, almost unbearable. You mean so much to me, darling, and I need you so very much. I often lay at night imagining that great day when I will return home to you. It is so vividly clear in my mind, I see it all as clearly as if it is actual fact. You, as sweet and lovely as ever with your arms outstretched to embrace me, your smile of welcome and the ecstasy of your kiss. I miss you, darling, miss you more than words could ever convey. You are lovely, the loveliest and sweetest being in creation. I adore you and worship you, sweetheart. Everything about you is adorable from the top of your hair to the tip of your toes, you are perfect and superb. I could wish for nobody better, darling, as you are the one perfect thing in this world. I live only for the day when I can hold you in my arms once again, press you tight to my body, hear the pounding of your heart and to be able to kiss those ruby lips of yours over and over again. I want to hold you, never to let you go again. I long to tell you how much you mean to me and to hear you whisper that you love me. We will be wonderfully happy together I am sure of that, as we love each other so very much. Love such as ours will survive all partings. We belong to each other, completely.

Who knows what wonderful happiness is in store for us both when peace is here. A house of our own, maybe a couple of kiddies, but above all, you and I together. Whatever else we have, as long as we have each other, then we will be happy. Children, well we will wait and see, like you, my darling, I want a year or two at least just with you alone. I want to take you out, to give you those things that

I have never been able to give you up to the present, to try and make up for all those things you have missed, through marrying me. I have not given you hardly any of the things that a young woman like you should have. Even when we have been out anywhere, more often than not it has been you who took me out. Instead of having a good time given to you, you have had to provide the good time for us both. I hope, darling, that when I do get home I will be able to make up for all you have done. I could never repay you because the happiness you have given me is beyond all repayment, but I will do my best to make you happy.

You say that you know how much I like children as my mother and others have told you, but I don't think either you or they realise how much I love you. I don't want children, home, work or anything else, all I want is you and to make you happy. The other things I will have only to ensure your happiness. When you say I only want children when you do, I am not giving way to you. I am telling the absolute truth as you are my entire life and your happiness is my sole ambition.

Well, darling, I have just returned from dinner, and, boy, what a dinner. I can hardly sit here writing as I feel so full, it is only because at five o'clock I will be leaving to go on guard that makes me continue to write. I would like to finish this letter off this evening, but instead I must carry on now, as it is already three o'clock, so it only leaves a little under a couple of hours and I've got to have tea before then. To start our dinner we had a first course of soup, then pork, turkey, peas, carrots, salad, baked and mashed potatoes and sauce. For sweet, Xmas pudding, mince pie, pears and custard. Then a cup of coffee and some shortbread biscuits and oranges, apples, nuts, two pints of beer and fifty fags to complete the meal. The N.C.O.s [49], W.O.s [50] and officers acted as mess orderlies and brought each course round to us

263

and collect up all the empty plates.   The C.O. [51] gave a toast and we drank to 'all those at home' and before we started eating we had a minutes prayer for our loved ones. It was surprising how quickly a room full of noisy, boisterous lads became so quiet and thoughtful for that minute.   I guess the thoughts of each of us was back home during that time.   In your no.193 letter you tell me about your trip to the Palladium and how much you enjoyed Irving Berlin's show 'This Is The Army'.   I am very pleased that you enjoyed yourself and I want you to always continue to do so.   As for thinking you fresh by talking to a Yank, I could never think that because I would trust you with my life.   I know you are and always will be, true to me and even if I didn't, your complete frankness speaks for itself.   If you ever thought of doing something underhand I am sure you would not write about it.   No, darling, I know you are not fresh, I know that like myself you have only one person in your life and that you love me as I love you.

When I first came to the sad conclusion that I could no longer retain your letters as I had too many, I decided to retain all the airmails and every letter over ten pages.   Up to that time I had only two letters of ten pages and that was up to June.   Now, however, it looks as if I will have to increase the size to twelve pages before I keep them as lately every other letter is of ten or more pages.   As you said in one of your letters, I seem to have lost touch of letter writing, but you seem to have found it with a vengeance. It is wonderful to read such lovely letters and to know that you think so much of me, thanks a million for them, darling. I only hope that by you writing such letters you do not tie yourself in every night.   I know what it is to write a long letter – one letter and the whole evening is gone.   That is one reason why I don't write many of them now as, besides not having a lot of news, I have very little time.   By the time we have finished tea it is 6.00 pm and the lights go out at

264

10.15 pm, so I have four hours to wash, shave, clean my kit for the following morning, make my bed and have supper. Usually I manage to get all ready by supper at 7.30 pm, then back from supper at eight and then start writing. Two nights a week I go to the pictures and the remaining five I utilise for all my fan mail and also any reading and an occasional game of monopoly or darts. Since I have been in Italy the difficulty has been not in finding what to do, but rather finding time in which to do it.

Today I have had the whole day off and I have not stopped writing since nine thirty except to go to dinner. Yes, you're quite right. My wrist feels as if it is going to break off at any moment. I keep putting the pen down and stretching my hand and fingers to relieve the ache, but it still aches. Despite that, the ache in my fingers is very slight compared to the ache in my heart, darling. I love you so very much and would give anything to be with you now. Perhaps next year will see us together again. I hope so, although I am not banking on the war finishing quickly. Jerry can take a heck of a lot of punishment as is shown by the hammering they have taken in Russia. Despite the terrific losses in men and material, they still come back for more and I think they can stand a lot more before they crack. I much prefer to look forward to a very long war – then if it does end quickly, well and good – if it doesn't, then I won't be disappointed.

The news is keeping good, especially from the Russian front, if it still continues then who knows, we may soon be together again. I hope so, beloved, as I want nothing more than to be with you once more. Just think, darling, me sitting in my old armchair beside a roaring fire, you on my lap with your arm around me and the radio going, but both of us too wrapped up in each other to heed it. I long to ruffle up your hair again, or to play those other rather childish pranks we used to indulge in. I don't know exactly what I miss most (besides you, of course) but I think I look forward to being able to lie down in a bath of hot water, just lying completely covered and let myself soak. It is well over a year since I last had a bath. I have had many showers and wash downs, but, oh, for a long hot soak and to soak all the filth and rottenest of war right out of my system.

There is something else that I have not had for well over a year, darling – the medicine that only you can supply. I guess I have almost forgotten what it is like after being without for so long. However, having waited for so long I can continue to wait until that great day of our reunion. I have endured that long awful parting and I have remained true to you, darling. No matter how long I am away, now I know that no other woman could possibly attract me. The time one is away does not matter because the longer it is, the easier it becomes to ignore any urges. During the first two or three months away from you I went through living hell, night after night. I longed for your presence, but in the passing of time those urges become less frequent and a lot weaker, until now they hardly ever occur.

Well, darling, I am afraid I must come to a close now, as in a very few minutes I will be on guard. Give my love to all at home, all my love to you, beloved. Look after yourself and, above all, don't worry over me. Let's hope that next Christmas will see us home together again. Cheerio, my sweet, remember I love you always and am very proud and happy to be your ever loving husband,

Bill

xxx

LIVING FOR YOU DARLING

[44] A yo-yo is an axle connected to two disks and a length of twine looped around the axle. It works by holding the free end of the string (by inserting one finger in a slip knot), allowing the force of a throw to spin. The yo-yo unwinds the string allowing it to wind itself back to the hand, exploiting its spin. First invented in ancient Greece, it became popular in the 1920s as a popular pastime of many generations and cultures.

[45] Hovel is a small humble dwelling.

[46] V cigarette is Viceroy, a low cost brand and the first filter with a cork tip produced in 1935.

[47] Senior Service is a cigarette brand named after the nickname of the Royal Navy with the brand's logo of a sailing ship.

[48] Bill stayed with Mrs. Jeram in Brighton when on his motor mechanic course in July-August 1942.

[49] N.C.O.s – Non Commissioned Officers', i.e.: Lance Corporal, Corporal, Sergeant, Staff Sergeant.

[50] W.O. – Warrant Officer.

[51] C.O. – Commanding Officer.

(Below) the photo of Gladys sitting on a chair with her arms folded to Bill is 'the best of the whole lot and the photo by which all others are judged'

(Above & Below) Gladys, aged 20, 1943

(Left) Bill, aged 24, July 1944
(Below) Bill (right) with Alec making adjustments to the engine of the lathe truck

January – February 1944

On Tuesday, 4th January 1944 the Battle of Monte Cassino begins. Cassino is the strongest German defence located south-east of Rome. To the west of Cassino is the Benedictine Monastery, a natural fortress on a high mountain primarily as a lookout post, overlooking Highway 6. To the south of the town are three rivers gaining access to the Liri Valley, the Gateway to Rome. It is imperative to capture and keep the town. It is where Bill is to later fight

Tuesday, 11th January 1944 – A week later is the 'first' Battle of Monte Cassino: the Americans retreat. Mussolini's son-in-law, Count Galeazzo Ciano, with four other fascist ex-leaders, are tied to chairs and shot in the back in Verona, Italy. Ciano left behind five diaries of his views of the war, first published in 1946. Bill's 15th Army Group, formed on 11th July 1943 with the 8th British and 7th U.S. Armies (8th + 7th = 15th Army) is re-designated successively Allied forces in Italy.

Wednesday, 12th January 1944 – Winston Churchill and Charles De Gaulle begin a two day wartime conference in Marrakech, Morocco.

Saturday, 15th January 1944 – American bombers drop 1,400 tons of bombs onto the monastery. The destruction and rubble provide better protection from aerial and artillery attacks, so, two days later, German paratroopers take up positions in the ruins. General Eisenhower arrives in London, England to take command of the Allied Invasion Force.

Monday, 17th January 1944 – Monte Cassino is attacked when the British forces cross the Garigliano River in Italy. Two days later the British 46th Division attacks from the right of the river.

Thursday, 20th January 1944 – For two days the American 36th Infantry Division tries to cross the Gari River in an attempt to establish a bridgehead near Sant'Angelo in order to launch attacks on the Gustav Line near Monte Cassino.

Friday, 21st January 1944 – German bombs attack London in the Little Blitz. Meanwhile, the Allied invasion force, heading for Anzio, sails from Naples.

Saturday, 22nd January 1944 – The Allies begin the assault on Anzio, western Italy, known as Operation Shingle. Against fierce enemy fighting the American 45th Infantry Division maintains their hold. Over the next few days Allied units push inland to a depth of seven miles against increasing German resistance.

Monday, 24th January 1944 – Monte Cassino is attacked across the flooded Rapido valley north of Cassino into the mountains behind with the intention of then wheeling to the left and attacking Monte Cassino from high ground. Whilst the task of crossing the river would be easier in that the Rapido upstream of Cassino is fordable, the flooding made movement on the approaches each side very difficult. In particular, armour could only move on paths laid with steel matting and it took eight days of bloody fighting across the waterlogged ground for the 34th Division to push the German infantry back and establish a foothold in the mountains.

Between Wednesday, 26th and Saturday, 29th January 1944 Allied progress is halted on the beachhead of Anzio for a general consolidation and reorganization to take place. Allied forces and the landing of reserves pushed the total troop strength to over 61,000.

Saturday, 29th January 1944 – 285 German bombers attack London. The H.M.S. Spartan is sunk off Anzio.

Monday, 31st January 1944 – The abbey of Monte Cassino, 80 miles south of Rome, is in ruins. Americans are still struggling to protect the beachhead at Anzio, 35 miles south of Rome.

At the beginning of February the battles at both Monte Cassino and Anzio intensify. After an unsuccessful three day attack on Monastery Hill and Cassino town, the Americans withdraw. They are replaced by the 2nd New Zealand Division and the British 8th Army on the Adriatic front.

Tuesday, 8th February 1944 – The plan for the invasion of France, Operation Overlord, is confirmed.

Bill is now near Naples and his next letter dated on Saturday, 12th February 1944, is number '13'. The 15th Army Group is renamed Allied Forces in Italy on Tuesday, 11th January 1944 and then Allied Central Mediterranean Force on Tuesday, 18th January 1944. This letter is written on an American Red Cross headed paper.

Bill is 24 years and 5 months old: Gladys is 21 years and 9 months old.

PTE. POWELL T/69083.
W/S PLATOON.
G.H.Q. CAR COY R.A.S.C.
H.Q. A.C.M.F

Saturday 12 February 1944.

My own darling beloved wife,
    Hello my sweet, here I am once again, writing to tell you how very much I love you and how much I miss you. I hope and pray that you are keeping in the best of health and that all is OK both at home and at work. I am pleased to say that I am keeping fit and well, also quite safe and sound, so there is absolutely no need for you to worry about me.
    For a change I have something to write about today, as I told

(Above) Bill's letter to Gladys written on Saturday, 12th February 1944

Mrs. Gladys Powell
84a London Road
North Cheam
Surrey
England

(13)
PTE. POWELL T/69083
W/S PLATOON
G.H.Q. CAR COY. R.A.S.C.
H.Q. A.C.M.F.

Saturday 12 February 1944

My own darling beloved wife,

Hello my sweet, here I am once again, writing to tell you how very much I love you and how much I miss you. I hope and pray that you are keeping in the best of health and that all is ok both at home and at work. I am pleased to say that I am keeping fit and well, also quite safe and sound, so there is absolutely no need for you to worry about me.

For a change I have something to write about today, as I told you in my air letter on Wednesday I went out for the day on Tuesday. I had a really grand time, one of the most interesting days I have ever spent. We went by lorry to the town of Pompeii and spent the day sightseeing. Although I have been through the modern Pompeii several times, this was the first time I had ever had an opportunity of visiting the old Roman town that was wiped out by the eruption of Vesuvius. It is almost beyond all belief that over 2000 years ago such a fine civilization could have been in being. I am going to do my best to describe it for you. Before I do so, I had better tell you a little about its history. It dates back to the old Roman Empire (some years before Christ) and is popularly supposed to have been wiped out by an eruption of Vesuvius in the year 79 A.D. Actually it was completely buried up to a height of over 20 feet in hot ashes when the volcano Somma erupted. Somma is a sister volcano to the more famous Vesuvius and both are just to the rear of Pompeii. While Vesuvius is still an active volcano, with its ever present smoke and rumblings at the top, Somma is now extinct.

Pompeii itself lies seventeen miles from Naples and one mile from the sea. It was first discovered some four hundred years ago whilst digging a canal through to Naples. Excavations were started at once and the long lost city was discovered. The excavations were still being carried on up to the outbreak of this war and no doubt they will be continued when the war is over. Where necessary the town has been rebuilt – using only the bricks and tiles, etc. from the original town. The only artificial part of it all is on one or two houses, they have entirely rebuilt them so as to give one the full impression of what they were like. Nowadays there is another Pompeii, a few hundred yards from the old Roman town. The modern town is just a typical Italian town except for a beautiful cathedral, of which I will tell you more later. The old Roman town is completely walled off and to enter it one must go through one of its eight gates and pay the admission money. Guides are available to show you around and describe everything to you and we availed ourselves of their services.

After paying our admission fee and getting our English speaking guide we entered the iron gates into Pompeii – or rather just outside, because the next thing we came to were two huge pillars set in the side of a twenty foot wall, these were the old gates to Pompeii itself. Passing through these we come to the huge amphitheatre – the oldest known in the world. To look at, it is like a modern football ground – except in football grounds one has to stand whilst in this amphitheatre there was seating accommodation for over twenty thousand people. It was here that the Romans watched their gladiator fights, chariot racing, or the spectacle of Christians being fed to the lions. Further up the cobbled road we came to the baths. There are altogether six of these baths in Pompeii, three large public ones and three smaller private ones. The sides were marked off for ladies and gentlemen and separate changing rooms were allocated for them. Along one side are the remains of the cubicles where hot baths were available to the Romans. In the middle were the swimming pool and also a games room, Turkish bath and rest room.

Also, one can see the elaborate hot water system they had evolved, complete with lead pipes to carry the water into the baths. It seems as if the Romans knew almost as much as we do today, as houses were equipped with stone storage tanks to catch the winter rain and save it for the summer draught. The streets were paved and a form of drainage was in operation. The houses themselves were large and wonderfully painted inside. Some of the paintings were still in a very well preserved condition and one house had a large inscription painted inside which our guide translated as follows: 'Take your fill of food, woman and wine' and another telling one to: 'Eat till it hurts then retire to the vomit room'. Most of the houses had this vomit room. It appears you were not a good host unless you fed your guest until he was sick.

Along the main road of the town we see many shops and houses, mostly taverns or other eating and drinking houses. Outside these shops are holes bored in the stone pavement which presumably held awnings in front of the shop. Over the doorpost one can still see the signs denoting the trade of the owner, such as a dice for a gambling saloon, kettles for the coppersmith, jars for the grocers, iron keys for the ironmonger and a bundle of wheat for the baker. All these signs are cut in the stone above the doors, but the most peculiar of all was the man's penis – denoting a brothel. It seems as if the trade of sex and prostitution is indeed the world's oldest profession, for inside this 2000 year old brothel were rooms containing a stone bed and a jar. Around the walls were painted and carved pictures of men and women having intercourse together, all in different positions and no fewer than 69 altogether.

Outside the door of each room was a picture of the girl who used to live there and a notice telling one how she satisfied your wants. It also seems as if the Romans looked on sex with a far franker outlook that we do. Outside almost every house was a carving of a penis with either wings or legs, which was their good luck charm. Also in a great many of the houses there were pictures of men and women together in the nude. Also on a great many walls were paintings of the various gods and goddesses, such as Juniper, Mars, Othello, Venus and many others, all denoting or portraying some story or fable. It appears that the Pompeian's had very little furniture, but instead relied on these paintings to decorate and furnish their houses. There are many temples, theatres and even gymnasiums all in a fair state of presentation, but the two things that impressed me most was the water system, houses, furniture, sprays and baths all being supplied by lead pipe – some of which is still visible. The other things was the wonderful paintings, many of which are in a marvellous state of presentation, each one a wealth of colour and detail had a perfect masterpiece of art.

To finish off my narrative of Pompeii, I must tell you a little of the life of the citizens of that town – remember this is 2000 years ago. Bronze beehives were found, so they knew all about beekeeping, oil was sold by weight and in the same sort of jars as are used in Italy today. The streets were paved with volcanic lava – the same as Naples is today. The marriage rites were also interesting. The law forbid an engagement to last longer than two years, even breach of promise suits could be brought against anyone who broke off an engagement. Tables of affinity were prepared to prevent the marriage of near relations. There were two forms of marriage – one before a priest and divorce was hard to get, but the other was by mutual consent and, to divorce your wife, all that was necessary was to turn her out. The Pompeian's were only allowed one wife at a time, but as the second form of marriage and divorce was very easy, this was no handicap to them. A man went into mourning by not showing or cutting his hair for a week and a woman by wearing white and no ornaments. Even a form of paper and ink was known to them and they left many verses and books in their houses. These of course, with their utensils, are all in the museums – mostly in the museum at Naples. It all goes to prove that we aren't as clever as we imagine we are.

After a most interesting morning I left the old Roman city, went out through the gate along a couple of hundred yards of road into the Italian town of Pompeii where we had left the lorry. There we proceeded to light a fire, make some tea and cook our dinner – in the centre of the town's square.

Whilst we were thus engaged we were besieged by the town's population, who descended on us with pleas, entreaties and urges to buy "souvenir Pompeii" and fruit of all kinds – all at a price that would equal or excel my month's pay. I did get some fruit – by the usual method of helping myself then paying what I thought it was worth. That is now the most common way of getting things, the local price lists are published in our paper, so we help ourselves to goods and pay as per the price list. This way we neither rob them – nor get robbed. If they were dealing with Jerry they would get a few kicks instead of money, so they can't grumble – much.

After dinner I had a stroll round the town itself, but did not find anything of interest until I came to Pompeii Cathedral. This is supposed to be the second finest church in the world, surpassed only by the church of St. Peter's at Rome. I can say personally that it's the finest and most beautiful building I have ever seen. It is far too great for me to attempt to describe, all I can tell you that may help you get some idea of what it is like is this, it is decorated with solid gold, silver and marble, has some of the world's best paintings of saints, etc., also a solid gold organ, a tower with over fifteen huge bells and even the bells are made of an alloy of gold, silver and bronze. The organ alone cost well over 250 thousand pounds [£9,379,650.00p in 2013]. Solid gold altars and crucifixes, gold chandeliers and silver rails were round the pews and altars. The ceiling is richly carved and painted – the painting alone taking over three years to complete. The Italian name for the church is Santa Maria – or St. Mary's, but it is known more popularly as Pompeii Cathedral. If St. Peter's at Rome is supposed to be better than this, I will have to see it to believe it.

By the time I came out of the church it was getting dark and time to be getting home again. To complete a very interesting day we were able to see Vesuvius outlined against a dark sky, belching vivid red flowers and clouds of smoke and with that our day ended.

Despite all this, darling, I have yet to see anything as beautiful as you, or any sight that thrilled me as much as the day at Nonsuch Park when you were standing against a background of roses and the sun was sending rivers of gold running through your hair. You stood there, a perfect vision of exotic beauty, against which even the display by nature seemed very shoddy. You were so wonderful, my beloved, that I was frightened, I did not think it possible that a being so lovely could ever fall in love with me.

However, the gods were on my side and I have never

been so proud and happy as that day a few months later when you stood by my side in church and became my wife. I love you, darling, with all my heart and soul. I love you with a love so great that mere words are powerless to express my feelings. I love you far more than you could ever realize. I only wish I were able to put into writing all the things that I long to say to you. They are so jumbled up in my mind though, that I would sound crazy to write them. Sounds crazy – I am crazy, crazy about you, sweetheart. I live only to hold you in my arms once again, to feel the ecstasy of your kiss and to be able to tell you how very much I love you and how much I miss you.

Darling, I worship you, I love you, I need you, I miss you, I long for you, nothing can ever take your place, you are more necessary to me than the sun is to the earth. I cannot live without you, my beloved. All I want from life is a home and you to share it with me. I pray that before long my dreams will be realized and I will be home with you once more. Well, darling, I must come to a close now. Look after yourself, keep smiling, enjoy yourself as much as you can and please don't worry about me. Give my love to all at home and here's hoping they are all ok. All my fondest love to you, sweetheart. Goodnight, my darling, I am always your ever loving husband,

Bill

xxx

I LIVE FOR YOU ALONE

February 1944 – February 1945

On Monday, 14th February 1944 – General Dwight D. Eisenhower establishes S.H.A.E.F. (Supreme Headquarters Allied Expeditionary Force) as his headquarters in Great Britain. In the four battles at Monte Cassino from Monday, 17th January 1944, Allied casualties amounted to about 21,000 including 4,100 killed in action and two German armies are defeated. Bill is to move south to fight at Monte Casino. The soldier in the conflict next to Bill is shot dead.

Tuesday, 15th February 1944 – The 'second' Battle of Monte Cassino begins and the monastery on top of Cassino is destroyed by Allied bombing.

Friday, 9th March 1944 – In Italy the Allied Central Mediterranean Force is renamed Allied Armies. The army group is commanded by Field Marshall Sir Harold Alexander.

Wednesday, 15th March 1944 – The historic Benedictine monastery at Cassino, Italy, which the Germans used as an observation post and artillery position, is bombed by Allied aircraft in the 'third' battle and now stands demolished.

Friday, 24th March 1944 – 335 Italians are killed in Rome in the Ardeatine Massacre, including 75 Jews and over 200 members of the Italian Resistance from various groups.

Tuesday, 4th April 1944 – Photographs of part of Auschwitz concentration camp are taken by Allied surveillance aircraft. Two prisoners escape and manage to provide detailed information about the mass murder that is taking place. Charles de Gaulle takes command of all Free French forces.

Thursday, 27th April 1944 – Secret preparations are going

on all over the south of England in a rehearsal exercise to prepare for the D-Day landings exercise. Slapton Sands beach in Devon is a replica of the Utah gravel beach where the U.S. Army is to land. An unexpected German torpedo attack results in 946 Americans killed. This tragedy is given strict secrecy because of the D-Day preparations.

Tuesday, 2nd May 1944 – Gladys' 22nd birthday.

Saturday, 6th May 1944 – Bill passes his Trade Test examination and is remustered as a vehicle mechanic in group A, class 2 (AII).

Tuesday, 9th May 1944 – The battle at the Gustav Line near Monte Cassino continues without resolution.

Thursday, 11th May 1944 – In a 'fourth' Battle of Monte Cassino the British cross the Rapido River concurrent with the opening of an offensive campaign toward Rome.

Thursday, 18th May 1944 – Finally, after appalling wet and cold weather conditions, the Germans evacuate the town and the monastery of Monte Cassino. Polish troops hoist their red/white flag on the ruins. Prisoners are taken, three defence lines are smashed and vast quantities of German material are destroyed.

Tuesday, 23rd May 1944 – The Allies advance towards Rome. Other Allies begin an offensive from the beaches of Anzio, Italy. Two days later the Germans retreat and American forces break out of the beachhead and link up with the 5th Army; both then begin their advance on Rome.

Thursday, 25th May 1944 – The Germans are now in retreat in the Anzio area. American forces break out of the beachhead and link up with the 5th Army; both then begin their advance on Rome.

In June 1944 Bill joins the 128 Petrol Depot, R.A.S.C. C.M.F. and is stationed in France until July 1944.

Sunday, 4th June 1944 – British, American and French troops enter Rome, the first Axis capital to fall to the Allies.

Monday, 5th June 1944 – More than 1,000 British bombers

drop 5,000 tons of bombs on German gun batteries on the Normandy coast in preparation for D-Day the following day. By midday, five Allied divisions (two British, two American and one Canadian) are safely ashore. On the Omaha Beach (the codename for one of the five sectors located on the Normandy beach) there are high casualties due to strong German resistance along the coast. By nightfall of the longest day the Allies have nowhere near achieved the depth of penetration planned, but they have succeeded in landing 155,000 fully equipped soldiers on the continent of Europe. Rommel believes the result of that first day will determine the outcome of the campaign and even of the war. Although no major battles have been fought, the German forces have nevertheless lost the day.

Tuesday, 13th June 1944 – Germany launches their first V-1 Flying Bomb (also known as the Buzz Bomb or Doodlebug) attack on London in revenge for the invasion. Adolf Hitler believes in Germany's victory with his 'secret weapon'.

Wednesday, 14th June 1944 – General Charles de Gaulle makes a triumphant return to France.

Sunday, 18th June 1944 – Elba is declared liberated and the Allies capture Assisi, the birthplace of St. Francis, Italy.

In July 1944 Bill has left France where he has been stationed for one month to return to Italy where he is stationed until the end of the war.

Thursday, 20th July 1944 – Adolf Hitler survives an assassination attempt by Claus von Stauffenberg. Four people are killed and almost all the survivors are injured. Hitler is shielded from the blast by a heavy, solid oak conference table leg and is only slightly wounded. Stauffenberg and the conspirators are tracked down and overpowered. For his involvement Stauffenberg is shot the next day.

Friday, 4th August 1944 – The Germans destroy historic

bridges and buildings before Florence, the Tuscany capital in Italy, is liberated by the Allies. The trials of the bomb conspirators against Hitler begin. A tip from an unidentified Dutch informer leads the Gestapo to a sealed off area in an Amsterdam warehouse where they find Jewish diarist Anne Frank, her family and others in hiding.

Saturday, 5th August 1944 – Polish insurgents liberate a German labour camp in Warsaw, freeing 348 Jewish prisoners who join to fight the Germans.

Tuesday, 8th August 1944 – The plotters in the bomb against Hitler are hanged, their bodies hung on meat hooks with reprisals made against their families.

Saturday, 12th August 1944 – The oil pipeline laid between England and France, known as Operation Pluto, begins operating.

Tuesday, 15th August 1944 – The Allies reach the Gothic Line, the last German strategic position in North Italy.

Thursday, 24th August 1944 – Following the success of Operation Overlord the Allies enter Paris. The Germans surrender Paris to the Allies in defiance of Hitler's orders to destroy it. Hungary decides to continue the war together with Germany.

Friday, 1st September 1944 – Anne Frank's last diary entry; she and her family are placed on the last transport train from Westerbork, Holland, to Auschwitz concentration camp in Poland, arriving three days later.

Sunday, 3rd September 1944 – The Allies liberate Brussels. A day later the British 11th Armoured Division liberates the city of Antwerp in Belgium.

Tuesday, 5th September 1944 – Russia invades Bulgaria: Bulgaria declares war on Germany.

Thursday, 7th September 1944 – The Belgium government in exile from London returns to Brussels.

Saturday, 9th September 1944 – The first V-2 rocket attacks London.

Wednesday, 13th September 1944 – Bill's 25th birthday.

Monday, 18th September 1944 – The Channel port in Brest, France, falls to the Allies.

Tuesday, 19th September 1944 – An armistice between Finland and Russia is signed, ending the Continuation War.

Monday, 9th October 1944 – British Prime Minister Winston Churchill and the Russian Premier Joseph Stalin begin a nine day Tolstoy Conference in Moscow to discuss the future of Europe.

Saturday, 14th October 1944 – German Field Marshal Erwin Rommel, under suspicion for participating in the 'July 20 Plot' to assassinate Adolf Hitler, is approached at his home by Wilhelm Burgdorf and Ernst Maisel, two generals from Hitler's headquarters. Burgdorf informs Rommel of the charges and offers him a choice: he could face the People's Court or choose to commit suicide quietly. If he chooses the court, his staff will be arrested and his family will also suffer even before the predicted conviction and execution. If Rommel chooses suicide, the government would assure his family full pension payments and a state funeral claiming he died a hero. Burgdorf has brought with him a cyanide pill for the occasion. Rommel decides to choose to end his own life and explains his decision to his wife and son. Carrying his field marshal's baton, Rommel is then driven away from his home where he takes the cyanide pill.

Wednesday, 18th October 1944 – Hitler orders a call-up of all men between the ages of 16 to 60 years for Home Guard duty.

Monday, 23rd October 1944 – The Allies recognise Charles de Gaulle's cabinet as the provisional government of France.

Monday, 6th November 1944 – Despite his declining health since 1940, Franklin D. Roosevelt becomes the only American president to win a fourth term when he wins over republican challenger Thomas E. Dewey.

Friday, 10th November 1944 – V-2 rockets continue to hit Britain at the rate of about eight a day.

Monday, 20th November 1944 – Adolf Hitler leaves his wartime headquarters at Rastenberg, East Prussia, to go to Berlin to establish himself in a bunker.

Tuesday, 21st November 1944 – San Marino declares war on Germany.

Thursday, 23rd November 1944 – Metz, France, is taken and Strasbourg, in eastern France, is liberated by French troops.

Sunday, 26th November 1944 – With heavy rain, the war in Italy is stalemate.

Sunday, 3rd December 1944 – The British Home Guard is stood down.

Tuesday, 5th December 1944 – The Allies control Ravenna, Italy, an inland city once the capital of the Western Roman Empire.

Monday, 11th December 1944 – General Mark W. Clark takes command of the Allied Army Group and the title of the headquarters is reverted back to 15th Army Group. Allied Armies in Italy controlled the land forces for some of the hardest fighting of the entire war. Operations carried out include: the long stalemate on the Gustav Line with the hard fought Battle of Monte Cassino; the Anzio landings; the capture of Rome; and ending with the Allied forces stuck again just south of the Po Valley and the Alps.

Thursday, 14th December 1944 – Bill passes another Trade Test examination and is upgraded to a vehicle mechanic, group A, class 1 (AI).

Friday, 15th December 1944 – A private airplane carrying band leader Glenn Miller disappears in heavy fog over the English Channel while flying to Paris.

Saturday, 16th December 1944 – The Battle of the Bulge, Germany's last desperate attempt for success on the western front, uses its remaining reserves to launch a massive counter-offensive in the Ardennes to try to split the Western Allies, encircle large portions of their troops and capture their primary supply port at Antwerp in order to prompt a political settlement. A week later, on 23rd December, the skies clear over the Ardennes to allow Allied aircraft to begin their attack on the German offensive and the American counter-attack begins with The Battle of the Bulge reaching its deepest point in the Belgium village of Celles and the furthest point the German army are to advance.

Sunday, 24th December 1944 – V-1 flying bombs reach Manchester.

Friday, 29th December 1944 – The Russians launch the Battle of Budapest against the German and Hungarian forces. Two days later Hungary, now led by a Russian controlled government, declares war on Germany.

Sunday, 7th January 1945 – British Field Marshall Bernard Montgomery holds a press conference at Zonhoven describing his role at the Battle of the Bulge.

Monday, 8th January 1945 – The Russian army hands over the power of West Berlin to the British and American armies.

Tuesday, 16th January 1945 – Adolf Hitler takes residence in the Führerbunker (Leader's bunker), an air raid shelter in Berlin.

Wednesday, 17th January 1945 – The Soviet Union occupies Warsaw, Poland.

Saturday, 20th January 1945 – President Franklin D. Roosevelt is inaugurated for his fourth term. Harry S. Truman is sworn in as Vice President. Evacuation of Auschwitz and Birkenau concentration camps begins and the Red Army liberates the death camps. Hungary agrees to an armistice with the Allies.

Thursday, 25th January 1945 – Bill is S.O.S. posted on

admittance to hospital. Two days later Bill is discharged from the hospital. [No known reason]

Saturday, 27th January 1945 – The Soviet Union liberates Auschwitz.

Tuesday, 30th January 1945 – Adolf Hitler gives his last speech.

Between Sunday, 4th and Sunday, 11th February 1945 Winston Churchill, Prime Minister of the United Kingdom, President Franklin D. Roosevelt and Russian leader Joseph Stalin hold the Yalta Conference to agree on the occupation of post-war Germany and when Russia will join the war against Japan.

Friday, 16th February 1945 – Venezuela declares war on Germany.

Bill has moved from W/S Platoon, General Headquarters Car Company to 128 Petrol Depot in the Royal Army Service Corps stationed in Sparanise, a municipality in the Province of Caserta in the Italian region Campania, located about 40 km northwest of Naples and about 25 km northwest of Caserta. Its surrounding communities are the villages of Francolise, Calvi Risorta and Pignataro Maggiore. Bill's next letter is number '78'.

Bill is 25 years and 5 months old: Gladys is 23 years and 9 months old.

78.   PTE. POWELL T/69083
        128 PETROL DEPOT
        R.A.S.C.   C.M.F.

Monday 18 Feb 1945.

My own darling beloved wife,

    Hello sweetheart, here I
am at the beginning of
what I hope will be my
last week in the army —
and I hope that by this
time next week I will
be on my way home to
you — for keeps.
    I have just asked our
O.C. if I can have the

(Above) Bill's letter to Gladys written on Monday, 18th February 1945

289

Mrs. Gladys Powell
84a London Road
North Cheam
Surrey
England

(78)
PTE. POWELL T/69083
128 PETROL DEPOT
R.A.S.C.
C.M.F.

Monday 18 Feb 1945

My own darling beloved wife,

Hello sweetheart, here I am at the beginning of what I hope will be my last week in the army – and I hope that by this time next week I will be on my way home to you – for keeps.

I have just asked our O.C. [52] if I can have the rest of my time here off duty – and he has said I can do so – so now I am officially finished, a gentleman of leisure.

I hope to try and get out either tomorrow or Wednesday to see if I can buy a couple of small presents to bring back with me. I don't know whether I will be successful or not – but I hope to get something for you this time, as I felt very mean in not bringing you back a present when I came home on leave last time.

It is pretty certain now that I will be home on or before Sunday week – the 3rd March. Up to now I am still down to go from here on Thursday – and even if that gets delayed it will only be for 48 hours, then about four days in the assembly area and four days travelling home. Even for allowing any hold-ups the 3rd of March should be the latest date – and if all goes well the 27th February should be the great day.

In any case now it will only be a case of a couple of day's hold-up – so it won't make much difference.

I expect you will just about get this letter by the time I get home – but in case it does get home quickly and thus beat me, you will know now that you can expect me any time between say Tuesday the 26th February – until Sunday 3 March – the most likely days to be Wednesday 27th or else Thursday 28th February.

It will hardly be worthwhile to write you another letter after this – so this will be my last letter, darling. If I am held up, I will write again. If not then I will send you an airmail when I go to the assembly area – and that will be the last letter you will have from me – and I hope it will also be the last letter that I will have to write to you my, darling. It's not that I am fed up with writing to you – although I don't exactly like writing – but when I have to write it means we are apart – and I never want to be away from you again.

I love you, my darling, love you with all my heart and soul and miss you far more than I could ever tell you. My whole life is bound up with you and I need you more than life itself. Indeed, darling, you are my life. All I ever want is to hold you close in my arms and feel your lips on mine, to know that you love me as I love you and above all to give you the same happiness that you have given me, beloved.

It seems almost too good to be true that by the time this letter arrives I will probably be indoors to receive it – and that six and a half years of soldiering will be over.

I know we will be very happy, sweetheart – and I only hope that I am able to get a decent job that will enable us to live as we both like.

I love you, darling – and in a few more days I will be able to tell you how much instead of trying to write it.

Until then, my darling, I will say cheerio – and hope that the next ten days go by very quickly.

All my love and fondest regards, I am always very proud and happy to be your ever loving husband,
Bill
xxx

GOD BLESS YOU DARLING

[52] O.C. – Officer Commanding.

February – March 1945

Bill did not return home.   Instead he remained stationed in Sparanise, Italy, with the 128 Petrol Depot in the Royal Army Service Corps (R.A.S.C.).

Sunday, 18th February 1945 – One O.R. (Ordinary Rank or Junior Rank; O.R.s are generally Privates, i.e.: not N.C.O.s or S.N.C.O's or Officers) is posted to no.3 transit camp ready to be sent home to the UK on the grounds of long service.

Monday, 19th February 1945 – Normal depot routine in Bill's 128 Petrol Depot is carried out throughout the day. One ordinary rank soldier has been admitted to no.2 General Hospital.

Tuesday, 20th February 1945 – At 00:01 hour 705 Engine Petrol Display Company, an operational committee of U.S. petrol point at Calvi Risorta, is taken over by Bill's 128 Petrol Depot in the Royal Army Service Corps.   At 07:30 hour a rehabilitation of the petrol point at Calvi Risorta commences in order to cope with the heavier volume of traffic consequent upon the closing of the U.S. Army Point. Calvi Risorta is a municipality in the province 25 km northwest of Caserta, Italy.   The village was scheduled to be bombarded by the Allied forces on Monday, 18th October 1943.   Air support has been requested against the German positions, but a message delivered from 'G.I. Joe', a homing pigeon, arrived in time with the information that the British have captured the village avoiding the bombing and saving the lives of up to a thousand men, including the British troops occupying it.   Pigeons had long played an important role in war.   Due to their homing ability, speed, and altitude, they were often used as military messengers. They ceased being used as of 1957.   'G.I. Joe' was housed at the U.S. Army's Churchill Loft at Fort Monmouth in New

Jersey along with 24 other heroic pigeons. He died aged 18 and was mounted and displayed at the U.S. army Communications Electronics Museum.

Wednesday, 21st February 1945 – At 09:00 hour the petrol point at Calvi Risorta has a visit by the O.C. (Officer Commanding, normally a Major). At 11:15 hour 31 tons packed P.O.L. (petrol, oil and lubricants – normally packed in jerry cans and 10 gallon drums) are received by rail from 8 Petrol Depot, R.A.S.C.

Thursday, 22nd February 1945 – At 07:30 hour routine depot maintenance and issues to the area units are carried out throughout the day. At 16:30 hour ten tons of bulk M.T. 80 is received from the petrol point at Calvi Risorta. M.T. 80 is low octane petroleum; bulk because it is in a tanker. They are decanted into barrels to replace the depot packed stocks by R.T.W. (Road Tanker Wagon) and not decanted into jerry cans. Meanwhile today marks the end of the Battle of Monte Castello, situated southwest of Bologna in northern Italy. The battle began on Saturday, 25th November 1944. After nearly three months of fighting between the Allied forces advancing into northern Italy and the German defenders, the Brazilian Expeditionary Force manages to expel the German forces in the (Tuscan) North Apennines where their artillery is impeding the advance of the British 8th Army towards Bologna. There are six Allied attacks against the German forces, four of which are strategic failures. Both sides sustained large casualties due to several factors, including the extremely low temperature existing at the time. Uruguay declares war on Germany and Japan.

Friday, 23rd February 1945 – A normal depot routine takes place throughout the day from 07:00 hour. At 16:30 hour 16 tons of bulk M.T. 80 is received by a unit road tanker wagon from the petrol point at Calvi Risorta.

Saturday, 24th February 1945 – At 09:00 hour the petrol

point at Calvi Risorta is visited by the Officer Commanding. A satisfactory progress is noted on rehabilitation. At 16:30 hour 16 tons of bulk M.T. 80 is received by a unit road tanker wagon from the petrol point at Calvi Risorta. At 16:30 hour 16 tons of bulk M.T. 80 is received by a unit road tanker wagon from the petrol point and decanted into barrels.

Sunday, 25th February 1945 – At 10:00 hour one sergeant is despatched to Perugia in the central part of Italy to attend a unit educational instructors' course. At 15:00 hour 2 I/C (Second in Command) is despatched to R.A.S.C. T.D. (Royal Army Service Corps Training Depot) to attend a no.6 short petrol duties course. [The appointments and Ranks are: C.O. (Commanding Officer) = Lieutenant Colonel; O.C. (Officer Commanding) = Major; 2 I/C (Second in Command) = Captain.] At 16:30 hour 16 tons of bulk M.T. 80 is received by road from the petrol point at Calvi Risorta. Turkey declares war on Germany.

Monday, 26th February 1945 – At 07:30 hour starts with a normal depot routine maintenance and issues to area units is carried on throughout the day. At 16:30 hour 16 tons of bulk M.T. 80 is received by road from the petrol point at Calvi Risorta. Syria declares war on Germany and Japan.

Tuesday, 27th February 1945 – At 11:00 hour there is a visit by a G.T. Coln. At 14:30 hours the petrol point at Calvi Risorta is visited by the Officer Commanding. A satisfactory progress is noted on all the road making and rehabilitation carried out by the unit personnel and civilian labour. At 16:30 hour ten tons of bulk M.T. 80 is received by the unit transport from the petrol point.

Wednesday, 28th February 1945 – At 07:30 hour there is a normal depot routine maintenance and issues of packed petrol, oil and lubricants is carried out throughout the day. At 13:15 hour 90 tons of packed petrol, oil and lubricants are received at Sparanise railhead from 8 Petrol Depot. The unloading commenced immediately with 3-3 ton vehicles and is completed by 16:45 hour. At 16:30 hour 10½ tons of bulk M.T. 80 is received by road in a unit road tanker wagon and decanted into barrels to replace the depot packed stocks.

Thursday, 1st March 1945 – At 12:00 hour a petrol, oil and lubricant report is rendered to S.T. (Supply and Transit) in the 56 area. At 14:00 hour one ordinary rank soldier is collected from 'B' transit camp on return from 28 days leave in the U.K. At 15:00 hour 203 returnable cans of M.T. 80 are recovered from the Carabinieri at Cancello and taken into stock on an instruction received from their S.T. 56 area. The Carabinieri is the national military police of Italy, policing both military and civililian populations. Although the Carabinieri assisted in the suppression of opposition during the rule of Benito Mussolini, they were also responsible for his downfall and many units were disbanded by Nazi Germany, which resulted in large numbers of Carabinieri joining the Italian resistance movement. San Felice a Cancello is a municipality in the province of Caserta, located about 14 km southeast of Caserta and about 30 km northwest of Naples. At 16:30 hour 16 tons of bulk M.T. 80 is received from the petrol point at Calvi Risorta. In the unit road tanker wagons are decanted into barrels to replace depot stocks. Franklin D. Roosevelt gives what will be his last address to a joint session of the United States Congress, reporting on the Yalta Conference. Former American Vice President Henry A. Wallace starts his term of office as U.S. Secretary of Commerce, serving under President Franklin D. Roosevelt.

In March Anne Frank dies in the Bergen-Belsen concentration camp of typhus a few weeks before the camp is liberated by British troops on Sunday, 15th April 1945. Anne Frank gained international fame posthumously after her diary, given as a 13th birthday gift, was published. It starts on Friday, 12th June 1942 until Tuesday, 1st August 1944 when her life in hiding was exposed.

Bill has now moved from his camp in 128 Petrol Depot to 'A' Platoon, 717 Company, in the Royal Army Service Corps, General Headquarters Car Company, based in the Central Mediterranean Forces in Florence, Italy. Bill's next letter is number '17'.

Bill is 25 years and 6 months old: Gladys is 22 years and 10 months old.

17

Pte. Powell T/169083
A. PLATOON
717 COY. R.A.S.C.
G.H.Q. CAR. C.M.F.

Friday 2 March 1945,

My own darling beloved wife,

Hello once again my sweet heart, ever hoping
that this letter finds you in the very best
of health and that everything at home
is alright. I am quite fit and well so
there is no need for you to worry about me.
I am very pleased to say that your letters
are still arriving OK, today I have received
No 17 and 18 sealetters, yesterday No 3 parcel
and on Wednesday No 13, 14, 15 and 16 sealetters
also one from your mother. I have briefly
answered some of these letters in my long
airletter to you on Wednesday evening, but
now I will endeavour to answer them all
fully. I won't answer each one seperately
but answer the whole lot together (13 & 18.)

First of all I am so very pleased to know
that my letters are reaching you so very
quickly darling and I hope they will always
continue to do so — until I am home again
and letters no longer necessary. Its rather
funny about the time taken for our
letters to reach each other. I recieve your
air letters in three or four days, yet it

(Above) Bill's letter to Gladys written on Friday, 2nd March 1945

298

Mrs. Gladys Powell
84a London Road
North Cheam
Surrey
England

(17)
PTE. POWELL T/69083
A. PLATOON
717 COY. R.A.S.C.
H.Q. 15 ARMY GROUP
C.M.F.

Friday 2 March 1945

My own darling beloved wife,

Hello once again my sweetheart, here's hoping that this letter finds you in the very best of health and that everything at home is alright. I am quite fit and well so there is no need for you to worry about me.

I am very pleased to say that your letters are still arriving ok, today I have received no.17 and 18 sea letters, yesterday no.3 parcel and on Wednesday no.13, 14, 15 and 16 sea letters, also one from your mother. I have briefly answered some of these letters in my last air letter to you on Wednesday evening, but now I will endeavour to answer them all fully. I won't answer each one separately but answer the whole lot together (13 to 18).

First of all, I am so very pleased to know that my letters are reaching you so very quickly darling and I hope they will always continue to do so – until I am home again and letters no longer necessary. It's rather funny about the time taken for our letters to reach each other. I receive your air letters in three or four days, yet it takes three times as long for my airletters to get home to you, on the other side of the scale you receive my sea letters in a week or ten days, yet yours take a month or six weeks to get out here. Still, the main thing is that we both get them and as long as we continue to do that, neither of us should grumble.

As for my posting them in England, you needn't worry about that as I don't suppose you will get any letters from me when I arrive in Blighty *[53]* again. I will only need a few minutes to find out the next train to London and I will be on my way home. Perhaps the army may have different ideas – but I am rather used to getting my own way and nobody will be able to keep me long in England before I am on my way home to you once again. When that day does eventually arrive – as one day it will, then again I am afraid a lot of your calculations will go astray. You say you will be there to meet me at the dock – or, if that is impossible, then you will meet me at the station – but I don't think so, darling. What is more likely to happen is that one day – yes I did say one day – you will get a telegram from me saying I have arrived back in England and will be home in a few days and the next thing you will know will be seeing me walking in a couple of days later. Even if I was to know where I would land – or even what station in London I would arrive at, I would not want to meet you there. Anything could happen to delay things and I would not like to think of you having to hang about waiting for me – perhaps for hours on end. No, when that day does come, you just sit tight – put the kettle on so that it will be ready for a cup of tea for me. You are quite right in one thing – when you say that you will bet 100-to-1 that we both cry with happiness. It will be the day I have lived for, dreamed of and pictured in my mind for the past two years or more, darling, and I know how I will feel and have more than a good idea that you will feel just the same.

Perhaps on the whole this has had some good points

about it, for if there had been no war you would never have gone to Cheam to live, I would not have been at Ewell, there would have been no dance – and we wouldn't have met each other. Even this very long separation has served a good purpose, for it has proved how strong and loyal our love for each other and shown us both how mutual love and trust can surmount any obstacle. Without this separation we would never have known how much we really mean to each other, how we are each essential to the others happiness. I always knew that I loved you, my darling. I knew that I would always be happy whilst I was with you, but I never realized how great that love was and how very much I needed you – or how much you, in your turn, loved me. I miss you, my sweetheart, more than anything else in the world and live only for the day when we will be reunited once again. I hope that when that great day comes, darling, you will not be disappointed in me and that I will be able to give you the same ecstatic happiness that you have given me. My one ambition is to make you happy, darling, to be able to provide you with the things you deserve and to make up for all that you have missed since I have been away, my beloved.

In your letters you say that you will be happy anywhere, even in a single room as long as I am there to share it with you. I often wonder whether we will have to content ourselves with one room, darling – at least for a time, as the housing situation seems to be very serious. Despite all the promises of houses, it really appears that very little is being done to ease the situation. The way things are progressing, I would not be a bit surprised to see a repetition of the 1918 'Land fit for heroes to live in', just a hell of a lot of rash promises which amounted to precisely nothing. Already the danger signal has shown, as a few weeks ago the president of the Master Builders Federation [54] – an organisation of the building trade employers – said that they were prepared to cooperate with the housing scheme on two conditions – that the rents were increased and that the government allow them a substantial subsidy. Also, in his speech he had quite a lot to say about the present chaotic conditions of labour and the peril of the bonus system, the lack of any need for any prefabricated houses [55] and he finished up with the demand that all controls must go and that private enterprise be given an entirely free hand. What he really meant was that nothing must be allowed to interfere with the profits of the building industry – they must remain firm, even if it means thousands of families being forced to live in one room flats or – even no home at all.

I am sorry to hear that you are still worrying yourself about me, darling, there is no need for it as I am really quite safe and sound. You say it doesn't look as if I am far from the front, well it is about seventy odd miles away – and over a range of mountains at that. For all we know here the war could be over, as all I know about it is what I read in the daily papers. We are miles out of the shell range – and I haven't seen a Jerry plane for almost a year now. If I am always as safe as I am now, then I will be lucky, very lucky. As I have told you, this place is used as a leave town – the same as Rome – and they wouldn't do that if there was any danger, would they?

I have already told you how pleased I was to hear that you have made a start towards the furniture for our home. You are a silly fool, darling – fancy writing to ask if I agree and hope I am not annoyed. How could I be when you are doing so much to make our dream home an actual fact? I can imagine how proud you felt when you got it home and saw before your eyes the beginning of your own home. I, in my turn, am also very proud, proud to have such a wonderful wife as you, sweetheart. I love you even more – if that is at all possible – for all you have done and are doing to make our future happy, darling.

I have just had some more mail arrive from you, sweetheart. This time no.19 and no.20 sea letters, also no.19 airmail and no.5 parcel – so I will also answer them in this letter that makes this letter answering nos.13-20 letters. I do think you are getting even crazier, my darling. I couldn't help smiling at your wrangle with Mum about the cash from the penny bank *[56]* – and about how proud you felt when you knew that the furniture was really yours. I certainly don't blame Mum not allowing you to have the money from the penny bank – in fact, I think you had a hell of a cheek to even ask for it – anyone would think we had no cash. I still think your excuse for not using our cash account pretty weak – but you're the boss, darling, and I am more than proud to know you look after our cash so well. That is the reason why I make over as big allowance to you as I can, because I know you can be trusted to look after it. I could bank it myself, but sending it home to you in the form of increased allotment means it gets saved just the same – and it is at home in case you need it at any time. Don't forget, my darling, if you ever need any cash for anything, please don't hesitate to use that. I can and do, trust you completely – always.

I received the paper about the new war gratuity scheme in your no.19 letter. We have had it published already in our own newspaper, darling – so I am really fully acquainted with all its details. I will try and explain it all clearly and show you exactly how we stand. First of all, the gratuity itself amounts to 10/- [£18.27p in 2013] for each month of war service – so I will get 10/- for each month I have been in the army since 3rd September 1939.

Then there is our deferred pay – or post-war credit, which is 6d [91p in 2013] a day since 1st February 1942, add to this 56 days pay and ration allowance for the discharge leave and also a day's pay and a day's ration allowance for each month served overseas and finally your allowance will continue throughout my leave period. So, if I were discharged in September – now I don't say I will be – but, if I was, then I would get a total of –

	£- s- d	[in 2013]
Gratuity pay 72 months at 10/- a month	30-00-0	1,095.97
Post-war credit – 3 years 9 months at 6d day	35-00-0	1,278.63
56 days leave at 3/3 a day	9-02-0	332.44
56 days ration allowance at 3/- a day	8-08-0	306.87
34 days leave at 3/3 a day (overseas leave)	5-10-6	201.84
34 days ration allowance at 3/- a day	5-02-0	186.31
Your allotment – 13 weeks at £3	39-00-0	1,424.76
Making a grand total of –	132-02-6	4,826.82

I hope that makes it clear to you. Now one other point – you ask whether I will get paid as a driver or as a tradesman. Well, darling, my money is now 9/1d [£16.59p in 2013] a day – but 4d [61p in 2013] a day of that is overseas allowance, the rest is my rate of pay. So I will be paid at the rate of 8/9d [£15.98p in 2013] a day, of this 5/6d [£10.05p in 2013] a day will be in your allotment and 3/3d [£5.94p in 2013] a day in my leave pay – ok (I hope).

Now for a subject which I think will interest you more than anything else, whether or not I will be sent anywhere else after the war with Germany is over. Of course I can't give a certain answer – but it will be of some interest for you to know that yesterday we had published a list of people who are eligible for posting to the Far East. No names, but rather a classification of people who are likely to go, they are a person of an A1 medical category, in release group over no.24 and having less that 2½ years overseas service. It appears that men with a 3 years and 9 months overseas service are being repatriated from the Far East – and they will not send anyone who has less than fifteen months to go – otherwise they will no sooner get out there than it will be time for them to come home. As you can see, I am just about eligible to go – I am in release group no.25 and have two years and four months overseas service – so let's hope Jerry holds on for another couple of months. In any case, the order says that any man who is sent will definitely have 28 days leave at home first, so that is something worth knowing.

I don't know how it would really affect me, darling. You know I am such a funny bloke and get some weird ideas – but I really think I ought to go out there. You see, darling, after all I am strong, fit and an experienced and fully trained soldier. I have been in sub-tropical climates and have not suffered any of the diseases associated with them and I am still quite young. That is my convictions, but if the army doesn't send me, I don't think I would have the courage to volunteer. I just feel that I couldn't face another two years or more like this, sweetheart. Yet I hate the Japanese as much, if not more, than I do the Germans and feel deep inside me that I would be quitting and shirking to pull out before they are beaten. What I would really like is for the Japs to quit before Jerry, as that would save me a lot of worry – and I would not have anything nasty on my conscience. I know you will say I have done my bit, darling – but that is not enough for me. You know really, sweetheart, you made a mistake in marrying a fellow with such a funny conscience – but I feel that as I have spent so much time in politics, in telling others how rotten is the fascist, Nazi or imperialist (they're all the same basically) systems then I ought to keep on fighting until they are all finally smashed. I know just what it would mean if ever these people imposed their vile creed on us, darling – and knowing that, I should be in the fore front of the fight to smash them. Despite all this, however, I can't see myself being able voluntarily to leave home, to go away again into the filth of war – and above all, to leave you for another year or more.

In your letters you say that if I was to be sent you would try to endure that, as you have this parting – as you say that, you know in your heart I would not be able to settle down knowing the war was still on. I think you are right, darling – but I only hope I am either sent out there, or else the war with Japan ends before I have to make a choice. I love you so much, my beloved, and miss you more than life itself and if I volunteered to go out East I would curse my foolishness all the time I was out there – and think I had let you down and if I stayed at home, I would be cursing myself and calling myself yellow. In the words of the late Syd Walker, "Now what would you do, chums?" [57]

So you are all in favour of having that injection I told you about when you have our first boy. As for your idea about a woman having to be conscious in order to help herself – well, that can't be so, because I have since found out that my suggestion is already very late. The injection is called twilight sleep [58] and is now widely used in cases of childbirth in quite a lot of the leading hospitals. So, you can have it if you like, darling. Now, you needn't be scared about having children – anyway it's only the first one you need worry about – all the rest after that come easy and if you keep up one a year, I believe you don't notice the twentieth. Seriously though, beloved, like yourself I don't want to have any children for the first two years of our reunion. If we get our first child just about two years after our reunion, then it will give us eighteen months together, darling. But, if we are apart much longer, then we may have to cut down on our schedule – otherwise we will be getting rather on the old side.

It rather amused me to read about the idea of doping our tea – I often wish they would, it would save me a lot of sleepless nights. I don't know where that story started, but quite a few people at home have that idea, but there is absolutely no foundation to it, sweetheart. I have made enough tea so I ought to know and to see the way some of the fellows act out here I should say that if any dope was used it would excite rather than dull their sex urges. We do get nasty tasting tea quite often – but due to the fact that the cooks forgot the sugar – or that the tea has been stewed for hours, but as for any dope pills – well, just forget it.

You seem to think it quite possible that Jerry will attempt to pull out of Italy – well, he may try it – but if he does we will do all in our power to stop him. While he has to keep troops here, he can't use them in action against the Red Army or in France. If he succeeds in retreating from here to the Alps, we will have an even harder job to shift him. Our task is to destroy the Nazi army if we advance, then we kill Jerries as we do so. If he voluntarily retreats, then we must stop him so that we are still in a position to kill him. The capture of large areas of territory means nothing at all. The main thing is to wipe out the army that is opposing you. You remember in Africa Jerry and us went backwards and forwards right across Africa – but each side was still able to push back again because they had kept their armies intact – until we got Jerry cornered at Tunis – and his African Corps went bust. The same in Russia, Jerry drove the Russians back to Moscow and Stalingrad, but did not succeed in destroying the Russian army as they retreated before him and they were in a position to attack themselves. No, it does not matter if Jerry wants to back out or not – our sole objective is to destroy him.

Thanks a lot for your no.5 parcel, darling. It arrived just in the nick of time. Last week I was getting very short of toothpaste and the only stuff they had in the N.A.A.F.I. was some Yankee mush that tasted like nothing on earth. So I cut down my teeth cleaning from twice to once a day, but even then I ran right out last night. This morning I brushed my teeth with brush alone and I intended to buy a tube of the Yankee mush tonight – but as your parcel arrived with some Pepsodent *[59]* – well, I'm ok again. Somehow it seems that Pepsodent is the only stuff that really cleans my teeth, up to recently we were able to buy Pepsodent toothpaste from the N.A.A.F.I. and although it's not quite as good as the powder, it's the next best thing. But lately it's only been this Yankee stuff – Dr. Kyles *[60]*, or some such name and it's a terrible mush. Also, thanks for the soap, that too is awfully handy and, although I still have some left from the last lot you sent, it was beginning to run out. Don't worry about sending any ordinary soap, darling, as I have plenty. Also, I am still well stocked up on aspirins, shaving soap, flints *[61]* and such like stuff. The powdered milk that you sent I may waste – as I am going to use it in an attempt to make some milk chocolate. I have still got some cocoa that your Mum sent me – so now I will go to it. I will let you know whether my experience works after I have tried it out – so wish me luck.

I am pleased to know that your photo is on the way – and I hope it arrives soon. Did you get the photo that I sent you in my air letter, I hope so as it is the nearest I can get to the one I liked best from your latest batch. When I sent off my first and second choice for enlargement before, I didn't include that one because it was almost the same as my first choice. It is not quite as good – but as near as I can get it.

Glad that you got my photo enlarged ok and thanks for getting one for my mother. It is very sweet and thoughtful of you, darling – just like you, sweetheart, always thinking of others and as unselfish as ever.

Letter writing now has become quite a problem, as under the new regulations, we are not allowed the declaration on the back of our air mails. Only the blue triangle air letters or the green envelopes are allowed to go censor free, every other letter has to be censored by the platoon officer first. We get an issue of two censor free letters a week, we can either have two green envelopes, or two blue triangle air letters or one of each and. As I usually send you two air letters and two sea letters each week, I am going to be two short. It won't make much difference just now as I have a small stock put by, but later on either my sea or air letters will have to go through the censor – what would you prefer. I won't cut down on the letters, darling, but I will have to cut down on what I put in them when they go for censorship.

I have told you all about my new watch, it is really a lovely one and I am very pleased with it. It keeps smashing time. I set it right by the wireless on Monday night at nine o'clock and this evening at six o'clock it was just one minute slow. I still can't get over the price though, it seems such a hell of a lot to pay for a watch, but I have wanted one for a long time and think it was worth the eight pounds [£292.26p in 2013]. I have been offered ten pounds [£365.32p in 2013] for it already, but now I have got it, I will hang on to it. My credits just about stood for it and with the money I drew this week for my pay, it left me about ten bob [62] [10/- = £18.27p in 2013] in credit, but inside a few weeks my balance will look a lot healthier. That is one reason why I like to keep ten pound or so in credit – if I want anything, then I can have it and no worry about being able to pay for it. What do you think about me paying all that for a watch – I bet you think I am a fool and wasting good cash.

The puppy is still with me and growing more cheeky and lovable every day and has already learnt that my room is not the place to deposit his unwanted food and not to be mistaken for a lavatory. At the moment he is asleep at the foot of my bed, also everyone else seems to be asleep. It is getting rather late as it is well turned eleven o'clock. I have been all the evening writing this letter, but although it is only 20 pages, it is a good bit longer than usual because the pages are larger and my writing a lot smaller. Anyway I guess it's about time I started to ring off, darling. I think I have just about answered all your letters. If there is anything that I have missed out, then I will answer it next time.

Before I finally close down, darling, I must remind you once again that I love you with all my heart and soul and miss you far more than I could ever tell you. I live only to be home with you again and to hold you in my arms and tell you how wonderful and lovely you are and how much you mean to me, sweetheart. My whole life is yours and yours alone, nobody else could ever interest me. I live for you and you alone can give me the happiness I desire. Take very great care of yourself, my beloved, as I love you so very much and please try not to worry about me as I am quite safe and well. Enjoy yourself as much as you can and let's hope that the very near future will see us together in each other's arms once again. Cheerio for now, darling, give my love to all at home. I hope everyone is keeping in the best of health and all at home ok.

Goodnight, my sweet, I love you now and always and am very proud and happy to be your ever loving husband,

Bill

xxx

[53] Blighty is a slang for Britain derived from the Hindustani word 'bilāti', later used to refer to home.

[54] Federation of Master Builders (F.M.B.) is a UK trade association established in 1941 to protect the interests of small and medium sized building firms.

[55] Prefab homes is often referred to as specialist dwelling types of prefabricated buildings which are manufactured off-site in advance, usually in standard sections easily assembled, to be used as a temporary replacement for housing that had been destroyed by bombs, particularly in London.

[56] Penny bank is a savings account.

[57] 'Now What Would You Do, Chums?' is a 1939 British dram film starring actor Syd Walker who plays himself, using the title as his catchphrase. He died on 13th January 1945.

[58] Twilight sleep is an amnesic condition characterized by insensibility to pain without loss of consciousness, induced by an injection of morphine and scopolamine, especially to relieve the pain of childbirth. This combination induces a semi-narcotic state which produces the experience of childbirth without pain, or without the memory of pain.

[59] Pepsodent is a popular brand of American minty flavoured toothpaste also available in powder.

[60] Dr. Kyles is an American brand toothpaste.

[61] Flints are a small piece of metal used to produce a spark to ignite fuel in a cigarette lighter.

[62] Bob is a British slang term for a shilling.

March – May 1945

Bill is now attached to the 'A' Platoon, 717 Company, R.A.S.C., General Headquarters Car, with the 15th Army Group, stationed in Florence, the capital of the region of Tuscany in Italy. His Commanding Officer is Major F.E. Townson.

Sunday, 4th March 1945 – Finland declares war on the Axis Powers.

Thursday, 15th March 1945 – V-2 rockets continue to hit England.

Friday, 23rd March 1945 – Germany is under attack from all sides.

Saturday, 24th March 1945 – Montgomery's troops cross the Rhine at Wesel.

Tuesday, 27th March 1945 – The Western Allies slow their advance and allow the Red Army to take Berlin.

Wednesday, 28th March 1945 – Argentina declares war on Germany, the last western hemisphere country to do so; its policies for sheltering escaping Nazis are also coming under scrutiny.

Friday, 30th March 1945 – (Good Friday) the Red Army pushes most of the Axis forces out of Hungary into Austria.

Saturday, 31st March 1945 – General Eisenhower broadcasts a demand for the Germans to surrender.

Sunday, 1st April 1945 – Normal duties in Bill's 'A' Platoon, 717 Company, R.A.S.C. headquarters, 15th Army Group, are carried out. Two officers and 60 O.R.s (Ordinary Rank or Junior Rank) attend a special church parade at headquarters 15th Army Group.

Monday, 2nd April 1945 – Normal duties are carried out, otherwise nothing to report for today and also for the next day.

Wednesday, 4th April 1945 – In Bill's 'A' Platoon, 717 Company, R.A.S.C. headquarters, 15th Army Group, a visit by a catering adviser in the Florence command who made an urgent request for two cooks to be made available at Command Training Centre. This is arranged with difficulty owing to a shortage of personnel and wide dispensation of the cookhouse. The American troops liberate Ohrdruf, the first Nazi concentration camp, in Germany.

Thursday, 5th April 1945 – In Bill's 'A' Platoon, 717 Company, R.A.S.C. headquarters, 15th Army Group, the cooks are despatched to Command Training Centre as arranged, but then later in the day they return as there are no vacancies. The cookhouses are re-organised and the two cooks are wasted for 1½ days to no purpose. These facts are represented to the headquarters at Florence Command. Normal duties are carried out. The Po Valley Campaign begins in northern Italy. This is the last campaign in Italy and results in a complete surrender of the German forces that are occupying the country.

Saturday, 7th April 1945 – Lieutenant N.J. Hawkins reports for duty from the U.K. to Bill's 'A' Platoon, 717 Company, R.A.S.C. headquarters, 15th Army Group.

Sunday, 8th April 1945 – The non-availability of vehicle spares are now causing concern in Bill's 'A' Platoon, 717 Company, R.A.S.C. Headquarters, 15th Army Group and, with all efforts to obtain through normal channels having failed, the case is now represented to Allied Forces Headquarters.

Monday, 9th April 1945 – An audit board on all regimental accounts and proceedings are forwarded to the Officer Commanding at R.A.S.C., Florence Command. Lieutenant H.H. Jenkins reports for duty after his leave. Captain W. Halstead reports from Caserta for an interview with the Deputy Director Services Transport at 13 Corps.

Tuesday, 10th April 1945 – There is a special detail in Bill's 'A' Platoon, 717 Company, R.A.S.C. Headquarters, 15th Army Group, for the visit of His Grace the Archbishop of York. Captain Halstead returns to Caserta. The serious spares position is getting worse with seven Ford 4-seaters now off the road awaiting half shafts. The Allied Forces liberate Buchenwald concentration camp.

Wednesday, 11th April 1945 – One officer and 50 O.R.s attend a special service at headquarters 15th Army Group conducted by the Archbishop of York.

Thursday, 12th April 1945 – 79 O.R.s from Caserta are posted to 296 Company, R.A.S.C. General Headquarters Car. American President Franklin D. Roosevelt, aged 63, dies suddenly from a massive stroke at Warm Springs, Georgia, America. Vice President Harry S. Truman becomes the 33rd President.

Friday, 13th April 1945 – Normal duties are carried out with nothing to report in Bill's 'A' Platoon, 717 Company, R.A.S.C. Headquarters, 15th Army Group.

Sunday, 15th April 1945 – Bergen-Belsen concentration camp is liberated by British and Canadian forces.

Tuesday, 17th April 1945 – All company personnel in Bill's 'A' Platoon, 717 Company, R.A.S.C. Headquarters, 15th Army Group are blood grouped and ten men give blood. There are queries on their statements regarding spares raised by the S.T. 15th Army Group who inspect their workshops procedure and examine the large number of indents returns. The S.T. expresses full satisfaction that all effort has been made by the unit.

Thursday, 19th April 1945 – Switzerland closes its borders with Germany (and former Austria). The Soviets advance towards the city of Berlin.

Friday, 20th April 1945 – Hitler spends his 56th birthday in the bunker.

Sunday, 22nd April 1945 – Adolf Hitler concedes defeat in

his underground Berlin bunker after learning Felix Steiner could not mobilize enough men to launch a counter-attack on the Soviets who have just broken through Germany.

Monday, 23rd April 1945 – Captain W.H. Halstead and Lieutenant R. Fielding are posted to 296 Company, R.A.S.C. General Headquarters Car. The 15th Army Group headquarters in Bill's 'A' Platoon, 717 Company, R.A.S.C., have official photographs taken of the whole company for pictorial records. A warning order is received for a move to Bologna, in northern Italy.

Tuesday, 24th April 1945 – Captain R.P. Raithby and Lieutenant H.H. Jenkins proceed to a new area. All available officers report at headquarters 15th Army Group to attend a staff film.

Wednesday, 25th April 1945 – Captain R.P. Raithby and Lieutenant H.H. Jenkins' party return and report the location reserved for the unit is just big enough to accommodate the workshop only. This position is usual and the case is represented to the U.S. headquarters and the 15th Army headquarters. The Po Valley Campaign ends. Most cities and towns, notably Milan and Turin, are freed by the Partisans days before the Allies arrived.

Thursday, 26th April 1945 – Russian troops link up at the Elbe River cutting Germany in two. The Nazi surrender means the British and Canadians now control the German border with Switzerland from Basle to Lake Constance. This is followed by the Western Allies rejecting any offer of surrender by Germany other than unconditional on all fronts.

Friday, 27th April 1945 – Captain R.P. Raithby and his advance party move forward to an area in Bologna. When they arrive, they report the location found is suitable and it is requisitioned. It is reported that a lot of cleaning and preparation is necessary before occupation. In the meantime fascist leader Benito Mussolini ('Il Duce') with total defeat looming attempts to escape north, but is quickly captured. He is taken with Miss Clara Petacci, Mussolini's mistress, and fifteen other fascists to the small village of Giuliano di Mezzegra, Italy.

Saturday, 28th April 1945 – Benito Mussolini and Miss Petacci are executed. Their bodies, with the other executed fascists, are taken south to Milan in a van.

Sunday, 29th April 1945 – At 3.00 am Benito Mussolini and Miss Petacci are dumped on the ground in the old Piazzale Loreto town square in Milan. After being shot, kicked and spat upon, the bodies of Benito Mussolini, Miss Petacci, Colonel Giuseppe Gelormini, Nicola Bombacci, Minister of Interior and Mussolini's friend; and Alessandro Pavolini, ex-Ministry of Popular Culture (propaganda) and editor of Rome's 'Messagero', are hung upside down on meat hooks from the roof of an Esso gas station situated on the corner of Via A. Doria and Buenos Aires. This is done both to discourage any fascists from continuing the fight and as an act of revenge for the hanging of many partisans in the same place by Axis authorities. Achille Starace, Secretary of the Fascist Party from 1931-1939 is captured later in Milan and sentenced to death. He is first taken to the Piazzale Loreto town square and shown the body of Mussolini. Starace, who once said of Mussolini: "He is a god", saluted what is left of his leader just before he is shot on the spot before being hung next to the body of Mussolini. The angry civilians then stone the corpses from below. As Miss Petacci's body swayed, her skirt fell to revealed she had no underwear, having no time to dress fully. One Partisan stood on a box and tucked her skirt between her roped legs.

On the very same day Adolf Hitler marries his long-time mistress, Eva Braun, in a closed civil ceremony held inside the Fühererbunker in Berlin. A day later they both commit suicide as the Red Army approaches the Führerbunker in

Berlin. Grand Admiral Karl Dönitz succeeds Adolf Hitler as President of Germany; Joseph Goebbels succeeds Hitler as Chancellor of Germany. The Reichstag, the Parliament of Third Reich from 1933 to 1945, is captured, signalling the military defeat of the Third Reich.

Monday, 30th April 1945 – In Bill's 'A' Platoon, 717 Company, R.A.S.C. Headquarters, 15th Army Group, a copy of a reply regarding spares from Allied Forces Headquarters is received; the letter holding out little hope of any improvement in the situation and it is anticipated that within 3,000 miles the unit will be 60% V.O.R. (Vehicle off Road). Orders are issued for a move of the company to a new area in Bologna.

Tuesday, 1st May 1945 – Hamburg radio announces that Adolf Hitler has died in battle "fighting up to his last breath against Bolshevism." Joseph Goebbels and his wife, Magda, commit suicide after killing their six children. Karl Dönitz appoints Count Lutz Graf Schwerin von Krosigk as the new Chancellor of Germany. The war in Italy is over, but some German troops are still not accounted for. Meanwhile, in Bill's 'A' Platoon, 717 Company, R.A.S.C. Headquarters, 15th Army Group, normal detail duties is carried out and the company Officer Commanding visits the proposed new location in Bologna.

Wednesday, 2nd May 1945 – (Gladys' 23rd birthday) the Russians arrive in Berlin with an unconditional surrender of the Germans. Russian soldiers hoist the Red flag over the Reich Chancellery. Lübeck, a prisoner of war camp for officers from 1940 until April 1945, is occupied without resistance by the British 2nd Army. The surrender of Axis troops in Italy comes into effect. Low category men from the infantry unit are posted in and report for duty into Bill's 'A' Platoon, 717 Company, R.A.S.C. Headquarters, 15th Army Group. The end of hostilities is announced in an Italian theatre.

In May Bill is now in Rome, Italy.

Friday, 4th May 1945 – German troops are surrendering unconditionally to Field Marshall Bernard Montgomery throughout Europe. Denmark is liberated; Holland is liberated by British and Canadian troops.

Saturday, 5th May 1945 – German forces officially surrender. Prague rises up against occupying Nazi forces. The American 11th Armoured Division liberates the prisoners of Mauthausen concentration camp. From 1938 to 1945, one of the first massive concentration camp complexes in Nazi Germany was set up to the west of Mauthausen. In early 1940 a large number of Poles were transferred to the complex and an estimated 30,000 died. Inmates were subjected to barbaric conditions, the most infamous of which was being forced to carry heavy stone blocks up 186 steps from the camp quarry. The steps became known as the Stairway of Death. Canadian soldiers liberate the city of Amsterdam from Nazi occupation. In Bill's 'A' Platoon, 717 Company, R.A.S.C. Headquarters, 15th Army Group nine drivers are posted to the Infantry Regimental Training Depot for transfer to infantry in place of low category replacements. Some are 'of bad military character', but some can drive. It is thought it will be difficult to abort satisfactorily. Bill visits the Roman Forum, Rome, Italy.

Sunday, 6th May 1945 – Bill visits the Coliseum, the Ponte Vittorio Emanuele II Bridge and the Vittorio Emanuele II Monument, Rome, Italy.

Monday, 7th May 1945 – Bill is at the Vatican, Rome, Italy, and sees the Pope. General Alfred Jodl signs the unconditional German Instrument of Surrender at Reims, France, ending Germany's participation in the war. The document is ratified on Tuesday, 8th May in Berlin. This becomes Victory in Europe Day (V.E. Day) as Nazi Germany surrenders marking the end of World War II in

Europe with the final surrender being to the Soviets in Berlin, attended by representatives of the western Powers. Canadian troops move into Amsterdam after German troops surrender. The Surrender of the Dodecanese is signed in Symi, a Greek island. The British 8th Army together with Slovene partisan troops and a motorized detachment of the Yugoslav 4th Army arrive in Klagenfurt, the capital of the federal state of Carinthia, the southernmost of Austria.

Tuesday, 8th May 1945 – German Army Group Centre resists in Prague until Friday, 11th May. Between 8th and 29th May 1945 thousands die as French troops and released Italian P.O.W.s kill an estimated 6,000-40,000 Algerian citizens.

Wednesday, 9th May 1945 – Hermann Goering is captured by the American Army. The German occupation of the Channel Islands ends with the liberation by British troops. While the war is at an end in Europe, war with Japan continues.

Bill is still with the 717 Company in the Royal Army Service Corps, General Headquarters Car Company based in the Central Mediterranean Forces in Rome. Bill's next letter is number '37' dated Saturday, 12th May 1945.

Bill is 25 years and 8 months old: Gladys has just turned 23 years.

37.

PTE. POWELL T/69083
717 coy. R.A.S.C.
(C.H.Q. CAR.) C.M.F

Saturday 12 May
1945.

My own darling beloved wife,
Hello sweetheart, once again it
is time for my usual letter to
you — and once again I am stuck
for anything fresh to say so I must
revert to the same old topic - of
how much I love and miss you.
You are all that matters to me
my beloved, my only ambitions and
aims in life is to be home with
you again and to be able to hold
you tight in my arms. I love you
so very much darling, love you
far more than I could ever
manage to describe, my only
thoughts are of you, if where

(Above) Bill's letter to Gladys written on Saturday, 12th May

Mrs. Gladys Powell
84a London Road
North Cheam
Surrey
England

(37)
PTE. POWELL T/69083
717 COY. R.A.S.C.
(C.H.Q. CAR) C.M.F.

Saturday 12 May 1945

My own darling beloved wife,

Hello sweetheart, once again it is time for my usual letter to you – and once again I am stuck for anything fresh to say so I must revert to the same old topic – of how much I love and miss you.

You are all that matters to me, my beloved, my only ambition and aim in life is to be home with you again and to be able to hold you tight in my arms. I love you so very much darling, love you far more than I could ever manage to describe, my only thoughts are of you, of where you are and what you are doing. Of whether you are happy, whether you still miss me – and above all, whether you still love me. I just couldn't live without you, my own darling. My whole life is yours and yours alone. Nobody else could ever interest me. As long as I have you, then I am happy. Every day is one day nearer to that great day when we will be in each other's arms once more. Just to picture it in my mind sends a tickling feeling running up and down my spine, beloved, to be there in the flesh will be beyond all imagination. I need you so very much, darling, my whole mind and body cries out for you. It's you and you alone I want from life and I want you far more than words can ever express. Words were never designed to convey the love I have for you, my sweet, no matter how I try my efforts will always remain just a feeble travesty of the real inner most feelings I hold in my heart. God alone knows just how much you mean to me, your love is all I ever want from life and I am living only for the day to come when I will once again know the ecstasy of your wonderful love in all its beauty and glory. If only I could tell you just what I try so hard to convey, my dearest, it would help so much, but the harder I try the more inadequate my efforts seem. Much as I want to be home with you again and to feel your firm yet soft supple body against mine, much as I want to experience the thrill of your wonderful kisses and to feel your arms around me, holding me tight and close to you. Much as I want to enjoy all this again, beloved, above all I want it with you and you alone. No one else could ever interest me. It's you and you alone I want to share my life with me – and as long as I have you then I have everything that really matters, sweetheart. Your love is the greatest asset I could ever wish for and as long as I have that, my life could not be richer.

Now, darling, the war in Europe has come to a close. It's been five years and eight months of bitter struggle – but we have emerged victorious. Let us hope that we will also succeed in winning the ensuing peace. Having defeated the Nazis on the battlefield – and dispelled the idea once and for all of the German superman and the decadent democracies, we must now ensure that Germany – or any other nation, is not in a position to wage war again. The United Nations [63] must above all remain united, for only in our strength and unity can peace be kept. All over the world, in the desert of Africa, the hills of Tunisia, in Sicily, Italy, France, Belgium, Holland, Greece, Crete, Norway, Finland, Poland, Czechoslovakia, Rumania, Hungry, Estonia, Latvia, Bulgaria and even in England itself, there are bodies of those of the Allied nations who have died in

322

order to win this victory against Nazi tyranny. We must never forget them, this time we must ensure that they did not die in vain. It is up to us, we have won the war – now on to win the peace.

Perhaps it is really a little too early to congratulate ourselves on victory – as up to now it is only half won – we have still got to apply the final sunset to the land of the rising sun. But, the war in Europe coming to an end had meant that no longer are we worried over the safety of you at home, for no longer will sirens scream their warnings, no longer will you have to listen to the drone of enemy bombers, or the thump throb of the V-bombs – or just the blinding explosion of the rockets. Now you are safe – and we can fight better for that knowledge. Everyone at home has shared with us in the great victory, for you have produced the weapons without which we could never have won and you have produced these weapons whilst under bombardment yourselves. It is a victory we all share and let's hope that soon we will be able to rejoice in the final victory – the defeat of Japan.

When I look back, the past six years seem almost a lifetime – in a lot of ways they are – as children have grown into men and women during the war. Others are growing up now who have never known a world of peace. I have now been longer in the army than I was at work in Civvies Street. I left school just before I was fifteen – I was in the army before I was twenty. This is the longest job I have ever had – and I wonder how I will settle down to normal life again. I don't even know what sort of work I will be employed at, as I was driving before the war – but now there are thousands more drivers than will be required in peace time. I have learnt a little of motor mechanics – but the motor industry has stated that it can offer no opportunities for any new intakes into the industry as they will have more men than they will need by restricting their old employees. The army have laid the foundations of an educational scheme – but can offer no suggestions on a likely job to train for. I don't care two hoots what I work at – or where – but I want a job that will pay enough cash for us to live on in reasonable comfort and security. I think that our efforts and sacrifices during the past six years have earned us the right to that chance.

The war for one has been one of different aspects and periods. There was first the period between August 1939 and May 1940, the period of the so called Phoney War [64] when it was just a holiday in uniform. Nobody took any notice of the war. It was just an excuse to have a d– good time. Then came Dunkirk and the awakening. From then on for a year it was just hard work with Jerry bombers doing their utmost to blow us off the map. This period was brightened very considerably for me in October, for then it was that I met you, my darling – and learnt how great and wonderful love was. From the whole of that time of air raids, bombs, etc., for me it was one long grind. Driving all hours of the day and night and living just for the lovely breaks when I was able to see you.

Then came the German attack on Russia – and with that the raids at home – and now the aspect of the war changed from one of hard work to that of complete boredom. Gone had the urgency of the days of the blitz [65] and somehow one could never manage to recapture the holiday effect of the wars earlier days – it was just a period of waiting and training for bigger things to come. Again the hellish monopoly was broken by the wonderful times that we had together, our wedding, our honeymoon and our evenings, weekends and odd leaves that we could snatch at happiness together. Then the period was further brightened by my being sent to Brighton – where I was to learn the job I am now doing – and above all, be able to see you regularly. I spent four lovely months there at Brighton, seeing you every weekend and during the midweek as well. It was like heaven, but a heaven that was to draw to an end in the November when I said my last goodbye to you at Newmarket and sailed for the inevitable period of real war.

For me now the period of waiting had changed to that of action, but for you a long period of patiently waiting had begun. Time passed and we went from the landing in Algiers to the African victory at Tunis, from Tunisia to Sicily and then on to the long Italian campaign. For over a year and eight months the campaign dragged on – over mountain range after mountain range. We no sooner captured one mountain then we found Jerry even more strongly entrenched in the next. Big battles were fought. The names of Reggio, Salerno, Cassino, Anzio and the Liri Valley will go down in history. And then, at long last, we achieved what we set out to do – we licked Jerry and, on your birthday, we made fame by being the first army to get the unconditional surrender of a German army. Then a few days ago the period of warfare ended with the full surrender of the German army and the war in Europe came to an end. Now I begin a new period again, a period of waiting once more – this time – for who knows what. Maybe for a home coming, or maybe for the Far East – or perhaps, even for the army of occupation – time alone will tell. I am living in hope that when this period of waiting is over, that the next period would be one of adjusting myself to civilian life once again – but that rests in the lap of the gods, so I must just trust to luck and keep my fingers crossed hoping for the best. In any case, I don't mind doing my share to defeat the Japs – but I want some leave at home with you before I go. It is two and a half long years now since I last saw you, darling – and that is more than enough for me. My one and only ambition now is to get home again as soon as I can, nothing else matters. I don't care what I have to do afterwards – I can worry about that

325

when the time comes, but now I have one aim only – to see you again soon.

Now, for a brief description of my leave, darling. It began last Thursday, with a three hundred mile trip on a lorry to Rome. Phew, what a journey, up and down one mountain after another. It was like a scenic railway and I was really and truly seasick when I arrived at Rome. A short rest, a good meal and a bath soon had me straightened out, however and I was none the worse for the journey.

Friday I spent in the camp – writing letters, reading and generally lazing about. Saturday I went into town for a sight-seeing tour – there was not much that I had not seen before – but I went to help pass the time away and to brush up my memory. It was on this tour that I met my old pal, Ralph, I have already described the luck and coincidence of our meeting – so I won't go into that again, but you can imagine how surprised and pleased I was at seeing him. We spent the rest of the day together – visiting a show in the evening.

On Sunday morning I met him again in the town and we had a walk round, I showed him over the town – and almost walking his feet off in the process. The afternoon we also spent together on a tour of the old Roman ruins – this time in an official party complete with a guide. The evening was spent in the cinema – where we saw 'Mutiny on the Bounty' starring Charles Laughton, Clark Gable and Franchot Tone. It was a re-issue of the old film – but, as I had somehow missed it before, it was new to me and I enjoyed it a lot. We arranged to meet the following day – but Ralph could not make it as he was on duty and I have not seen him since as he has moved.

Monday morning I spent on a tour of the Vatican City and its museums, also I had an audience with the Pope himself – but I have also described that in my last letter – so I will not dwell on that again. In the afternoon I had arranged to meet Ralph – and that was more or less wasted hanging about waiting for him. Or perhaps I shouldn't really say it was wasted as I had told him to meet me in the Alexander Club ice cream bar at two o'clock – well, I got there about a quarter to two and didn't leave before six – and I was stuffing ice cream all the time. It was delicious, lovely, smashing, very tasty – very sweet – in fact, just the job. If that song 'A Little Of What You Fancy Does You Good' [66] is correct then, boy, oh boy, am I getting fit and strong. This is the first place I have seen any ice cream this year and believe me I have made the best of it while I have been able. Now let's see, where was I before I got a little distracted by describing the ice cream – oh, yes, I was telling you about my leave and I had reached Monday afternoon. Well, in the evening we got the first official news of the war's end. During the afternoon I heard the B.B.C. report that a message from the Jerry H.Q. had announced the unconditional surrender of Germany – but it was not until 20 past eight in the evening that the official news came through – although the Eyeties had it all in their papers early in the evening. But at twenty past eight the radio programme was broken by the announcement from S.H.A.E.F. [67] that the war in Europe was over – and that Mr. Churchill and the King would broadcast on the following day – which would be known as V.E. Day. Well, a party of us decided that it was an event worth celebrating in the traditional style and we set out to do so. But two hours later we had given it up as a bad job – as the only signs of a celebration I had seen was when a press photographer arrived at the Alexander Club [68]. He issued a few papers around and asked us to wave and cheer for the benefit of the camera.

So, as everything seemed to be as normal we decided to return back to camp and forget the whole thing, but on our way back in the lorry we passed a floodlit café – from which came the sound of singing, so we bailed out and joined in the fun. It was about ten o'clock when we landed at the café - and somewhere in the early hours of the morning when we left. No, I was by no means drunk - not even merry, but I had enjoyed myself - and awoke next morning - not with a sore head - but a sore throat from the singing. Most of Tuesday on V.E. Day I spent in writing and sleeping - with just a little reading. At three o'clock I went downstairs to hear the Prime Minister's peace declaration then continued writing and reading up to nine o'clock when I again went downstairs to hear the King's speech. I indulged in an orgy of drinking whilst listening to the King - as beer was on sale in the N.A.A.F.I. - one pint per man.

Wednesday I overslept in the morning and got up too late for breakfast so had a wash and went into town for some eats. It was very hot - far too hot to walk about in comfort, so I returned to camp for dinner - and spent the afternoon writing. In the evening I again went into town to the local cinema and saw Irene Dunne in 'The White Cliffs of Dover' [a 1944 World War I film] - which I thought was awful - it bored me to tears, but as the ice cream parlour was next door to the cinema I passed the time slipping from the cinema to the ice cream parlour. Being V.E. Day 2, the N.A.A.F.I. Alexander Club was opened for an extra hour and a half - until eleven o'clock instead of 9.30 pm. So, we stayed there on coming out of the cinema until about half past ten and again celebrated the victory - in tea. There was about half a dozen of us together and we kept buying rounds of tea "Have another boys", "OK, Signorina [Miss], Ancora [brand] tea." Then at 10.30 having drunk ourselves almost tea silly we returned to camp - and so to bed.

Thursday morning I got up about 9 am, had a wash and breakfast and then spent the morning on the camp skating rink. I am afraid I can't truthfully say I spent the morning skating - as at least half the time I spent sitting down -

accidentally. I don't know what's wrong with my skating – I can skate all day – in a straight line, but when it comes to turning or stopping – well, that's a different story. It's like my dancing – do you remember when I used to dance with you – straight up the hall, stop – then turn round – wait for the correct beat and then straight down again? Well my skating is very much the same – only I can't fit the stop in. I just skate like hell straight down the rink – grab at the rail at the end – turn myself round and skate like hell back again – and if anyone gets in my way – God help them, as I can do nothing to avoid them. The funny part is, whenever I hit anyone, it's always them and not me who go over, the only time I ever fall down is when I try to turn or stop. I have been told that the correct way to stop on skates is to place one foot behind the other – but when I do this, one foot goes one way and the other foot goes the other way – and I sit down – hard. Still, it's a good laugh and I enjoyed it and that's all that matters.

After leaving the skating rink I had my dinner and then went up on the terrace and spent the afternoon reading. From where I was sitting I could hear the music coming from the band in the dance hall opposite. There were dances every afternoon, but I never went to one. Yet, I would rather like to learn to dance – but I will leave it until I get home and get you to teach me, darling. Somehow I don't fancy holding any other girl in my arms – even only while dancing. My only wish is to be by your side once again and to tell you how lovely you are – and how much I love you. I not only love you, darling, I adore and worship you and will always do so until the day I die.

Thursday evening I went to a variety show in the camp – it was not bad at all and passed the evening – my last evening – pleasantly. I got into bed about 10.30 pm and on Friday morning I was up at six o'clock to prepare for the journey back. We left about 8.30 in the morning and the

ride back was no better than the ride down.   I got back to
our camp about eleven o'clock at night – with a splitting
head ache and feeling as sick as hell.   I didn't even bother
to draw my kit out from the stores – instead I just threw my
blankets down on the bed and got down to sleep.

Saturday afternoon is usually half day here – so I didn't
think it was worth going in just for the morning – and
besides, I had a lot of unpacking and sorting out to do – so I
took the day off and spent most of it writing this letter to
you, darling.

Now for a few words about the rest camp itself, it was
quite a large place – it used to be an Italian hospital –
situated on the outskirts of Rome.   The amenities inside the
camp are very good and one would have quite a nice time
without leaving the camp area.   There is a dance hall where
dances are held every afternoon from 3 pm until 6 pm, the
camp arranges for girls to be present at these dances – in
conjunction with the local Italian youth organisation.   Then
there is a decent sized sports field – which usually has a
football match in progress, a really smashing swimming
pool – which unfortunately was in the process of being
cleaned whilst I was there – otherwise it would have seen
quite a lot of me.   Also there was a library, reading rooms,
dart boards, billiard and table tennis tables, a skating rink,
cinema and a theatre.   Then there were shops in the
courtyard – run by Eyeties – but for our use only.   They
were very dear – but not quite as dear as in the town.
These shops consisted of 'Selfridges' which sold souvenirs,
gifts, etc., 'Burtons' which were the camp tailors, 'W.H.
Smith', the newsagents, 'Pullars of Perth' for cleaning and
pressing our clothes, 'Wallace Heaton' for photographs and
a couple of fun fairs – containing pin tables, etc. – but at 6d –
not a penny – a go.   Then there was the 'Grosvenor House
Club' run by N.A.A.F.I. where we could get snacks and
refreshments.   The 'Crown and Anchor Hotel' which was

the same sort of place – but for sergeant and warrant officers only. Add to this showers, hair dressers, boot blacks and general information rooms, you can see it was quite a decent place. There were no rules or regulations to bother about and we could do as we liked, go out and come in when and how we pleased, although if we wanted to go to town we had to be properly dressed – but in the camp area and the vicinity we could walk about how we liked. There was a good system of transport into town – lorries left the camp area every five minutes and go to the Alexander Club in Rome – and they return every five minutes from the club to camp. The first lorry in the morning used to leave camp at 7 am (although I am afraid I was never around to see it go) – and the last lorry left the Alexander Club to return to camp at half past eleven – and there was always a supper waiting when it got back, as supper never closed until the last lorry was back in camp.

On the whole it was a pretty decent place – which is a lot more than I could say for Rome itself. I never imagined that a place could change so much in so short a time, it had altered from being the best, cleanest and finest town I had ever seen – to that of being one of the filthiest and unmoral places in Europe. Vice is terrific. Providing you have enough cash, one can buy everything and anything – or even anybody. All day long one is accosted by people wanting to buy or sell something or other – and at night – phew – Piccadilly, isn't in it. Girls and women of all ages literally besiege one with offers to come and sleep with them – and ask for 40 dollars (£10) for the so called privilege. I can perhaps understand a bloke taking a prostitute for a night – but to pay that price, they must be raving mad – yet they must do so, as they always seem to get plenty of clients.

Another point about that is that, unlike most places, the prostitutes here do not stick to any one quarter. In nearly every large town there is always a certain area which is quite notorious for that sort of thing – but in Rome it is all over the town – any main street is the same, the town is lousy with them – but at £10 [£365.32p in 2013] a time – boy, it must be a very profitable business. Everything else in the town was on a similar exorbitant scale. It cost me nearly five pounds [£182.66p in 2013] for photos, I had six taken which cost £2-10s-0d [£91.33p in 2013]. Then later on I had another three which cost 25/- [£45.67p in 2013] then one or two odd snaps at 5/- [£9.13p in 2013] each. It was a hell of a lot of cash – but that was about all I spent any money on – as I thought they would be about the best gift to send you home. I know you always like to receive a photo of me, darling – for some unbeknown reason – perhaps because for some equally unknown reason that you happen to be in love with me.

I often wonder just why you fell in love so completely with me, my beloved. When I first met you I fell head over heels in love with you – but I knew then that my love was not returned, darling. The first five months I knew you, I am sure that you only liked me – and not love me. Even when we became engaged on 28th December 1940 I still knew that, although you liked me a lot, that liking had not developed into love. But a little under three months later I realized that you did really and truly love me.

The realization was brought home to me after I came out of hospital from that motor cycle accident. Your entire attitude towards me had changed – and I knew that my love for you was then fully returned. From that day onwards it has grown into the great love that you now have for me and a love that is equalled only by my love for you, my sweet. We have had some wonderful times together in the past – and we will have some even better times in the future. We have lived through these past years of separation and our love for each other has proved itself strong enough to overcome any temptation and emerged pure and whole – perhaps even stronger, as it has been tested and tempted by the time apart. When that great day of reunion comes, darling – as it surely will one day soon now – we will be able to hold our heads up, to look each other in the face knowing that we have both remained true to our wedding vows. That is something we can be proud of, darling, the knowledge that our love for each other has remained pure and untarnished by any illicit relations.

I love you so very much, my precious – I cannot live without you. All that makes this parting bearable is the certain knowledge that you are at home patiently waiting to welcome me when I return once more. I am always thinking of you, dearest. Whenever I close my eyes for a second, I see your beautiful image before me. I see your sweet face looking so radiantly beautiful and it seems to tell me to be patient – to hold on and that it won't be long before 'All the Things You Are' [69] – are mine once again. If ever I get fed up, my darling, I can feel you cheering me up and encouraging me. When things appear to be tough and everything against me – you are there to give me inspiration and to help overcome my difficulties. I love you, darling. I love you far more than I could ever tell you. I love you with every breath in my body – now and always.

Well, darling, now for news of the mail that I have received from you – phew, it's hard to know where to begin as I had such a lot. As you know, I have not received a letter all the time I have been on leave – and I arrived back too late last night to get my mail from the post corporal – but I was down there first thing this morning. There were nine letters and three parcels for me, darling – seven of the letters and all the parcels from you, one letter from my mother and one from Ivy. Here are the numbers, etc. of the letters I got from you – first of all airletters no.33 dated 25 April, no.34 dated 2 May – quite a big event that date – and I don't mean the end of the war in Italy. No.35 dated 4 May and no.36 dated 7 May. Also, the following sea letters no.57 dated 29 April, no.58 dated 1st May and no.5 dated 3rd May. As for the parcels – well, one contained the shoes, darling – which are a very good fit and with which I am extremely pleased and the others I believe contain papers, but up to now I have not had a chance to open them, so I can't tell you what numbers they are yet.

I won't answer your letters one at a time, but I have made a note of all the questions, etc. and will deal with each item separately. First of all, I was very pleased to hear that you have had such a good week for mail and parcels and so very glad that my record, air mail birthday greetings, flowers and parcels all arrived at such a nice and appropriate time and that they brought you so much pleasure. I only wish I had been able to send you a decent present for your birthday, darling – but am afraid my credit wouldn't stand the strain. Regarding the airmail – yes, it is hand painted but not by me. It was done by a famous Italian artist – although I never even saw it. He did one for a pal of mine for 5/- [£9.13p in 2013] so I gave him the same amount and your address and told him to do one for me. But, I bet he would be annoyed if you confused my work with his.

Dear, oh, dear – have my ears been pinned back. I ask a simple little question and get one hell of a lecture on the duty of a husband. Phew – well, I'll try and explain it all again now – in case you don't know what I am talking about, it is this subject of Burma – and boy, has it got under your skin. First of all, get it into your thick head that I am fed up to the teeth with war – I have had more than a bellyful – and I also live only to get home with you once again. The position is this – if I had volunteered, I would have been home inside a month or six weeks for a month's leave – then away to the Far East for no more than a year – and home again for good. If I don't volunteer, I may be home in a couple of years – then there is still the chance of going out East and for *three* years. It wasn't any question of wanting to leave you – it was just a question whether to choose a month at home and another year away – or take a chance on home for good soon – or away for years to come. I only thought that by volunteering I would know *exactly* where I stood. OK. That's clear – I hope. Now, for revision – I'm not going to volunteer – because I think – yes, I only said think – that I stand a chance of demobilisation soon. Up to now there is no official information – but the Yanks have announced their demob plans and if I was in the American army I would be in the first batch out. At a guess – and again I must stern it is only a guess – I may be miles out – but, I should say I will be home in about three or four months – and, with a bit of luck, another six months should see me in civvies – I hope.

Just one other thing, darling, before I leave this subject. I am afraid I did not like your reference to your being entitled to some home comforts, as whilst I fully appreciated that you deserve and have earned a home of your own, you must realize that on the whole you – and I, have been very lucky. There are a hell of a lot of people who will never experience any more home comforts – some will be left out here and others scattered in lonely graves all over the world and as long as force rules and might is right, there can be no security for anybody. Remember, darling, that although Japan seems very far away from England, she is next door to the Soviet Union. If she was to attack and conquer Russia she would then be in Europe and only a stone's throw from home. There can be no peace until the war is over and the war will not be over until Japan is smashed – unconditionally.

About this furniture business, my darling – I am not quite sure whether you have already bought any more or not. But, as to whether I mind dark oak – well, don't worry about that, as I don't mind in the slightest. I would like to be able to go with you to choose all the stuff we need for our home, but that will be impossible, so I must leave the entire choice to you. You have the opportunity to see and compare different articles and I know you are sensible enough to select that which will be best for our purpose and the greater value for money. I will respect your judgement – and be proud to have such a sensible wife. Whatever you choose, will be ok by me – it will not be fair for me to judge without being able to compare articles – and, in any case, colour is the least thing that counts. I am so very pleased and proud though, darling, to hear how our home is growing and hope that it won't be long now before we share it together.

You ask whether or not I want the enlargement of the photo you sent out here or not. Well, darling, the photo is really wonderful – and last week I would have certainly said yes to your question – but now – you can keep it – burn it, throw it away, or do as you like with it. The reason for my change of mind is that whilst I was at the rest camp I had the photo copied by an artist and the result is – no, darling, I just can't think of words to describe it as it is so wonderful and life-like. Really, he has made your hair a little too light – almost blonde, yet in a way that makes it better still, as it is almost the exact image of how you looked that day at Nonsuch Park. Do you recall the occasion – we were walking through the flower garden together, then you turned – and as you did so, the sun caught your hair sending chimers of gold run through it and lighting you into the most beautiful sight I ever have seen. I will never forget it, as you stood there against a background of lovely flowers. You were so lovely, that you made the flowers and nature itself seem dull and tawdy. This picture I have now seems to recapture that occasion – and as such, it has pride of honour in my pin-up collection – always.

As a matter, of fact I nearly sent it home to you as I did intend to get one done of myself and send them both home for framing. But, I am sorry to say things didn't turn out as I hoped and instead of finishing it as I asked on Thursday, the fellow said it would be done by eight o'clock Friday morning, but he hadn't turned up with it when I left the rest camp – so you've had it – and I have – also, the photo he was copying it from. So it's no good my sending you home a photo of yourself – or rather a painting – so I will keep it, get it framed and bring it home with me when I return. My darling, you are getting very forgetful – you say in your letter that on May 2 you celebrated your second birthday away from me. What happened to the other year – you were only twenty when I left, you know. I have been away for your 21st, 22nd – and 23rd birthdays, but perhaps we can celebrate them all on my 26th in September.

A rather funny thing happened this afternoon, darling – do you remember some time ago sending me a parcel containing some sweets in a powdered milk tin. Well, today we were making some tea and my mate went to open a tin of milk when I said "Don't open that, I have some of the powdered milk in my kit bag and we had better use it up before it gets all over my kit." Well, he waited until I had gone through my kit and found the tin – which I handed to him – he opened it and found the sweets – which I soon grabbed back again. I had taken the tin to contain what it said on the label – but it meant I have established a record for keeping sweets, as usually I eat them as soon as they arrive. Oh, needless to say, the sweets are gone now. In fact, they had gone within half hour of their discovery.

From today, darling, our letters are no longer subject to unit censorship, so I can send or rather write what I like without having to worry about our war officer reading it. Of course, up to now letters are still liable to be censored at the base – but I don't mind that – and even that is likely to be discontinued very soon. One thing though, darling, I would now like a few envelopes sent out – no, not in batches of a hundred – but I am getting a little short. Perhaps you could send out a few as you did the writing pad – by air mail. Well, believe it or not, but I am beginning to get very tired, darling, so I will draw to a close – besides, I've probably bored you enough already.

One item of great interest has received very little attention, the defence regulation 18B *[70]* is now discontinued? It is very quick work and Morrison *[71]* is to be greatly congratulated. I was very afraid that it would be one of those so called emergency measure that would be kept after the war – and so be a divert menace to the liberty that we have fought so hard for. But I suppose I should not have worried for, although Morrison is sometimes very chary of criticism and vent to treat his criticism with open contempt – he has never sought to surpass that criticism. He has always been first and foremost a democrat. I raise my hat to him for the speed in which he abolished that very un-English regulation that was only adopted under extreme circumstances. Congratulations, Bert [Herbert Morrison] – but it is about time Ernie Bevin *[72]* followed his example and got down with the service chief to release some statement on the men to be demobilised. Then I would know for certain what my chances are of coming home.

I will be sending this letter – if one can call it a letter – in five different envelopes and I will number them on the back 1-5. You see, in order to go by air, they must weigh no more than one once and there are approximately twelve pages to the ounce. I would still send it by air if I was to pay the postage for the excess weight – but that would cost no less than eight – yes, eight shillings [£14.61p in 2013]. You see, this note will weigh about five ounces – the first ounce will go free and then sixpence [91p in 2013] for each additional half ounce. So, four ounces over the weight at six pence half ounce will be eight shillings – which I think you will agree is expensive for a letter. Of course, I am afraid it will be rather awkward if one of the instalments go astray – but if so you will have to guess what was in those twelve pages.

A few days ago, darling – on V.E. Day to be exact, I wrote you a letter in which I said that I was sorry it was not longer, as I thought V.E. Day merited a long letter. But, owing to the fact that I was away on leave – and thus had received no mail from you to answer, I promised I would write a long letter on my return to camp. Well, here it is and, if you have the patience to read it, then you are better than me – because I don't intend to do so. So, if there are too many mistakes, you can blame the fact that I am too tired to sit and check through it, darling.

Well, sweetheart, I am afraid that is about all for now so I will come to a close – it's now two o'clock on Sunday morning and I have been writing since ten this morning – so you can imagine what my wrist is like. Take great care of yourself, my darling, remember I love you with all my heart and soul and live only to see you once again.

Give my love to all at home and all my fondest love to you. Goodnight, beloved – until tonight when I will be with you again with my usual air letter – I hope. I am always proud and happy to be your ever loving husband,

Bill

xxx

GOODNIGHT LOVE

[63] The United Nations is an international organisation founded in 1945 to replace the League of Nations whose stated aims include promoting and facilitating

cooperation in international law, international security, economic development, social progress, human rights, civil rights, civil liberties, political freedoms, democracy, and the achievement of lasting world peace.

[64] The Phoney War is a phase early in World War II that was marked by a lack of major military operations by the Western Allies (the United Kingdom and France) against the German Reich. The phase covered the months following Britain and France's declaration of war on Germany (shortly after her invasion of Poland) in September 1939 and preceding the Battle of France in May 1940. War was declared by each side, but no Western power had committed to launching a significant land offensive, notwithstanding the terms of the Anglo/Polish and Franco/Polish military alliances, which obliged the United Kingdom and France to assist Poland.

[65] Blitz is known as the lightning war (in German: blitzkrieg).

[66] 'A Little of What You Fancy Does You Good' recorded by Marie Lloyd in 1915.

[67] S.H.A.E.F. is Supreme Headquarters Allied Expeditionary Force of the Commander of Allied forces in northwest Europe from late 1943 until the end of the war with General Dwight D. Eisenhower in command throughout its existence.

[68] The Alexander Club is named after Field Marshal Harold Alexander, 1st Earl Alexander of Tunis who served with distinction in both world wars. It is situated at XX Via Settembre, Rome, Italy, is a N.A.A.F.I. run canteen and resting place where service people could have a good meal: bangers and mash etc., a bath/shower, shave, haircut, beer and meet friends. It was a converted six storey department

store building in the heart of Rome with six mezzanine floors with a huge candelabra in the centre of the ceiling, the subject of a bet between a party of Commandos and Paratroopers as to which could do a Tarzan act by lassoing the candelabra and swinging to and fro. This was all good fun until after a while the bolts loosened and in the middle of one swing by a paratrooper, the bolts departed the ceiling and the candelabra came crashing down the six floors to the ground, pinning the paratrooper underneath, who said after he was uncovered that it was probably his last jump. It was. He had broken his back.

[69] 'All the Things You Are' (see words below) is a song composed by Jerome Kern, with lyrics written by Oscar Hammerstein II and adopted as Bill and Gladys' personal love song.

[70] Defence Regulation 18B, often referred to as simply 18B, is the most famous of the Defence Regulations used by the British Government during World War II. The complete technical reference name for this rule was: Regulation 18B of the Defence (General) Regulations 1939. It allowed for the internment of people suspected of being Nazi sympathisers. The effect of 18B was to suspend the right of individuals to habeas corpus.

[71] Herbert Morrison is a Labour politician and the Secretary of State for the Home Department. During World War II several leading fascists, including Oswald Mosley, were imprisoned without trial. In November 1943 Morrison controversially decided to order Mosley's release from prison resulting to large scale protests describing the decision as "a slap in the face of anti-fascists in every country and a direct betrayal of those who have died for the cause of anti-fascism."

[72] Ernest Bevin is a Labour Politian and Minister of Labour and Labour National Service in the war time coalition government. Although Bevin was not actually an M.P. at the time, a parliamentary position was found and Bevin was elected unopposed as an M.P. (Member of Parliament) for the London constituency of Wandsworth Central. Bevin did not get on with Morrison. When once told "the trouble with Herbert [Morrison] is that he is his own worst enemy", Bevin replied: "Not while I'm alive, he ain't!" During the war Bevin was responsible for diverting nearly 48,000 military conscripts to work in the coal industry. These workers became known as 'the Bevin Boys'. He also drew up the demobilisation scheme that ultimately returned millions of military personnel and civilian war workers back into the peacetime economy.

'ALL THE THINGS YOU ARE'
Time and again I've longed for adventure,
Something to make my heart beat the faster.
What did I long for? I never really knew.
Finding your love I've found my adventure,
Touching your hand, my heart beats the faster.
All that I want in all of this world is you.
(Chorus)
You are the promised kiss of springtime
that makes the lonely winter seem long.
You are the breathless hush of evening,
that trembles on the brink of a lovely song.
You are the angel glow that lights a star,
the dearest things I know are what you are.
Some day my happy arms will hold you, and
Some day I'll know that moment divine,
When all the things you are, are mine!

(Above left) Bill, aged 25, at the Roman Forum,
Rome, Italy, on Saturday, 5th May 1945
(Above right) Bill at the Coliseum, Rome, Italy, on Sunday, 6th May 1945

(Above) Bill by the Ponte Vittorio Emanuele II Bridge, Rome, Italy

(Above) Bill outside the Vittorio Emanuele II Monument, Rome, Italy, on 6th May 1945

(Above) Bill ('x') at the Vatican, Rome, Italy, on Monday, 7th May 1945

May – December 1945

While Bill is in Rome, Italy, his 'A' Platoon, 717 Company, R.A.S.C. Headquarters, 15th Army Group, remains in Florence.

Monday, 14th May 1945 – The Battle of Poljana, the last major battle of World War II in Europe, is fought in Yugoslavia (now Slovenia).

Wednesday, 23rd May 1945 – The President of Germany, Karl Dönitz, and Chancellor of Germany, Count Lutz Graf Schwerin von Krosigk, are arrested by British forces at Flensburg, an independent town in the German state of Schleswig-Holstein. They are respectively the last German Head of State and Head of Government until 1949. Heinrich Himmler, former head of the Nazi SS, commits suicide by taking a cyanide pill whilst in British custody. In May 1945 Flensburg was the seat of the last government of Nazi Germany, the so-called Flensburg government led by Grand Admiral Karl Dönitz, which was in power from 1st May (Hitler's death) until its dissolution on 23rd May. The nearest larger towns are Kiel (86 km south) and Odense in Denmark (92 km northwest). Irish/American fascist politician William Joyce ('Lord Haw-Haw') is captured. He was later charged with high treason in London for his English language wartime propaganda broadcasts on German radio. Convicted, he is hanged on Thursday, 3rd January 1946 at Wandsworth Prison.

Wednesday, 30th May 1945 – The Iranian government demands that all British and Russian troops leave the country.

Sunday, 3rd June 1945 – Still under Commanding Officer Major F.E. Townson, the 'A' Platoon, 717 Company, R.A.S.C. Headquarters, 15th Army Group, leaves Florence and arrives in Verona on Monday, 4th June.

Tuesday, 5th June 1945 – Allies agree to divide Occupation Zone Germany into four areas of control governed by the four powers of occupation: America in the south, Britain in the northwest, France in the southwest and the Soviet Union in the east. Berlin, which geographically lies in the Soviet Zone, is divided into four sectors. Germany is stripped of its war gains and the territories in the east to Poland and the Soviet Union. Seven million prisoners and forced labourers leave Germany; most die either during their emigration of starvation, harsh conditions, or are worked to death. Over 10 million German-speaking refugees arrive in Germany from Western Europe. Many German POWs become forced labourers to provide restitution to the countries Germany had devastated in the war and some industrial equipment is removed as reparations. The British take over Lebanon and Syria and the Allied Control Council, the military occupation governing body of Germany, formally takes power.

Tuesday, 19th June 1945 – The United Kingdom begins demobilisation.

Sunday, 24th June 1945 – A victory parade is held in Red Square, Moscow.

Sunday, 1st July 1945 – Germany is divided between the Allied occupation forces, Occupation Zone Germany into four military occupation zones.

Thursday, 5th July 1945 – The Philippines are declared liberated.

Friday, 6th July 1945 – Norway declares war on Japan.

Sunday, 8th July 1945 – President Harry S. Truman is informed that Japan will talk peace if it can retain the reign of the Emperor.

Saturday, 14th July 1945 – Italy declares war on Japan.

Monday, 16th July 1945 – A train collision near Munich,

Germany, kills 102 prisoners of war. The world's first atomic bomb is detonated in New Mexico.

Tuesday, 17th July 1945 – Several changes have taken place since the Yalta Conference in February, affecting the relationships between the Allied leaders. The Soviet Union occupied Central and Eastern Europe, the result of the British election which had the leadership changing hands, and Vice President Harry S. Truman assumed the presidency after President Roosevelt died on 12th April. Participants are Communist Party General Secretary Joseph Stalin from the Soviet Union, President Harry S. Truman from the United States, and from the United Kingdom Prime Ministers Winston Churchill and Clement Attlee, who participated alongside Churchill while awaiting the outcome of the 1945 general election held during the conference in the United Kingdom. Stalin, Truman, Churchill and Attlee gather in Germany for a Potsdam Conference to confirm earlier agreements for the demand for the unconditional surrender of all Japanese forces and to decide how to administer punishment to the defeated Nazi Germany, which had agreed to unconditional surrender nine weeks earlier, on 8th May (V.E. Day). The occupation of Germany by the Allies, the division into four occupation zones, the prosecution of Nazi war criminals, the reversion of all German annexations in Europe (including Sudetenland), and the 'orderly and humane' expulsions of the German populations from Poland, Czechoslovakia and Hungary are all agreed.

Saturday, 21st July 1945 – President Harry S. Truman approves the order for atomic bombs to be used.

Thursday, 26th July 1945 – Winston Churchill resigns as Great Britain's Prime Minister after his Conservative Party is soundly defeated by the Labour Party in the 1945 general election. Clement Attlee becomes the new Prime Minister. It is the first time that Labour has governed Britain with a majority in the Commons. Attlee replaces Winston Churchill at the negotiating table at Potsdam. The Potsdam Declaration is issued.

Monday, 30th July 1945 – The heavy cruiser U.S.S. Indianapolis is hit and sunk by torpedoes from a Japanese submarine in the Philippine Sea. Some 900 survivors jump into the sea and are adrift for up to four days. Nearly 600 die before help arrives. Captain Charles B. McVay III of the cruiser is later court-martialed and convicted.

Monday, 6th August 1945 – As Japan continues to ignore the Potsdam terms the United States B-29 Superfortress, the Enola Gay, drops an atomic bomb codenamed Little Boy, on Hiroshima, Japan, at 8.15 am (local time). Bill's ex-'A' Platoon, 717 Company, R.A.S.C. Headquarters, 15 Army Group, remains in Verona under the Commanding Officer of Captain W.I.S. Craig until Major R. Bennett (R.A.S.C.) takes over command of the unit and they arrive in Milan.

Tuesday, 7th August 1945 – While in the middle of the Atlantic Ocean returning from the Potsdam Conference aboard the U.S. Navy heavy cruiser U.S.S. Augusta, President Harry S. Truman announces the successful bombing of Hiroshima with the atomic bomb.

Wednesday, 8th August 1945 – Russia declares war on Japan.

Thursday, 9th August 1945 – A United States B-29 Bomber, Bockscar, drops an atomic bomb, codenamed Fat Man, on Nagasaki, Japan, at 11.02 am (local time) forming a mushroom cloud that rises 18 km into the air.

Friday, 10th August 1945 – Japan offers to surrender to the Allies, 'provided this does not prejudice the sovereignty of the Emperor'. The Allies reply that Emperor Hirohito will be subject to the authority of the Supreme Commander of the Allied Forces. Emperor Hirohito decides to accept the terms stated in the Potsdam Declaration.

Monday, 13th August 1945 – The Zionist World Congress

approaches the British government to discuss the founding of the country of Israel. The wars of national liberation ensue, leading to the creation of Israel, together with the decolonisation of Asia and Africa.

Wednesday, 15th August 1945 – Emperor Hirohito announces Japan's surrender on the radio, although the surrender seems to be 'unconditional', the Emperor's status is still open for discussion. This ends the period of Japanese expansionism and begins the period of occupation of Japan. The United States calls this day V.J. Day (Victory over Japan Day). Korea gains independence.

Sunday, 19th August 1945 – Mao Zedong and Chiang-Kai-shek meet in Chongqing to discuss an end to hostilities between the Communists and the Nationalists.

Saturday, 25th August 1945 – Bill is granted a 28 day L.I.A.P. to return home next month. Whilst the war was on, the Army has operated a scheme whereby anyone who has served overseas for four years is repatriated. This is known as Python, a reference to the Army eating its own tail. Towards the end of 1945 a new scheme is introduced named L.I.A.P., which letters denote 'Leave In Addition to Python'. Under L.I.A.P. any person who would have served overseas three years before being demobilised is to be given a short home leave.

Thursday, 30th August 1945 – Vietnam's capital Hanoi is over-thrown by the Viet Minh which ends the French occupation in what becomes North Vietnam: the south becomes South Vietnam.

Friday, 31st August 1945 – Allied troops arrest Field Marshall Walther von Brauchitsch, the commander-in-chief of the German army.

Sunday, 2nd September 1945 – World War II officially ends. The Japanese surrender documents are signed aboard the deck of the American battleship U.S.S. Missouri in Tokyo Bay, ending the war. Japanese forces surrender on Wake Island after hearing word of their country's surrender.

Wednesday, 5th September 1945 – Singapore is liberated by British troops.

Wednesday, 12th September 1945 – The Japanese Army formally surrenders to the British in Singapore.

Thursday, 13th September 1945 – Bill's 26th birthday.

Friday, 28th September 1945 – Bill is detached home to Gladys. Bill is also pleased to see his mother, Tilly looking so well.

Between Monday, 1st and Monday, 15th October 1945 is the Operation Backfire where the Allies acquire German technology. Three A4 rockets are launched near Cuxhaven in order to show Allied forces the rocket with liquid fuel.

Tuesday, 16th October 1945 – Bill returns to Italy and is now attached to S.O.S. in 128 Pit Depot near Genoa.

Wednesday, 24th October 1945 – The United Nation is formed. The undivided country of India joins the United Nation. Pakistan is formed and joins later, followed by Colombia.

Tuesday, 13th November 1945 – Charles de Gaulle is unanimously elected president of France by the provisional government.

Thursday, 15th November 1945 – Only a month after Bill left England to return to his service in Italy his mother, Matilda 'Tilly' Louise, dies, aged 54. The cause of death is myocardial degeneration (heart attack) and mitral regurgitation. Most of the women in the Fraser family had died very young from heart trouble. William has moved his wife and daughter, Ivy, to Southend as Tilly had preferred the air there. However, Tilly had returned to London after the war had ended and died at the family home, 34 Kenmont Gardens, College Park, London, NW10. Bill is never to see his mother alive again.

Clement Attlee, Harry S. Truman and Mackenzie King

call for a United Nations Atomic Energy Commission to share nuclear information.

Tuesday, 20th November 1945 – Matilda 'Tilly' Louise's burial is at Streatham Cemetery, Garratt Lane, London. Among the mourners with William Senior and daughter, Ivy, are Gladys, her mother, Hilda, Mr. and Mrs. Fraser (Matilda Louise's older brother and her sister-in-law), Mr and Mrs. Wallace (sister, Dulcie Rose and brother-in-law, Will), Mrs. Prince and Mrs. Nye, their friends. Also attending the funeral is June Alston who the Powell family fostered as a baby, her mother having mental problems and her father unable to cope on his own. Soon after Bill and Gladys had married June's father had June evacuated to Newmarket, not wanting his daughter in danger living in London during the constant bombing. June's mother is still in hospital. June was then fourteen and had lived with William Frederick and Matilda Louise since she was a baby, leaving the Powell family to live in a safer area. She returned to be at the funeral of her foster mother. Amongst the flowers received are those from Matilda Louise's former neighbours on the Latchmere estate. The memorial card from William for his wife Matilda Louise's funeral read: "A light is from our household gone, a voice we loved is stilled, a place is vacant in our hearts, which never can be filled."

Also today the Nuremburg Trials begin; a series of military tribunals held by the Allied forces. Twenty-four of Germany's Nazi leaders, who have been charged with war crimes, including committing crimes against humanity of Germany's Nazi war criminals involved in the Holocaust and other World War II crimes, face an International Military Tribunal. The Tribunal is made up of four judges, one each from the United States, the Soviet Union, Great Britain and France and an alternative, as well as a prosecutor. The Russians wanted these trials to be held in

Berlin, as the capital city of the 'Fascist Conspirators', but Nuremberg is chosen as the city was the location of the Nazi Party's rallies and the laws stripping Jews of their citizenship were passed here. The Palace of Justice is spacious and largely undamaged (one of the few that has remained largely intact despite extensive Allied bombing of Germany) with already a large courtroom and a large prison as part of the complex. The majority of defence attorneys are German lawyers. The main counsels are supported by a total of 70 assistants, clerks and lawyers. The defence counsel witnesses included several men who took part in the war crimes during World War II, such as Rudolf Hoess, the Commandant of Auschwitz. The men testifying for the defence hope to receive more lenient sentences.

Tuesday, 25th December 1945 – Bill spends Christmas Day rescuing two soldiers' whose truck is stuck up in the mountains of Fontanigorda, near Genoa. Bill is attached to 128 Petrol Depot, R.A.S.C., Central Mediterranean Forces stationed near Genoa. Bill writes his final letter number '50' to Gladys on Friday, 29th December 1945 detailing his rescue.

Bill is 26 years and 3 months old: Gladys is 23 years and 7 months old.

(Above) Gladys, aged 23, alone at her home on 6th July 1945

(Above) Bill, aged 26, & Gladys, aged 23, in the back garden of their first home,
84a London Road, North Cheam, Surrey, on 23rd September 1945

(Above) Bill's letter to Gladys written on Friday, 29th December 1945

Mrs. Gladys Powell
84a London Road
North Cheam
Surrey
England

(50)
PTE. POWELL T/69083
128 PETROL DEPOT
R.A.S.C., C.M.F.

Friday 29 December 1945

My own darling beloved wife,

Hello my sweetheart, here I am at long last after the longest absence I have ever had from writing to you. I am really sorry my darling that I have been forced to make you go short of your letters, but honestly beloved I am afraid it has been out of my control. You know – or should do by now – that I would not miss writing to you if I could possibly avoid it. However this has been the one occasion when it has been really impossible for me to write and I hope you will forgive me, darling. Now, for the full story of why you have gone without a letter for the past few days – and after hearing this I feel more you will understand and agree that I just could not write your usual letters. It has been easily the worst Christmas I have ever had, altogether now this is my seventh Christmas in the army and it is the only one that I have not enjoyed. Even my first Christmas abroad is better than this one – at least then I was with the boys and we made our own fun by having a singsong and we got something to drink – but this time, well – I was luckier than the other blokes, however, as I did get my dinner – they didn't even get that.

The story started by one of our wagons having to take some of our civilian workers home to their families for

Christmas. They lived in a little village in the heart of the mountains about fifty miles from here. Whilst they have been working with us, they have also been living with us – but our C.O. decided that it would be a nice gesture to take them home for the Christmas – so, on the morning of Christmas, a truck left here for this village of Fontanigorda [73]. So far so good, he reached the village – being directed by the Eyetie civilians who he was taking – about dinner time, but it was snowing heavily and the road was covered in snow and ice – and he found he was unable to get back – every time he tried to move, he just sunk the truck deeper in the snow. The first we heard of it was about three or four o'clock when we got a phone call saying he was stuck – and could we send a truck out to get him back. Here the weather was lovely and sunny – so I was not prepared for what fate held in store for me. I got out a truck and taking another fellow with me, we set out for this village. The first fifteen to twenty miles was ok then we hit the mountains, the snow, ice and large clouds just like fog. Even then we managed to keep going until we left the main road and started along a small minor road – which was really only a glorified cart track. There were bridges blown up every few yards – and to get round them we had to go along some wicked diversions. At times I was really scared – a track only a little wider than the truck – ice covered and caving in under the weight of the snow and our wagon – and a sheer drop of hundreds – or, in some places, thousands of feet below. We could only go along at a walking pace as I could not see because of the cloud – and for some miles the fellow with me walked in front with a torch making sure the road was ok. Twice he stopped me only a few yards from a big hole where the bridge had pucked up. It was freezing cold – but, believe me, I was sweating like a pig. I was scared that any second the lorry would skid on the ice – and a slide of only a few inches would have meant going over a hell of a drop.

Most of the way I kept my fingers crossed – and kept repeating "Group 26, Powell old boy, just another month, for God's sake, go careful." At long last somewhere around midnight we found the village where we were supposed to go – but no signs of our truck. For some time I kept driving around looking for some signs of them, but no such luck. Even at that late hour, there were plenty of people about – owing no doubt, to it being Christmas Eve – but nobody had seen our vehicle. In fact they said it was the first time a lorry had ever come to the village during the winter. They said that from November until March the entire village is cut off from motor traffic and even horses are hard put to reach them. Most of them were amazed to think a lorry had got into their village.

Well, after another couple of hours I decided to return to camp – thinking that no doubt the others had got their truck going and gone back on their own. It was about ten thirty or eleven in the morning (Christmas Day) when I got back – but, only to find that the other wagon was still missing. The O.C. sent out yet another truck to look for them whilst I and my mate got to bed. However, we only had a couple of hours sleep as we did not want to miss our Christmas dinner – at two o'clock we all sat down to dinner – and at half past the phone went and we were told the second rescue truck had broken down a few miles down the road. The O.C. said leave it until after dinner and then go and pull it back – but a few minutes later the phone goes again, this time it's the blokes in the first truck who were stranded – and telling us that it wasn't Fontanigorda where they were – but a village called Canale in the district of Fontanigorda. I told them I would try and reach them and I got out the truck, loaded up some food, etc. for them and started out about three o'clock for the second trip.

On the way I stopped at the second truck which had

broken down – managed to patch that up and told him to return to camp – I went on to the wagon which was stranded. Well, to cut a long – very long, story short, the return trip was the same as the first – but not quite so bad, as there was no cloud – it was not snowing and the village was on a slightly better road and not so high up. On the other hand, it was thick ice instead of snow – and I was on my own and so had no one to warn me of any danger. But, being my second time over the road, I knew where the bridges were down and where the diversions were. Most of the way it was over the same road, but about five miles from the village I went to before, there is a fork road – the left fork goes almost straight up for five miles to Fontanigorda and the right fork goes up for about a mile to Canale where the wagon was stuck.

It was pitch dark by the time I found them and somewhere about nine o'clock at night. The lorry was stuck right in to the snow – so much so, that I would never had seen it had not the two blokes with it seen me first. The poor devils were frozen stiff, no food, no blankets and stuck there about 36 hours. I had brought a lot of wood with me – and in a few minutes we had a fire going and we got a brew of tea on and got down to some eating. They were also without any fags – but I had also brought some of them with me and so it was not long before they were feeling somewhat alive. We had a conference to decide what to do – and although it was not much use doing anything in the dark, we decided to make a start then at shifting some of the snow in order to keep warm. We worked for about two or three hours, then I took them on my wagon to the nearest village where we found a café and had a few drinks. This was about eleven and we stayed in the café until about half twelve or one when it closed – and I took the blokes back to the other truck. There we undid the blankets I had brought with me and settled down in the back of my truck for a few hours sleep.   It was a few – very few hours, as despite the fact that we were all dead tired, it was far too cold to sleep properly.

We were up before five am and working on clearing the rest of the snow from around the truck.   In a little under an hour this was accomplished and we tried to move away – however, the wheels just spun on the ice and that's all.   I then hitched my truck to him and we both tried – him driving his truck – and me pulling him – but then we both started skidding.   In the end we had to go out on my truck to a forest a couple of miles away, get bundles of bushwood, small trees, bushes, etc., bring it back to the stranded truck and build a road for it.   It was necessary to do this for three hundred yards before the truck was able to grip on the normal road again – that three hundred yards took us altogether four and a half hours to cover, as it was half nine before we got going properly.

Then the journey back was without incident – except I was even more worried than ever as I could hardly keep my eyes open – and I know the two in the other truck were as bad.   However, about twelve o'clock it looked as if everything would be ok as we were almost over the worst of the mountains – and then it happened.   The other truck – which was just in front of me, started slipping going up a hill.   The driver made a fatal mistake of trying to rev it up faster to keep it going – and consequently he skidded across the road into a ditch.   He was dead lucky – almost anywhere else he would have fallen down a terrific drop – but he skidded in about the only place where there was a grass verge and a ditch – and that ditch stopped him going any further.   The trouble was how to get him out, about the only way possible meant a slight slip or misjudgement and I would have to go on the grass verge (over the ditch) to tow him out.   I was not prepared to take the risk – but I offered both the others the chance of driving my wagon whilst I stood by and gave advice – but they were like myself and declined the offer. We tried for about two hours to move the truck without going over the verge – but only succeeded in making things worse – as both back wheels sunk in the ditch, instead of one as previously. Then I set out to the nearest village for help – and returned some time later with almost a dozen Eyeties – and with them, ropes, bars and my lorry we succeeded in putting the truck back on the road again.

The trouble now was that it was dark again – and up had come the clouds and snow again – so one chap walked in front with a torch – followed by the other fellow and his truck, followed by me with my truck. This went on for miles – and hours – until at long last we broke out of the snow and cloud – and from then on it was a straight-forward trip back to camp – and it was somewhere around two o'clock on Thursday morning by the time we got in. I did scribble you a few lines whilst one of the chaps was getting us some food – but, how I kept my eyes open, God only knows. I got to bed somewhere around three o'clock – and I did intend to get up in the evening and write again to you, darling. But instead, I am afraid I did not wake up. I did awake about two yesterday afternoon – and got out for a wash and a cup of tea. Then I thought I would just get back for a couple more hours – then get up and write you a letter – but, the next thing I knew it was seven o'clock this morning – and despite almost 30 hours sleep, I am still dead tired.

Well, so ends my story of Xmas 1945 – a real white Christmas – but, somehow I didn't appreciate the fact. Still, it's my last Xmas away from you – and one I will never forget. In just about five weeks from now I will begin my journey home, beloved – and am I living for that day to arrive, the day when we will be together forever and always, never more to part. Let's hope the next few weeks soon fly by, darling, and all our dreams are realized by our reunion once again.

I must come to a close now, my beloved, as it is getting late and I still think I am owed some sleep. Cheerio for now, my beloved, take very great care of yourself and keep smiling, here's hoping our reunion day will dawn in the very near future. Goodnight, beloved, all my love and fondest regards. I am always very proud and happy to be you ever loving husband,

Bill

xxx

YOU ARE THE PROMISED GIFT OF SPRINGTIME

[73] Fontanigorda is a commune in the province of Genoa in the Italian region Liguria, about 35 km northwest of Genoa.

January – December 1946

On the last day of 1945 the British Home Guard is disbanded.

Monday, 7th January 1946 – The Allies recognize the Austrian republic with 1937 borders and divide the country into four occupation zones.

Thursday, 10th January 1946 – The first meeting of the United Nations is held at Methodist Central Hall, Westminster in London.

Sunday, 13th January 1946 – Bill has a medical examination.

Wednesday, 16th January 1946 – Charles de Gaulle resigns as a head of a French provisional government: four days later resigns as President of France.

Friday, 1st February 1946 – The Kingdom of Hungary becomes a republic.

Thursday, 14th February 1946 – The Bank of England is nationalized.

Wednesday, 20th February 1946 – Bill's Notification of Impending Release card reads: 'Whilst this man has served with this unit, he has worked extremely hard – he is conscientious and straightforward – smart in his appearance and popular among his fellows'. Bill has had no accident for six years driving S.V. cars, 3 ton G.S. tank transporters, petrol tankers, 10 ton Macs jeeps. This is stamped with approval on Friday, 22nd February and for disembarkment on Thursday, 28th February 1946.

Friday, 1st March 1946 – Bill arrives at Dover, having left Italy to return home to Gladys after fighting in the war since November 1942.

Saturday, 2nd March 1946 – British troops withdraw from Iran according to the treaty: the Soviets do not. In North

Vietnam Ho Chi Minh is elected President. He signs an agreement with France which recognizes Vietnam as an autonomous state in the Indochinese Federation and the French Union.

Sunday, 3rd March 1946 – Bill is allowed home on leave. He has served in the army for 6 years and 180 days.

Tuesday, 5th March 1946 – In his speech at Westminster College, Missouri, America, Winston Churchill talks about the Iron Curtain, a term symbolised efforts by the Soviet Union to block itself from Europe into two separate areas from the end of World War II in 1945 until the end of the Cold War in 1991.

Sunday, 10th March 1946 – British troops begin withdrawing from Lebanon.

Friday, 15th March 1946 – Clement Attlee promises independence to India as soon as they can agree on a constitution.

Monday, 29th April 1946 – The trials against war criminals begin in Japan.

Thursday, 9th May 1946 – King Victor Emmanuel III of Italy abdicates and is succeeded by his son Humbert II.

Sunday, 2nd June 1946 – In a referendum, Italians decide to turn Italy from a monarchy into a republic. Women vote for the first time.

Tuesday, 4th June 1946 – Bill is finally discharged from the army. His military conduct is recorded as 'Exemplary'.

Monday, 10th June 1946 – Italy is declared a republic. Humbert II of Italy leaves the country and goes into exile in Portugal. Alcide de Gasperi becomes head of state. From 1945 to 1953 he was the prime minister of eight successive Christian Democratic governments. His eight year rule remains a landmark of political longevity for one leader in modern Italian politics. During his early successive governments Italy became a Republic (1946) and signed a Peace Treaty with the Allies (1947).

Tuesday, 1st October 1946 – The Nuremberg Trials which began in October 1945 end. All twenty-four of the men testifying on behalf of the defence are found guilty on several counts. Twelve are found guilty and hanged; three receive life imprisonment; two are sentenced to 20 years; one sentenced to 15 years; one sentenced to 10 years; three are acquitted, and two are not charged. Hermann Goering, the founder of the Gestapo (Secret State Police) and recently convicted Nazi war criminals, poisons himself before his scheduled execution.

Wednesday, 16th October 1946 – The Nazi war criminals convicted in the Nuremberg Trials are executed by hanging in the Nuremberg Palace of Justice gymnasium using the standard drop method instead of the long drop causing the condemned to die slowly from strangulation instead of a broken neck.

Tuesday, 31st December 1946 – President Harry S. Truman delivers Proclamation 2714 which officially ends hostilities in World War II: "Although a state of war still exists, it is at this time possible to declare, and I find it to be in the public interest to declare, that hostilities have terminated. Now, therefore, I, Harry S. Truman, President of the United States of America, do hereby proclaim the cessation of hostilities of World War II, effective twelve o'clock noon, December 31, 1946."

Part II.
(Details of operational service are to be completed by the applicant)

State ports and dates of embarkation for service overseas *LIVERPOOL OCT. 1942*

	(i) Army or Personal No., Highest Rank held, and Regiment or Corps during the period in Col. (iv)	(ii) UNIT with which served	(iii) Operational Area (i.e. actual country)	(iv) DATES from	to
(a) 1939-45 STAR (3.9.39 to {8.5.45 / 2.9.45 (Far East)})	*T/69083 PRIVATE*	*R·A·S·C*	*AFRICA SICILY ITALY*	*11·42*	*3·46*
(b) AFRICA STAR (10.6.40 to 12.5.43) 8th ARMY (23.10.42 to 12.5.43) 1st ARMY (8.11.42 to 12.5.43) H.Q.18 A.Gp. (15.2.43 to 12.5.43)	*T/69083 PRIVATE*	*1ST.T COY. R.A.S.C. H.Q. 18 A.G. CAR COY. R.A.S.C.*	*N.A. AFRICA*	*23.11.42 11·42 6·43*	*12.5.43 3·43 8·43*
(c) PACIFIC STAR (8.12.41 to 2.9.45)	*Home NA*	*3 9.39 03.11.42*		*22.11.42 28.2.46*	
(d) BURMA STAR (11.12.41 to 2.9.45)	*Home 2 TR*	*1. 3. 46 5.6.46*	*N.A.*	*4.6.46 23.11.42*	*8.5.45*
(e) ITALY STAR (11.6.43 to 8.5.45)	*T/69083 PRIVATE*	*H.Q. 15 A.G. 7A CAR COY.*	*SICILY ITALY*	*8·43 10·43*	*10·43 6·44*
(f) FRANCE AND GERMANY STAR (6.6.44 to 8.5.45)	*T/69083 PRIVATE.*	*128 PETROL COY. ADV. H.Q 15 AG 717.*	*ITALY FRANCE*	*7·44 6·44*	*3·46 7·44*
(g) ATLANTIC STAR (3.9.39 to 8.5.45)			*Reject after dates.*		
(h) AIR CREW EUROPE STAR (3.9.39 to 5.6.44)	*africa star 1st A/c BMF 5845/44*				

Signature of Claimant *W.T.Powell* Date *17·10·46*

Part III.
(To be completed by the *authority* who has duplicate copy of B199A/D420/B103)

(1) I am satisfied that he/she is entitled to the *1939 45* Star. Clasp.

Star. Clasp. Star. Clasp.

Star. Clasp. Star. Clasp.

(2) I am satisfied that he/she is not entitled to any of the above stars.

(3) I am unable to verify the service at and submit the same for consideration.

for Col. i/c R. A. S. C.

Signature of Authority referred to above RECORDS.

Overseas Command or Station Date

Award Published in Pt. II/III Orders No. *295* *18·12·46*

Recorded in A.F.B.200 A.F.B.200

For use only in War Office or Record Office

Stamp of 2nd Echelon or Unit publishing the Order.

R.A.S.C. RECORDS
28·DEC 1946
ORE PLACE
HASTINGS

R.A.S.C. RECORDS
22 OCT 1946
ORE PLACE

(Above) Bill's service record on release from the army

(Above) Bill, aged 28, & Gladys, aged 25 –
happy together again in their home in 1947

(Below) Gladys, aged 25, in 1947

(Above) Bill, aged 28, & Gladys, aged 25, in 1947

(Above) Bill's political election manifesto for the Sutton & Cheam Borough
Council election held on Saturday, 1st November 1947 from 8.00 am-9.00 pm

Sutton & Cheam Borough Council Elections – 1947

Polling Day: Saturday, November 1st
8 a.m. – 9 p.m.

WITH THE COMPLIMENTS OF

W.F. POWELL

W.F. Powell joined the North Battersea Labour Party, 1935, Chairman becoming Chairman, Sports Secretary and Organising Secretary of North Battersea Labour League of Youth, 1936 to 1939, Delegate to Battersea Trades Council and General Committee Labour Party, 1937 to 1939.   Secretary Latchmere Ward Association 1938 to 1939, eleven years membership to the Transport and General Workers' Union, always taken a keen interest in local Government.

Served in H.M. Forces July, 1939 to June, 1945.   A.A. Command London 1940 to 1942, since then has served in France, Italy, Austria, North Africa, Sicily, Tunisia, Gibraltar and Malta, 1942 to 1945.

Transferred membership of Labour Party to Sutton and Cheam on release from H.M. Forces, is now North Ward Assistant Secretary.

To the Electors of the North Ward of the Borough of Sutton and Cheam
Dear Neighbour,
I have been honoured, by being selected by the Sutton and Cheam Divisional Labour Party, to stand as their candidate in this Ward.   I do not intend to make rash promises, my policy is plain and straightforward, to do all in my power to increase the welfare of the Borough generally and of this Ward in particular.

HEALTH – Living and working in the North Ward, I know from actual experience the problems that beset us and will endeavour to secure a fair share of the Borough amenities for Worcester Park, not just its refuse and sewage.   I fully support the Hogsmill Valley Sewage Scheme, which will finally rid us of the smells and other unpleasant accompaniments of the sewage farm, by removing the farm itself from the district. I will continue the work that I am now doing in trying to send the menace to health caused by flies and crickets from the refuse dump. At the moment I am working as a private citizen, but as your Councillor, my hand will be strengthened and I will be able to bring more pressure to ensure that the incinerator is working and all other precautions are taken to prevent a recurrence of this Summer's invasion of these pests in the Boscombe Road, Conrad Drive and adjacent areas. The Green Lanes area is getting more like a rubbish dump every day, indeed a stranger of the Borough could be forgiven for mistaking the Brook and its banks for the refuse dump at the end of Boscombe Road. I will press for representations to be made to the County Council, to have this thoroughly cleaned up and restored to its old beauty.

COMMUNITY CENTRE – In co-operation with other democratic organisations, I strongly support the proposal for the construction of a Community Centre to serve the residents of Worcester Park. The lack of suitable meeting places is seriously retarding the growth of many beneficial organisations. I want to see a Community Centre that will become the centre of our "Social," "Cultural" and "sporting" activities. Owing to the urgent demand for houses, schools hospitals and other priority buildings, we must wait for the fulfilment of this plan, but as soon as men and materials are available, I will do my best to see that this project id realised.

LIBRARIES – The Library in Central Road is completely inadequate to serve a community the size of ours and I will support any scheme to improve this service, which is necessary to this area.

HIGHWAYS – I am in complete agreement with the scheme for the improvement and widening of Central Road. I will work to see that Central Road loses its cart track appearance and becomes worthy of being the main road of Worcester Park. I am determined to remedy the atrocious condition of our roads and footpaths, these are a disgrace to the Borough. It is well known that Sutton and Cheam is very backward in this matter and far behind the standard of neighbouring boroughs. I will ensure that, when our footpaths are disturbed to install new or repair old services of gas, water and electricity, that they are reinstalled as soon as possible.

HOUSING – Realising that it is impossible to build any more houses in this Ward, as we are already overbuilt, I would support my colleagues of the Labour group of the Council in their efforts to obtain land opposite the Borough, in order to provide accommodation for those of you without homes of your own, or are living under grossly overcrowded conditions.

FINANCE – I will closely watch the expenditure and ensure that you get full value in return for the rates you pay to the Council. Legislation of the Labour Government will shortly result in local authorities being relieved of expenditure on Health Services and Public Assistance; this should result in some reduction in local rates.

PARKS – I will endeavour to get more playing fields for the children of North Wards, keeping in mind the fact that the Croydon Sanatorium grounds may become one of our open spaces.

In conclusion, I would like to say that, if I am elected as your representative on the Council, I shall always be pleased to see you and discuss your problems with you.

Yours sincerely,
W.F. POWELL

84a London Road, N. Cheam

Toryism –Will all supporters please report to:-
  THE OLD WAY OF LIFE110, Buckland Way, Worcester Park,
  Labour –8, Beverley Gardens, Worcester Park,
  FAIR SHARES FOR ALL 84a London Road, Cheam
  Vote Labour on 1st November, 1947 THE PRESENT COUNCIL
  WORK & VOTE FOR LABOURLABOUR 13
  Anti-Labour, Tory & Independent 23
  VOTE LABOUR and so REDUCE THE ANTI-LABOUR MAJORITY
  Through Storm and Strife . . VOTE LABOUR . . . . to a Better Life

Post-War

In June 1946 Bill returns to Gladys at 84a London Road, North Cheam, Surrey; their first home together that Gladys prepared while Bill was at war.

One year later they expect their first child. On Monday, 10th March 1947 Robert William is born and Bill achieves an ambition: a son. Gladys knows how much she has pleased all the family by having a son, but this is marred by Bill's mother, Tilly, never living to see a grandchild she so desperately wanted.

Bill's father, William, hoped his son would succeed him as chairman of his Transport and General Workers Union branch. To do this, Bill would need to spend many hours and days away from Gladys and he is not prepared to undertake this commitment. Bill has spent four years away from Gladys and his priority is now to stay near his wife and their baby son. William is very disappointed with his son's decision. However, Bill becomes assistant secretary for the North Ward Labour Party and continues his involvement in politics.

Saturday, 1st November 1947 – Bill stands for the Labour Party in the North Ward of Sutton and Cheam Borough council elections. Bill receives 1,798 votes, but loses to Mr. Manning (Conservative) who wins with 2,664 votes; the Liberal candidate, Mr. Blandfold, receives 162 votes. Bill's political ambitions and interest is not deterred and he continues to commit his time to the Labour Party. Gladys spends many evenings with Robert playing cards while Bill is campaigning and despite Bill having a course in political management, Gladys is still able to achieve a more effective and simpler system than the one Bill has been taught for the election campaign.

Thursday, 13th January 1949 – Bill receives five medals for his army service during World War II sent from the Ministry of Defence: 1939-1945 Star, Africa Star with Clasp '1st Army', Italy Star, Defence Medal and War Medal 1939-1945.

Thursday, 12th May 1949 – Two years after first standing as a Labour candidate, Bill again stands for the Labour Party in the South East Ward of Sutton and Cheam Borough council elections. He fails to be elected, again losing to the Conservative candidate.

Monday, 11th September 1950 – With England now at peace, Bill is officially discharged from the army. One day later and one day before his 31st birthday, Bill enlists at Wandsworth Royal Army Service Corps Territorial Army in the rank of a driver and from 1951 attends annual camps.

Sunday, 29th July 1951 – After Gladys' younger sister, Eileen Lilian Elliston, returns to live with her parents, Hilda and George Elliston, and her brother Sonny, at 41 Becton Road, London, E16, Eileen marries Alfred 'Charles' Large at St. Mathias Church, Canning Town. Bill is Charles' best man at the wedding.

Thursday, 1st November 1951 – Bill is transferred to the Royal Electrical Mechanical Engineers in the rank of a craftsman.

With Bill's political ambitions finally over, he is now able to concentrate on family life. Much to Gladys' horror she discovers she is expecting a second child. Although Bill is delighted with the news, Gladys is not. Robert has given her and Bill many sleepless nights and after a bad birth with him, Gladys fears for her life. However, her doctor convinces Gladys that she is carrying life inside her and not, as many of his patients, carrying death.

Nearer the time of the birth Bill arranges for all the home comforts for his wife. Gladys, convinced after her first birth that she will die in childbirth, insists on dying at home. The luxury television they bought is placed in front of a bed Bill has brought downstairs for Gladys to watch in comfort. On Wednesday, 6th February 1952 King George VI dies, resulting in only mourning music being transmitted. Five days later at 9.00 am on Monday, 11th February the baby is ready to be born. The midwife has yet to arrive. Bill is lighting the fire, but has to stop to help deliver their second child: this time a daughter, Eileen Gladys. For Bill it is yet another ambition fulfilled: now having a daughter. Eileen proves to be little better than Robert, but together Gladys and Bill share and finally conquers their sleepless nights.

Wednesday, 1st October 1952 – Bill is appointed as Lance Corporal.

Monday, 20th April 1953 – Bill is promoted to Sergeant. On the same day Bill is granted the rank of War Substantive Sergeant.

Tuesday, 4th May 1954 – Gladys has a niece when Eileen and Charles produce their first child; a daughter, Patricia May.

Although 84a London Road was their first home, Bill and Gladys wanted their own house. Despite worried warnings from Gladys' father, they move in 1956 to 28 Albert Road, New Malden, Surrey, after they had saved for eleven years. Their mortgage in 1956 of £28 [£593.17p in 2013] quarter yearly worries Bill with the expensive commitment.

In December 1956 comes the news that Dulcie Rose, Bill's aunt, has died. Like many of the Fraser women, Dulcie dies at a young age: 46 years old.

In early 1958, at the age of six, Eileen contracts nephritis. In Bill's medical dictionary it describes this to be a deadly kidney inflammation. To his relief, the family doctor confirms this disease is now under control and is completely curable. After 13 weeks recovering in St.

Anthony's Hospital, Cheam, Surrey, Eileen is admitted in April to the Port Regis Convent for Delicate Children at Broadstairs, Kent, to convalesce. Bill and Gladys leave on their holiday unaware Eileen is desperately unhappy. Gladys' father, George, visits his granddaughter and observes she is "fretting." On return from their holiday, Bill and Gladys collect Eileen before the recommended recovery time to take her home in August.

Sunday, 1st June 1958 – Eileen and Charles have their second child, Graham Charles: Gladys now has a nephew.

Tuesday, 16th August 1960 – Bill's army records note that his religion has changed from Church of England to Agnostic (non-believer/pessimist).

Monday, 21st May 1962 – After losing his mother in 1945 Bill's father, William Frederick Snr., dies of stomach cancer at his home, 34 Kenmont Gardens, London, NW10, with Bill's sister, Ivy, present. William Snr. was 71 years old.

Gladys stopped working for Mary Workman's shop in London Road when they moved to New Malden. She works as a part-time cleaner at Burlington School opposite their house before working full time at Venners, assembling parking meters. Bill is working at Cheam Sanatorium, London Road, North Cheam, Surrey, maintaining all the hospital equipment and the hospital.

Tuesday, 14th September 1965 – Bill receives an Efficiency Medal, Territorial 1st Clasp; no.67/1965.

Bill and Gladys spend many happy years at 28 Albert Road, New Malden, Surrey, a home they have perfected. There they celebrate their 25th (silver) wedding anniversary in September 1966 with their family and many close friends. Holidays abroad are also now becoming more regular.

Bill remains with the Territorial Army as a senior Non Commissioned Officer attending two evenings a week, plus many weekends and two weeks at an annual camp. Bill is discharged from the T.A. Army on Friday, 31st March 1967. He joins the Royal British Legion at Worcester Park, Surrey, and is immediately elected on to the committee as membership secretary. The Royal British Legion is inside a pair of Nissan huts with less than 108 members before Bill, as part of the committee, arranges to move their premises to the nearby 69-75 Central Road, Worcester Park, Surrey, incorporating three shops to make one huge club.

Thursday, 20th July 1967 – After being admitted into hospital, Gladys' father, George dies of a heart disease, aged 73 years. Gladys loses a friend as well as a father, having always been so close and very alike.

Saturday, 7th September 1968 – A day after Bill and Gladys' 27th wedding anniversary, Robert and his fiancée, Phyllis, marry and their reception is held at Bill and Gladys' house. Robert and Phyllis then live at Ashford, Kent.

Saturday, 16th November 1968 – Bill and Gladys' first grandchild, Richard William, is born prematurely in Ashford, Kent.

Tuesday, 28th January 1969 – Gladys' mother, Hilda, dies. Although Gladys and Hilda would often disagree, they were still close and it is difficult for Gladys to accept so soon after losing her father.

Tuesday, 7th December 1971 – Robert and Phyllis leave Ashford, Kent, to live in Worcester Park, Surrey, and they produce a second grandson, Gary Robert.

For many years Bill and Gladys have enjoyed camping at home and overseas. After buying a caravan Bill and Gladys are able to experience a new freedom by weekend trips along the south coast and touring abroad.

Saturday, 22nd June 1974 – Bill gives his daughter, Eileen, away when she marries Alan Edwards. Bill and Gladys host the wedding reception in a hall; and Gladys, with the help of her friends, organises the catering.

Friday, 4th April 1975 – Bill's younger sister, Ivy, dies of cancer aged 53. Ivy's funeral is held on Friday, 11th April with the Salvation Army attending.

Thursday, 18th January 1976 – Bill and Gladys sell 28 Albert Road, New Malden, Surrey, for £12,995.00p [£79,321.48p in 2013] and move to 26 Sunbury Road, North Cheam, Surrey, they bought for £14,450.00p [£88,202.80p in 2013].

With both their children married and settled in homes of their own, Bill and Gladys receive the news that Robert and Phyllis are to part. Despite their regret, they invite Robert to stay with them until he finds a new home of his own when Phyllis returns to Scotland with Richard and Gary in April, 1976.

During June 1976 Bill and Gladys buy a chalet at Allhallows, no.250 'Hillbillsom' (their name-plate from Gladys' parent's house). Bill is a member of the boat club, owning a boat until it becomes too difficult to manage.

Wednesday, 29th June 1977 – Eileen and Alan present Bill and Gladys with their third grandchild and a first granddaughter, Julie Karyn.

Saturday, 9th June 1979 – Cathlyn Nicola is born. Cathlyn is Eileen and Alan's second child and Bill and Gladys' second granddaughter and fourth grandchild.

Gladys has left Venners to work in the laundry room at Cheam Sanatorium, the same hospital Bill works at in North Cheam, Surrey. She remains working there until she retires in May 1981. Bill is promoted to manage the planners' department at Belmont Hospital with an opportunity to earn a good wage.

Friday, 17th July 1981 – Robert marries Helen 'Jayne' Kusnierz.

Saturday, 6th September 1981 – Robert and Eileen with Gladys' sister Eileen and brother Sonny, hold a surprise party with a band for Bill and Gladys at Prince George's

Hall, Grand Drive, Raynes Park, London, to celebrate their 40th wedding anniversary. Guests attending are Fred Stagg, Bill's friend and best man when he married Gladys, and Gladys' close friend, Lily Kaufman.

Monday, 15th February 1982 – Bill and Gladys have their third grandson and fifth grandchild when Eileen and Alan produce Steven Charles. Bill and Gladys are Steven's Godparents, together with Alan's father, Charles.

Friday, 16th July 1982 – Exactly one year after they are married, Robert and Jayne have their first child, Laura Jayne. Laura is Robert's third child, Bill and Gladys' third granddaughter and their sixth grandchild.

With Gladys already retired, Bill also retires from the hospital planners' department in July 1983. Eileen and Alan hold a party for him at their house. Retirement proves to be a welcome for both Bill and Gladys with so many interests, enjoying even more time in their caravan in England and abroad.

Bill has become standard bearer, treasurer, secretary, vice chairman and poppy organiser at the Royal British Legion. He and Gladys dedicate many years service to the Poppy Appeal and sell poppies before Remembrance Sunday knowing they are one of the luckier families to have fought at war and returned home to a family life. On Monday, 16th August 1982 Bill and Gladys are awarded a certificate each 'in grateful recognition of distinguished voluntary effort on behalf of the Poppy Appeal. Upon such service fully and freely given, the success of the annual appeal depends' from the Royal British Legion Poppy Appeal.

For many years Bill has been eager to return to Italy to retrace the places that, forty years previously, he had fought. Now with the time, they leave in their caravan for a six week tour around Italy in May 1984. This time, armed with only a camera, they visit many war graves leaving behind their wreath of respect for those who died during World War II. It is a time for them to feel sad knowing so many men died at war and also a time to feel humble and just grateful to be alive. To Bill it is a relief to finally undertake this pilgrimage.

A year after Laura Jayne was born, Robert and Jayne separate.

Saturday, 21st July 1984 – Eileen and Alan give Bill and Gladys their seventh grandchild and fourth grandson, David William, named proudly after Bill.

Tuesday, 5th March 1985 – Gladys' brother, George William Elliston Jnr. (Sonny), the last in the Elliston dynasty, dies from a heart attack, aged 58. George had personally organised to donate his body to medical research, so a memorial service is arranged on Sunday, 24th March. A year later George's body is returned so his funeral and a Service of Thanksgiving is held on Friday, 9th May 1986.

Saturday, 6th September 1986 – Bill and Gladys celebrate their 45th wedding anniversary with a party held at Eileen and Alan's house and a professional female singer entertains their family and friends.

Bill receives a certificate from the Royal British Legion, Worcester Park, Surrey, 'as a mark of esteem and appreciation of his work as Secretary' from 1980 to 1986. On Saturday, 10th October 1987 Bill receives another certificate from the Royal British Legion Surrey Council 'in recognition of the outstanding and meritorious service rendered to the Worcester Park Branch Royal British Legion during the years 1955-1987'.

Monday, 22nd February 1988 – Bill is to be awarded medals from the King of Belgium, Albert II, as member no.13680. (Albert became king after his older brother, King Baudouin, died in 1993 of heart failure. King Albert later abdicated in favour of his son, Prince Phillippe of

Belgium.) Bill's membership card is initiated by Leopold III who reigned as King of Belgium from 1934 until 1951 when he also abdicated in favour of his son, Baudouin.

Monday, 9th January 1989 – Bill is elected president of the Royal British Legion Branch/Club at Worcester Park, Surrey.

Saturday, 16th September 1989 – Bill celebrates his 70th birthday with a party arranged by Robert and Eileen at Ruskin Lane Squash Club at Epsom.

Saturday, 20th October 1990 – Bill arranges a surprise meal for Gladys with their family to celebrate the 50th anniversary of when he and Gladys first met at the T.A. drill hall on Saturday, 19th October 1940. From the moment Bill first saw Gladys, he immediately knew he would marry her.

Friday, 5th April 1991 – Richard and his girlfriend, Tina Williams, present Bill and Gladys with their first great-grandchildren, twins William James and Leonard Christopher. Sadly, Leonard dies at one day old. William James, like his father, Richard, spends his first few months in an incubator fighting for his life; a battle he eventually wins. The same weekend Bill becomes a great-grandfather he holds a Ladies Night at Bournemouth as a Master of the Lodge.

Thursday, 2nd May 1991 – Gladys celebrates her 70th birthday.

Saturday, 7th September 1991 – Bill and Gladys celebrate their 50th wedding anniversary at the Royal British Legion at Worcester Park, Surrey, with a party. William James is safely out of hospital to join the four Powell male generations together for the first time: Bill, Robert William and Richard William.

With their daughter, Eileen, Bill and Gladys travel for six weeks from January 1993 to Singapore, Malaysia, Australia (Brisbane, Sydney and Melbourne where Eileen is tennis officiating) Fiji, Hawaii and America (Los Angeles). While they are travelling Gladys is in pain with her hip. On their return it is diagnosed that Gladys is in urgent need of a hip replacement. Arrangements are made and the operation is a success giving Gladys easy mobility again.

Wednesday, 14th December 1994 – Gladys' younger sister, Eileen, dies from a heart attack. Her funeral is held on Wednesday, 21st December at Slough. Gladys, the oldest, is now the only remaining member in the Elliston dynasty.

Tuesday, 14th March 1995 – With the upset of losing her younger sister, Gladys writes a note to Bill: *"My dearest Bill, If I go before you as one never knows – have a few words to say how much I've loved you for so many years. We have been so good for each other – few 'downs' – but thank God far more 'ups' in our lives. Only keep our good time we shared – our lives together. We have been so very lucky, one could not have asked for more. To reach our age has been a bonus, health-wise, cash-wise – had all we ever wanted from life. Take care. Look after yourself until we meet again. As ever, all my fondest love. Your loving wife, Glad."*

Gladys also writes a message to Robert, Eileen and her son-in-law, Alan: *"My dear Robert, Eileen and Alan. After the shock of Auntie Eileen leaving us all so quickly without any warning, thought I'll put pen to paper. I'm looking back on a great life Dad and I have spent together. I have no remorse or regret – enjoyed all the years we had 'time of writing'. 52 years, 7 months. Not bad, eh? I've lived life I wanted, done what I wanted, gone where I wanted. What more can one wish? I'm leaving behind a great family. My wish is that you will all keep close to each other. Keep in touch with each other and enjoy your lives as Dad and I have. Our grandchildren have been best part of our lives seeing them all grow up – very proud of them all. Extra bonus – lived to see William grow up – smashing little great, great-grandson after such a worrying start in life. What more can I wish for? Robert, Eileen, Alan – more so Bill. Thank you all for caring in last few years. Keep in touch with Pat, Chris, Graham, Lisa, Darren and Uncle Charlie – part of our family I've been so proud of."*

To Phyllis and John (Phyllis' husband after Robert): *"Phyllis and John – thank you both for letting Richard and Gary spend holidays with us while very young. A big hug to you. It meant so much to us both."*

To her seven grandchildren and one great-grandson: *"Richard, Gary and Laura. Julie, Cathlyn, Steven, David also William. Remember Grandad and me in years ahead. We loved you all."*

To Alan: *"Alan – take care of Eileen"*

To Robert: *"Robert – take care of Richard, Gary, Laura and Jayne"*

To John: *"John – take care of Phyllis"*

To Richard: *"Richard – take care of Tina and William"*

Have few tears, but much laughter in your years ahead. That's all, family. Goodnight, God bless you all. Much love, Mum."

Bill is still the president of both the branch and club of Worcester Park, Surrey, but he gradually allows other members to take control. He has proudly seen their Royal British Legion grow from a basic hut with 108 members to premises attracting over 1,700 members, for which Bill is mainly responsible. On Saturday, 20th April 1996 Bill is presented with a certificate as 'a Life Member of the Legion for Meritorious Service' for his dedicated services to the Worcester Park branch. He is presented with the award by David Knowles, the National Chairman of the Royal British Legion.

Tuesday, 14th April 1998 – Bill receives a certificate from the President and National Council of the Royal British Legion, 'as a mark of respect for the valuable service rendered on behalf of ex-Service men and women and their dependants'.

Gladys receives a certificate from the Royal British Legion, Worcester Park, Surrey, 'as a mark of esteem and appreciation of his work as a fund raiser' from 1985 to 1998. As the branch President, Bill signs Gladys' certificate.

Thursday, 7th January 1999 – For a Christmas gift, Eileen and Alan take Bill and Gladys away to Ostend, Bruges and Ypres where they visit World War I memorial sites and leave wreaths. Every evening at the Menin Gate since 1928 (except for a short time when Ypres was occupied by the Germans) at precisely 8.00 pm the traffic around the gate stops for the Last Post. As Bill has the freedom of the city of Ypres, he is awarded the privilege to proudly recite the Exhortation after the Last Post: "They shall grow not old, as we that are left grow old: Age shall not weary them, nor the years condemn. At the going down of the sun and in the morning. We will remember them."

Bill and Gladys have spent many enjoyable retirement years at their chalet at Allhallows. Reluctantly they sell the chalet in July 1999; the upkeep and travelling now becoming too much for them. Ironically, they sell the chalet to a Mr. Elliston (Gladys' maiden name) who also lives at Kingsland Road, Plaistow, London, E13 (the road Gladys' family had last lived). With the sale they also leave behind many happy memories where they would spend so much time with all their seven grandchildren. In place of their chalet Bill and Gladys often travel to Robert's holiday home in Torrievieja, Costa Blanca, Spain, where they enjoy the holiday complex, sun and friendship of many British locals living there.

Monday, 13th September 1999 – Bill celebrates his 80th birthday with a party held at the Royal British Legion. His family and close friends attend to enjoy the evening. It ends with the anthem, 'You'll Never Walk Alone'.

Saturday, 18th September 1999 – Bill and Gladys become proud great-grandparents again when their grandson, Gary, and Audrie Murray present them with a great-granddaughter, Fiona Murray Powell.

Saturday, 16th October 1999 – A month later at Epsom Registry Office, Surrey, Robert marries for the third time. Robert met Jenny Lyons early in 1999 and, after a whirl-wind romance, announces their engagement. Robert's brother-in-law, Alan Edwards, is best man. During the marriage service Bill reads a poignant poem to his son and new daughter-in-law: 'You Needed Me'.

After several visits to the doctor and hospital, Bill is diagnosed in December with bowel cancer. However, the cancer is at an early stage and treatable. Bill remains cheerful and optimistic.

Bill and Gladys celebrate the millennium at the Royal British Legion. Eileen and Alan then take Bill and Gladys to Slapton Sands in Devon, a place Bill and Gladys were keen to see, being of relevance during World War II.

When they return Bill is admitted to St. Helier Hospital, Carshalton, Surrey, for his operation on Wednesday, 26th January 2000. The operation is a complete success.

On Saturday, 29th January in Bill's diary Gladys writes: *"Saw and kissed Bill for very last time."*

On Monday, 31st January 2000 at 7.25 am, Bill dies of a heart attack. Gladys writes in Bill's diary: *"Bill left me for my life time."* (Each year on this day Gladys is to enter how many years Bill has left her, i.e.: in 2004, *"4 years ago Bill left me."*)

A military funeral is held for Bill on Thursday, 10th February 2000 complete with the union flag draped over his coffin and his medals and army cap Bill proudly wore placed on top. The funeral service is held at St. Phillips Church. The committal is held at the northwest crematorium and the final song is 'You'll Never Walk Alone' sung happily on Bill's 80th birthday only four months earlier. In Bill's diary Gladys on this day writes: *"Saying goodbye to Bill – harder than anyone could imagine."* (Each year Gladys will update the entry, i.e.: *"2003 – three years without you"* and *"2006 – six years without you"*).

Tuesday, 2nd May 2000 – On Gladys' 78th birthday she receives the deeds to their house, all formalities settled. To Gladys this is her final gift from Bill. Gladys writes in Bill's diary: *"1st birthday without Bill"*, and updates the number each year (i.e.: in 2002, *"3rd birthday without Bill"*).

Tuesday, 20th June 2000 – Gladys *"had Bill's gold badge received from the Royal British Legion made into a necklace I paid for myself, as Bill would have wished."*

Wednesday, 23rd August 2000 – To Gladys this is a *"very sad day – Bill's clothes collected and taken for a good cause to the Salvation Army. Cried most of the day. So miss him."* One blazer Gladys could not part with is the one Bill would wear with his war medals on. While sitting on the stairs crying, Gladys heard a thump from upstairs. A framed photo of Bill wearing the blazer Gladys had saved had fallen on to the floor in Bill's office.

Wednesday, 6th September 2000 – What would have been Bill and Gladys' 59th wedding anniversary, Gladys writes: *"2000 – 59 years. Now without Bill."* Gladys would update this entry each year (*"2004 – 63 years. Now without Bill"*).

Wednesday, 13th September 2000 – On what would have been Bill's 81st birthday, Gladys writes: *"Eleven of us went for a meal at Weatherspoons. Very pleasant evening. Miss you so much."*

Saturday, 16th September 2000 – Bill and Gladys' grandson, Gary, marries Audrie Murray. To Gladys it *"went off perfect. You would have been proud. Wanted to be with you so much."*

Sunday, 8th November 2000 – Remembrance Sunday and *"all attended service Saturday evening. Sunday laid wreath for you* [Bill]. *All family attended."*

Tuesday, 28th November 2000 – At the Worcester Park Branch Royal British Legion A.G.M. it is unanimously agreed to donate £50,000.00 to a planned Royal British

Legion retirement home in Weston-Super-Mare. In recognition to this generous amount, the home are to honour Bill by naming a bar area after him. Gladys writes: *"Eileen, Alan, Cathlyn, Robert, Richard, William and myself attended* [the A.G.M.]. *Dennis* [Clark] *took over from you* [as President of the Worcester Park branch]. *You were spoken of very much in honour. Eileen, your daughter alright, gave a super speech. Everyone had tears as she spoke on your behalf. She made the evening."*

Saturday, 14th July 2001 – Having lost her husband, Bill, Gladys writes another message for her family: *"Dear Eileen and Robert, Now is the time for Dad and I to put to rest together which is mine and Dad's wish – young and old together. Loved each other over 58 years which I am very proud of. God bless you both. Keep family very close to each other is all we wish for in our life. Goodnight to you both, Mum (also Dad)."*

Gladys leaves a message to each grandchild in order of birth: Richard, Gary, Julie, Cathlyn, Steven, Laura and David; and great grandchildren, William and Fiona. *"18 months since Grandad left us. Being close family – all he and me wanted."*

Richard – Sadly you and Tina parted, but Tina I only pray you find someone else to share your life with.

Trish – Welcome to our family. You never knew Grandad. He would have welcomed and liked you. Richard and Trish – have a happy life together. Look after each other.

Gary, Audrie and Fiona – Grandad was so proud to welcome Fiona. To be at your wedding would have been his greatest wish. Take care of each other.

Julie and Andy – Hope I shall be at your wedding. You have worked so hard for what you have made out of life. Just like Richard and Gary have done well. May it continue.

Cathlyn – One and only lovely Cathlyn – meet someone to care for you always. Enjoy your life. Most of all, be happy.

Steven – Hope you settle in life. Do your own thing. Enjoy your youth. Take after Dad and you won't go far wrong.

Laura – Wishing you, as everyone in family, always to stay close. Enjoy your life. Keep near Mum 'Jayne'. Both be happy.

David – One and only David. Don't wander too far from home as you have great family with Julie, Cathlyn and Steven.

William – You were so tiny when born, not having best start in life. But thank goodness grown into a lovely lad much loved by all.

Fiona – As of now, last of line in my lifetime. You are a little sweetheart. Do not change.

PS – Never leave out Pat and Chris – a lovely couple, but Pat is my sister Eileen's child.

Last word to Robert, Jenny, Eileen and Alan. Hope you all enjoy the happiness Dad and I had – you will never beat it. Much love, good health to all of you. Love Mum/Nan (also Dad/Grandad)."

Thursday, 2nd May 2002 – Gladys' 80th birthday: her family arrive at her house with food for a surprise party and later her friends attend to celebrate.

Saturday, 24th August 2002 – Gladys is Guest of Honour at the wedding of her oldest granddaughter, Julie Karyn, when she marries Andrew Astell. Several other members of the family are also involved: Alan gives his daughter away, Steven and David are two of Andrew's best men, Cathlyn is chief bridesmaid, William is page boy and Fiona is flower girl.

Sunday, 10th November 2002 – On Remembrance Sunday Gladys remembers Bill: *"Very good attendance. You would have been proud of us all. Poppy wreath laid on your behalf."*

Sunday, 10th November 2003 – On Remembrance Sunday Gladys writes: *"Bill, remembering you is easy, we do it every day. Missing you is the heartache that never goes away."*

Saturday, 6th September 2003 – Richard marries Patricia 'Trish' Casey on the exact day when 62 years earlier Bill had married *"the sweetest girl in the world."* Richard and Trish are to produce two more great-grandchildren for

Gladys: Katie Ann, born in 2005 and Jack Michael, born in 2008.

Friday, 4th May 2007 – Two days after Gladys' 85th birthday, Julie and Andrew produce Leanna Ellie, Gladys' fourth great-grandchild. 'Ellie' is short for 'Elliston', in remembrance of Gladys' maiden name and the Elliston dynasty.

Saturday, 3rd May 2008 – A party is arranged to celebrate Leanna Ellie's 1st and Gladys' 86th birthday. All of Gladys' family attend and also, as a special surprise guest, her long time friend, Lily Kaufman, now aged 94.

Gladys survives a serious burst aneurysm in her stomach and lives with Eileen and her family who care for her until she is able to return home. However, Gladys' health does not improve and returns to stay with her daughter. During the next few months Gladys needs constant care with her failing health.

Wednesday, 4th March 2009 – Eileen takes Gladys to the hospital. The doctor is shocked how quickly Gladys' health has rapidly deteriorated and informs her: "Things are catching up on you, ma'am" and that she is dying. Gladys knows. The doctor asks Gladys if she is scared. She replies she is not: she is ready to go and wants to go. Although she loves Eileen, she loves Bill more. And, if she did have a choice, she would choose to be with Bill any day: she still misses him so. Four days later Gladys gets her wish. Nine years after losing her beloved husband, Bill, Gladys dies at 12.15 pm on Sunday, 8th March 2009.

Tuesday, 31st March 2009 – Gladys' funeral service takes place. Like Bill's funeral service, Gladys' is held at St. Phillips Church, the adopted church where Gladys so happily married Bill 58 years earlier. Gladys' committal is also held at the northwest cremation and the same final song, 'You'll Never Walk Alone' is again chosen; embraced by the Powell and the Edwards family. A poignant poem is written for Gladys: 'God saw you getting tired and a cure was not to be, so he put his arms around you and whispered "come with me." With tearful eyes we watched you and saw you pass away, and although we love you dearly, we could not make you stay. A golden heart stopped beating, hardworking hands at rest. God broke our hearts to prove us He only takes the best'.

Gladys leaves behind her final message to Robert and Eileen: *"Dear Eileen, Robert, Alan and Jenny. Now at long last with Dad. I waited so long, so be happy for me. My fondest love to each and everyone. To all the family I've left. Thank you for your love and support you have given me since Dad left. But life without him has been meaningless. I've missed him beyond words can say. You'll never understand. My fondest love to all grandchildren who gave me lovely support. I've been so lucky. We will always try to take care of you in out-of-life. Care for each other. Always be happy. Our fondest love to you all. Mum and Dad."*

Bill is again reunited with Gladys: *"the finest, sweetest girl in the world."* It is *"Just like heaven to be with Gladys again"* and they are together *"till death do us part and even that will only be a temporary parting until we meet again in whatever life it is that follows this one."*

(Above) The Powell and Edwards family together, December 1999
(Below) Bill & Gladys' last photo together at Slapton Sands, January 2000

[During my wedding reception I returned to my parents' house to change and I left behind a letter for them when they returned home later that evening. When Mum gave me Dad's letters written to her during the war for safe keeping, amongst them is my letter. I would like to conclude with this letter to my parents. It says it all.]

28 Albert Road
New Malden
Surrey
KT3 6BS

22nd June, 1974

Dear Mum and Dad,

It seems the least I can do is to write this letter to you both – just to leave something behind for you when you return home from the excitement of our wedding reception. I have watched how you have thoughtfully arranged everything for our special day with such care and attention, giving us only the best there is. Alan and I would like you to know just how very thankful we are to you for all that you have done.

Looking back, there were times when it seemed that I wasn't the most loving of daughters to have, but I now feel that it is time to express my gratitude in every possible way. I really didn't realise how lucky I was to have a mother and father like you. There isn't a better pair in the world. It wasn't until these last few weeks that I suddenly began to appreciate all that you both have done for me. I never before wanted to leave home as I have been so very happy with you. But, although I love you both very much indeed, I love Alan just that little bit extra to now want to leave and start a new way of life as his wife and have a family of our own. But, I shall look back on these 22 years with you and treasure all the memories of us together. And, if Alan and I turn out to be half the parents you are, your grandchildren are going to have a very happy life too.

Thank you Mum and Dad so very, very much – for everything. God bless, love,

Eileen   xxx

APPENDIX
Films, Shows, Pantomime, Matches and Documentaries seen

FILMS SEEN
A Gentleman after Dark
A Modern Hero
A Night Alone
A Night in New Orleans
A Shot in the Dark
A Woman's Face
A Yank in the R.A.F.
Above Suspicion
Adventure in Sahara
Affectionally Yours
All This, and Heaven Too
Almost Married
Aloma of the South Seas
Angles Wash Their Faces
Arise My Love
Arizona
Back Street
Ball of Fire
Barricade
Behind the News
Bob's Your Uncle
Boom Town
Busman's Honeymoon
Buy Me That Town
Captains of the Clouds
Caught in the Draft
China Sea
Citadel of Crime
Come Live with Me
Comrade X
Convicted Woman
Dangerous Moonlight
Dark Streets of Cairo

Dead Man's Shoes
Dr. Jekyll and Mr. Hyde
Dr. Kildare's Crisis
Don't Get Personal
Down Argentine Way
Dressed to Kill
Edison, the Man
Emergency Landing
Escape
Flowing Gold
Flying Fortress
Flying Wild
For Beauty's Sake
49th Parallel
Forty Thousand Horsemen
Four Mothers (x2)
Four Sons
Gasbags
Gert and Daisy Clean Up
Gert and Daisy's Weekend
Give Us Wings
Gold Rush Maisie
Gone with the Wind
Great Guns
He Found a Star (x2)
He Stayed for Breakfast
Hello Sucker
Hell's Angels
Here We Go Again
Hi Diddle Diddle
Hi Gang!
Hit Parade of 1941
Hold that Woman!
Honky Tonk

I'm Nobody's Sweetheart Now
I Wanted Wings (x2)
International Lady
International Squadron
Invisible Agent
It's a Date
Johnny Eager
Jungle Book
Kathleen
Kid Glove Killer
Kitty Foyle
Let the People Sing
Ma, He's Making Eyes at Me
Maisie Was a Lady
Major Barbara
Man with Two Lives
Manhattan Madness
Manpower
Men against the Sky
Million Dollar Baby
Model Wife
Monkey Business
Mutiny on the Bounty
My Love Came Back
My Son, My Son!
My Wife's Family
Naval Academy
Nell Gwyn
New York Town
Niagara Falls
No, No, Nanette
No Orchards for Miss Blandish
No Time for Comedy
North West Mounted Police
Nothing but the Truth
Old Bill and Son
Old Mother Riley
On Dress Parade
One Night in Lisbon
Our Russian Allies

Paint and Powder
Pardon My Sarong
Paris Calling
Pride and Prejudice
Pride of the Blue Grass
Professor Mamlock
Radio Revels of 1942
Reap the Wild Wind
Return of the Thin Man
Ride 'Em Cowboy
Roamin' Wild
Saboteur
San Francisco Docks
Sandy Gets Her Man
Santa Fe Trail
Sea Raiders
Sergeant York
Skylark
So Ends Our Night
So You Won't Talk
South American George
Spare a Copper
Spooks Run Wild
Spring Parade
Strike up the Band
Sunny
Take It Easy
Target for Tonight
Tarzan's New York Adventure
The Ape
The Bank Detective
The Big Blockade
The Black Sheep of Whitehall
The Border Legion
The Bride Wore Crutches
The Case of the Black Cat
The Case of the Black Parrot
The Corsican Brothers
The Courtship of Andy Hardy
The Door with Seven Locks

The Farmer's Wife
The Fighting 69th
The Foreman Went to France
The Four Just Men
The Gay Caballero
The Gay Falcon
The Ghost of St. Michael's
The Ghost Train
The Glass Key
The Golden Fleecing
The Gracie Allen Murder Case (x2)
The Great Dictator
The Leather Pushers
The Man Who Came Back
The Man Who Came to Dinner
The Man Who Talked Too Much
The Man Who Wouldn't Die
The Mark of Zorro
The Marx Brothers Go West
The Mississippi Gambler
The New Adventures of Tarzan
The Phantom Submarine
The Scarlet Pimpernel
The Sea Wolf
The Smiling Ghost
The Son of Monte Cristo
The Spoilers
The Spy in Black
The Trail of Mary Dugan
The Under-pup
The Valley of the Sun
The Wagons Roll at Night
The Ware Case
The Way of All Flesh
The White Cliffs of Dover
They Came by Night
Thieves Fall Out
The Gun for Hire

Three Men from Texas
Tilly of Bloomsbury
Time Out for Rhythm
Tin Pan Alley
Too Many Girls
Trial of the Vigilantes
Uncensored
Underground
Wake Island
Wake Up and Dream
West Point Widow
When Ladies Meet
Whispering Ghosts
White Cargo
Yankee Doodle Dandy
Yesterday's Heroes
You'll Never Get Rich
Young People
You're in the Army Now

SHOWS SEEN
Alfredo and his Band
Auld Acquaintance
Belle of New York
Billy Cotton and Dorothy Ward
Black Vanities
Caroll Levis
Du Barry Was a Lady
Film show at Epsom
Forsythe, Seamon and Farrell
Gangway
Get a Load of This
Harry Parry's Sextet and comedian Ronald Frankau
Harry Roy and his Band
Henry Hall's Gust Night
Hippodrome comedy
Issy Bonn
Jay Wilbur and his High Class Band

Jeanie
Kenway and Young
Love Life and Laughter
Max Miller (x2)
Me and My Girl
Palais de Dance
Variety Show at London Palladium
Variety Show in a French theatre
Various shows at the Imperial Theatre
Vintage Cocktail
Wee Georgie Wood
Women Aren't Angels
Young Woodley

PANTOMIMES SEEN
Jack and Jill

MATCHES SEEN
Boxing match at Epsom baths

Stars of Radio
Sunday matinee
Thanks to Love, Fun and Games
The Western Brothers
Troise and his Mandoliers
Twenty To One
Inter Services: Navy vs. R.A.F. (boxing)
Tigers vs. Ramblers (hockey)
Tigers vs. Redwings (hockey)

DOCUMENTARIES SEEN
An Army film
Defeat of the Germans near Moscow
Mechanical Transport lecture
Nazi Germany lecture
Science in Modern War lecture

ABBREVIATIONS
Used from Bill's letters and diaries

A.A.C.	Anti Aircraft Company.
A.C.M.F.	Allied Central Mediterranean Forces.
A.D.	After Death.
A.E.C.	Associated Equipment Company.
A.F.S.	Air Formation Signals.
A.G.M.	Annual General Meeting.
A.N.Z.A.C.s	Australia and New Zealand Army Corps.
A.W.O.L.	Absent Without Leave.
B.B.C.	British Broadcasting Corporation.
B.N.A.F.	British North Africa Forces.
C.B.	Confined to Barracks, normally for a minor punishment.
C.H.Q.	Company Headquarters. Company and squadron both refer to sub-divisions of regiments: generally there are five companies to an infantry regiment or five squadrons to a tank regiment, transport regiment, cavalry regiment, etc.
C.M.F.	Central Mediterranean Forces.
C.O.	Commanding Officer.
CON	Convalescent.
COY	Company.
C.P.	Conservative Party.
D.C.G.	Could mean Deputy Commanding General (Roads), an official acronym associated with a component command, in this case roads. It could also mean Disaster Control Group or Defence Control Group.
D.S.O.	Distinguished Service Order – it is customary to refer to somebody by their rank, name and decorations.
D.T.s	Diamond 'T' 980 heavy tank transporter.
F.A.	Football Association.
G. Hospital	General Hospital.

G.H.Q.	General Headquarters.
G.P.O.	General Post Office.
G.R.T.D.	Could refer to the General Re-enforcement Training Depot. This is a special unit where injured soldiers slowly recovered and eventually recuperated enough to be discharged back to their units and back into the war. There is one depot 20 miles outside of Algiers, plus several elsewhere and in the UK.
H.Q.	Headquarters.
H.M.S.	His Majesty's Service.
L.I.A.P.	Leave In Addition to Python.
M.C.C.	Marylebone Cricket Club.
M.O.	Medical Officer.
M.P.	Member of Parliament.
N.A.A.F.I.	Naval, Army, Air Force Institutes is an organisation created by the British government in 1921 responsible with selling goods to servicemen.
N.A.T.O.	North Atlantic Treaty Organisation.
N.C.O.s	Non Commissioned Officers', i.e.: Lance Corporal, Corporal, Sergeant, Staff Sergeant.
O.C.	Officer Commanding.
O.R.	Ordinary Rank or Junior Rank; O.R.s are generally Privates, i.e.: not N.C.O.s or S.N.C.O.s or Officers.
P.O.L.	Petrol Oil and Lubricants, normally packed in jerry cans and 10 gallon drums.
P.O.W.	Prisoner Of War.
P.T.	Physical Training.
PTE	Private.
R.A.F.	Royal Air Force.
R.A.S.C.	Royal Army Service Corps.
R.A.S.C. T.D.	Royal Army Service Corps Training Depot.
R.E.	Royal Engineers.
R.E.M.E.	Royal Electrical and Mechanical Engineers.
R.M.P.	Remote Medical Practice.
R.O.P.	Restriction of Privileges or jankers, a term for an official punishment.
R.T.W.	Road Tanker Wagon, not decanted into jerry cans.

2 I/C	Second in Command.
Sec.	Section.
S.H.A.E.F.	Supreme Headquarters Allied Expeditionary Force, the Headquarters of the Commander of Allied forces in northwest Europe from late 1943 until the end of the war with General Dwight D. Eisenhower in command throughout its existence.
S.N.C.O.	Senior Non Commissioned Officer.
S.O.	S.O. initials are classic military which could have multiple meanings. This one could represent 'Staff Officer', normally someone who works in a brigade or divisional Headquarter; 'Station Office', the office responsible for a geographical Location with lodger units (i.e.: Donnington Station); or 'Senior Officer'.
S.O.S.	Save Our Souls.
S.T.	Supply and Transit.
S.W.A.L.K.	Sealed With A Loving Kiss.
T.A.	Territorial Army.
T.D.	Training Depot.
T.T.	Technical Training.
U.K.	United Kingdom.
U.S.	United States.
U.S.A.	United States of America.
U.S.S.	United States Ship.
U.S.S.R.	Union of Soviet Socialist Republics.
V.E.	Victory in Europe
V.J.	Victory over Japan.
V.O.R.	Vehicle Off Road.
W.O.	Warrant Officer.
W/S	Could be 'wounded and sick' platoon.

INDEX
Complete explanations from Bill's letters

[1] A.N.Z.A.C.s – Australia and New Zealand Army Corps.

[2] C.B. – Confined to Barracks, normally for a minor punishment.

[3] Roll call is the calling of names of soldiers to check attendance.

[4] M.O. – medical officer.

[5] Jerry is a World War II-era nickname for German soldiers.

[6] Pay parade is when soldiers would assemble and march up one at a time to the officer who would count out the cash to every soldier individually.

[7] C.H.Q. – Company Headquarters. Company and squadron both refer to sub-divisions of regiments: generally there are five companies to an infantry regiment or five squadrons to a tank regiment, transport regiment, cavalry regiment, etc.

[8] Music While You Work is a BBC daytime radio programme of continuous live popular music which started in June 1940 aimed to help workers become more productive.

[9] N.A.A.F.I. – Naval, Army, Air Force Institutes is an organisation created by the British government in 1921 responsible with selling goods to servicemen.

[10] Pot and pan is a Cockney slang for 'old man' (father or husband).

[11] Romeo and Juliet (two young lovers), Scarlett and Rhett (Scarlett O'Hara and Rhett Butler in 'Gone with the Wind'), Nelson and Hamilton (Lord Nelson and Emma, Lady Hamilton) and Elizabeth and Essex

(Queen Elizabeth I and Robert Devereaux, 2nd Earl of Essex).

[12] Eyeties is a World War II-era nickname for Italian soldiers.

[13] The Creed is a statement of belief that describes the beliefs shared by a religious community.

[14] Romeo and Juliet (two young lovers), (John) Darby and Joan (an elderly married couple), Napoleon and Josephine (Napoleon Bonaparte (Napoleon I) and his first wife, widow, Josephine de Beauharnais).

[15] The British government asked Sir William Beveridge to write a report on the best ways of helping people on low incomes. In December 1942 Beveridge published a report that proposed that all people of working age should pay a weekly contribution. In return, benefits would be paid to people who were sick, unemployed, retired or widowed. Beveridge argued that this system would provide a minimum standard of living 'below which no one should be allowed to fall'. These measures were eventually introduced by the Labour Government when elected in 1945.

[16] The Hoare-Laval Pact was a proposal made in December 1935 by British Foreign Secretary, Samuel Hoare, and French Prime Minister, Pierre Laval, for ending the Second Italo/Abyssinian War. Italy had wanted to take Abyssinia as part of its empire and have an empire like the Romans had and also to avenge previous defeats in the region. The Pact offered to partition Abyssinia (as Ethiopia was then called) and thus achieve Italian dictator Benito Mussolini's goal of making the independent nation of Abyssinia into an Italian colony.

[17] Neville Chamberlain was Prime Minister of Great Britain in September 1939 as Europe descended into World War II. Chamberlain paid a political price for

the failure of Britain in Norway in the spring of 1940 and resigned as Prime Minister to be succeeded by Winston Churchill. Chamberlain died shortly afterwards.

[18] David Lloyd George was a British Liberal politician and Prime Minister of the U.K. leading the Wartime Coalition Government between 1916-1922. After the armistice on 23rd November 1918 he promised the returning troops from World War I comprehensive reforms to deal with poor education, housing, health and transport: "What is our task? To make Britain a country fit for our heroes to live in." Lloyd George's post-war government raised the school leaving age to 14 and a total of 170,000 homes were built, a landmark measure. Although re-elected he remained dependent upon the coalition with the Conservatives, who had little intention of delivering such radical reforms. In place of this utopia they found a land blighted by unemployment and shortages. Inspired by the end of the war and the victory of the Russian workers and peasants, the spectre of revolution was taking on across the continent and Britain was no exception. In 1918 strikes had already cost six million working days. This exploded to almost 35 million in 1919, with a daily average of 100,000 workers on strike. In the face of such a crisis the ruling class split into two main camps: those who wanted an all-out assault against the working class, like Winston Churchill, soon to be Secretary of State for War. Alongside the struggle of the workers in industry, the armed forces and the police were to then take action. After years in the bloodbath of filthy foreign trenches, Churchill now expected British soldiers to fight a new war against the young workers state in Russia. This was unacceptable and the troops revolted.

Christopher Addison became the first Minister of Health in June 1919. Addison was responsible for the first Housing and Town Planning Act under which the state built 213,000 low-rent home (council houses) for the working class. He also presided over large increases in public spending until he was removed from Ministry of Health in April 1921 for his extravagance and it was then decided to halt the housing construction scheme.

[19] C.P. – Conservative Party.

[20] 'Oh, to be in England now that April's there' is from Robert Browning's poem, 'Home Thoughts, From Abroad'.

[21] Lily is Gladys' best friend. They have been friends since Gladys' mother, Hilda, and Lily's mother, Maggie Kaufman, were neighbours and also close friends. Most of Gladys' time was spent with Lily and her sister, Doreen Kaufman and was practically brought up by their mother and thought to be lucky with having two mothers, her own and also Mrs. Kaufman. Gladys was also friends with Doris who married Lily's brother, Reg Kaufman. Lily married Laurie Shrubsole and Doreen married Jack Braiden. Lily and Laurie had a baby girl, Pamela Doreen, born in February 1943.

[22] 'Wake Island' was a 1942 war film starring Brian Donlevy.

[23] MIZPAH means 'May the Lord watch between me and thee when we are absent from another' taken from Genesis 31:49 of the Bible – an emotional bond in separation (either when a loved one left for action or after death).

[24] Bill had previously seen 'Yankee Doodle Dandy' film with Don on Friday, 14th August 1942 when he was at his motor mechanic fitter course in Brighton.

[25] Billeted is lodging for a soldier to sleep.

[26] Boche is a World War II-era derogatory French word referring to the Germans.

[27] Macaronis is an Italian fighter plane.

[28] Lily's husband, Laurie Shrubsole, is also fighting in the war in the navy.

[29] Lin is Bill's affectionate nickname for Eileen, Gladys' younger sister, who Bill always had a soft spot for. Eileen is still living with her Aunt Elsie and Uncle Syd nearby at Worcester Park.

[30] After the victory at El Alamein, King George visited North Africa. From Pathé (1896-1976) Review of the Year – June 1943: Several shots of a great Allied army parade which marked occupation of Tunis. Generals Eisenhower, Giraud, Alexander and Anderson are standing at dais. There were various shots of King George VI chatting with troops during his visit to North Africa. The King is seen driving in an open car with troops cheering from both sides of the road.

[31] Although Bill was prepared to fight for 'King and Country', he is not a royalist. However, in his later years he was always the first to stand for the national anthem and passionately sing the words.

[32] Axis is an alignment of great powers that fought World War II against the Allies.

[33] When the King approached Bill he thought he is from India as Bill is so dark brown from the sun. The King stopped to speak to Bill and told him how pleased he is to see the Indian contribution to the war effort. Bill looked the King straight in the eye and replied in his broad Cockney accent: "Actually, mate, I'm from Battersea." (Cockney refers to people born within the sound of the Bow Bells, a church of St. Mary-le-Bow in the City of London, ringing at an estimated six miles to the east, five miles to the north, three miles to the

south and four miles to the west. Geographically and culturally, it is often used to refer to working class Londoners, particularly those in the East End. Linguistically, it can refer to the accent and form of English spoken by this group. The sound of the bells of St Mary's is credited with having persuaded Dick Whittington to turn back from Highgate and remain in London to become Lord Mayor. The church is also immortalised in the nursery rhyme, 'Oranges and Lemons' – "I do not know, says the great bell of Bow." The association with Cockney and the East End in the public imagination may be due to many people assuming that Bow Bells are to be found in the district of Bow, rather than the lesser known St Mary-le-Bow church. Thus while all East Enders are Cockneys, not all Cockneys are East Enders. Bill was born in the sound of the Bow bells; therefore classed as a true Cockney.)

[34] Latrine is a pit toilet.

[35] Monty is the nickname of Field Marshall Bernard Montgomery.

[36] Alex is the nickname of Harold Rupert Leofric George Alexander, 1st Earl Alexander of Tunis. He was a British military commander and field marshal who served with distinction in both world wars.

[37] General Dwight 'Ike' Eisenhower is a five-star general in the U.S. army during World War II who serves as Supreme Commander of the Allied Forces in Europe and is responsible for the planning and supervising of the invasion of North Africa in Operation Torch in 1942-43 and later for the successful invasion of France and Germany in 1944-45 from the Western Front. He became the first supreme commander of N.A.T.O. in 1951 and from 1953-1961 became the 34th President of

the United States of America following the simple but effective slogan, 'I Like Ike'.

[38] The 'Race to Berlin' refers mainly to the competition between two soviet Marshals to be the first to enter Berlin during the final months of World War II. On Wednesday, 2nd May 1945, with the war in Europe coming to an obvious conclusion, Soviet leader Joseph Stalin purposely set his two Marshalls, Georgy Zhukov and Ivan Konev, in a race to capture Berlin. Their separately commanded two armies competed against one another, ensuring that they would drive their men as fast and as far as possible to a quick victory. This led to a climax in the bloody Battle of Berlin. The Soviet advance and ultimate capture of the German capital was virtually unopposed by their allies. In an effort to avoid a diplomatic issue, Allied General of the Army Dwight Eisenhower had ordered his forces into the south of Germany to cut off and wipe out other pieces of the Wehrmacht, a unified armed forces of Germany from 1935-1945. It consisted of the 'Heer' (army), 'Kriegsmariner' (Navy) and the Luftwaffe (air force). The decision to leave eastern Germany and the city of Berlin to the Red Army eventually had serious repercussions as the Cold War emerged and expanded in the post-war era, but in doing so, the western Allies were also honouring agreements they made with the Soviet Union at Yalta.

[39] G.R.T.D. could refer to the General Re-enforcement Training Depot. This was a special unit where injured soldiers slowly recovered and eventually recuperated enough to be discharged back to their units and back into the war. There was one depot 20 miles outside of Algiers, plus several elsewhere and in the UK.

[40] Redcaps are the Military Police section of the allied Assortment who wore red caps.

[41] Rene is Gladys' friend, Irene.

[42] C.M.F. – Central Mediterranean Forcers.

[43] Benito Mussolini banned the sale of ice cream throughout Italy, the land that claims to have given birth to the ice cream. Mussolini would later complain that the people of Italy were a "mediocre race of good-for-nothings only capable of singing and eating ice cream."

[44] A yo-yo is an axle connected to two disks and a length of twine looped around the axle. It works by holding the free end of the string (by inserting one finger in a slip knot), allowing the force of a throw to spin. The yo-yo unwinds the string allowing it to wind itself back to the hand, exploiting its spin. First invented in ancient Greece, it became popular in the 1920s as a popular pastime of many generations and cultures.

*[45]*Hovel is a small humble dwelling.

[46] V cigarette is Viceroy, a low cost brand and the first filter with a cork tip produced in 1935.

[47] Senior Service is a cigarette brand named after the nickname of the Royal Navy with the brand's logo of a sailing ship.

[48] Bill stayed with Mrs. Jeram in Brighton when on his motor mechanic course in July-August 1942.

[49] N.C.O.s – Non Commissioned Officers', i.e.: Lance Corporal, Corporal, Sergeant, Staff Sergeant.

[50] W.O. – Warrant Officer.

[51] C.O. – Commanding Officer.

[52] O.C. – Officer Commanding.

[53] Blighty is a slang for Britain derived from the Hindustani word 'bilāti', later used to refer to home.

[54] Federation of Master Builders (F.M.B.) is a UK trade association established in 1941 to protect the interests of small and medium sized building firms.

[55] Prefab homes is often referred to as specialist dwelling types of prefabricated buildings which are manufactured off-site in advance, usually in standard sections easily assembled, to be used as a temporary replacement for housing that had been destroyed by bombs, particularly in London.

[56] Penny bank is a savings account.

[57] 'Now What Would You Do, Chums?' is a 1939 British dram film starring actor Syd Walker who plays himself, using the title as his catchphrase. He died on 13th January 1945.

[58] Twilight sleep is an amnesic condition characterized by insensibility to pain without loss of consciousness, induced by an injection of morphine and scopolamine, especially to relieve the pain of childbirth. This combination induces a semi-narcotic state which produces the experience of childbirth without pain, or without the memory of pain.

[59] Pepsodent is a popular brand of American minty flavoured toothpaste also available in powder.

[60] Dr. Kyles is an American brand toothpaste.

[61] Flints are a small piece of metal used to produce a spark to ignite fuel in a cigarette lighter.

[62] Bob is a British slang term for a shilling.

[63] The United Nations is an international organisation founded in 1945 to replace the League of Nations whose stated aims include promoting and facilitating cooperation in international law, international security, economic development, social progress, human rights, civil rights, civil liberties, political freedoms, democracy, and the achievement of lasting world peace.

[64] The Phoney War is a phase early in World War II that was marked by a lack of major military operations by the Western Allies (the United Kingdom and France)

against the German Reich. The phase covered the months following Britain and France's declaration of war on Germany (shortly after her invasion of Poland) in September 1939 and preceding the Battle of France in May 1940. War was declared by each side, but no Western power had committed to launching a significant land offensive, notwithstanding the terms of the Anglo/Polish and Franco/Polish military alliances, which obliged the United Kingdom and France to assist Poland.

[65] Blitz is known as the lightning war (in German: blitzkrieg).

[66] 'A Little of What You Fancy Does You Good' was recorded by Marie Lloyd in 1915.

[67] S.H.A.E.F. is Supreme Headquarters Allied Expeditionary Force, the Headquarters of the Commander of Allied forces in northwest Europe from late 1943 until the end of the war with General Dwight D. Eisenhower in command throughout its existence.

[68] The Alexander Club is named after Field Marshal Harold Alexander, 1st Earl Alexander of Tunis who served with distinction in both world wars. It is situated at XX Via Settembre, Rome, Italy, is a N.A.A.F.I. run canteen and resting place where service people could have a good meal: bangers and mash etc., a bath/shower, shave, haircut, beer and meet friends. It was a converted six storey department store building in the heart of Rome with six mezzanine floors with a huge candelabra in the centre of the ceiling, the subject of a bet between a party of Commandos and Paratroopers as to which could do a Tarzan act by lassoing the candelabra and swinging to and fro. This was all good fun until after a while the bolts loosened and in the middle of one

swing by a paratrooper, the bolts departed the ceiling and the candelabra came crashing down the six floors to the ground, pinning the paratrooper underneath, who said after he was uncovered that "it was probably his last jump." It was. He had broken his back.

[69] 'All the Things You Are' (see words below) is a song composed by Jerome Kern, with lyrics written by Oscar Hammerstein II and adopted as Bill and Gladys' personal love song.

[70] Defence Regulation 18B, often referred to as simply 18B, is the most famous of the Defence Regulations used by the British Government during World War II. The complete technical reference name for this rule was: Regulation 18B of the Defence (General) Regulations 1939. It allowed for the internment of people suspected of being Nazi sympathisers. The effect of 18B was to suspend the right of individuals to habeas corpus.

[71] Herbert Morrison is a Labour politician and the Secretary of State for the Home Department. During World War II several leading fascists, including Oswald Mosley, were imprisoned without trial. In November 1943 Morrison controversially decided to order Mosley's release from prison resulting to large scale protests describing the decision as "a slap in the face of anti-fascists in every country and a direct betrayal of those who have died for the cause of anti-fascism."

[72] Ernest Bevin is a Labour Politian and Minister of Labour and Labour National Service in the war time coalition government. Although Bevin was not actually an M.P. at the time, a parliamentary position was found and Bevin was elected unopposed as an M.P. (Member of Parliament) for the London

constituency of Wandsworth Central. Bevin did not get on with Morrison. When once told "the trouble with Herbert [Morrison] is that he is his own worst enemy", Bevin replied: "Not while I'm alive, he ain't!" During the war Bevin was responsible for diverting nearly 48,000 military conscripts to work in the coal industry. These workers became known as 'the Bevin Boys'. He also drew up the demobilisation scheme that ultimately returned millions of military personnel and civilian war workers back into the peacetime economy.

[73] Fontanigorda is a commune in the province of Genoa in the Italian region Liguria, about 35 km northwest of Genoa.